AMERICAN
SHOOTER

Related Potomac Titles

Lethal Logic: Exploding the Myths
That Paralyze American Gun Policy
by Dennis A. Henigan

AMERICAN SHOOTER

A PERSONAL HISTORY OF GUN CULTURE IN THE UNITED STATES

GERRY SOUTER

Potomac Books
Washington, D.C.

Library of Congress Cataloging-in-Publication Data
Souter, Gerry.
    American shooter : a personal history of gun culture in the United States / Gerry Souter. — 1st ed.
        p. cm.
    Includes bibliographical references.
    ISBN 978-1-59797-690-9 (hardcover)
    ISBN 978-1-59797-872-9 (electronic edition)
    1. Firearms ownership—United States—History. 2. Firearms—United States—History. 3. Firearms—Social aspects—United States—History. 4. Souter, Gerry. I. Title.

    HV8059.S63 2011
    683.400973—dc23

                                                    2011041758

Printed in the United States of America on acid-free paper that meets the American National Standards Institute Z39-48 Standard.

Potomac Books
22841 Quicksilver Drive
Dulles, Virginia 20166

First Edition

10 9 8 7 6 5 4 3 2 1

To the four great loves of my life:
Janet, Damienne, Allison, and Collin

Contents

Foreword   ix

Introduction   xiii

1   A New Culture Shaped by Old Fears   1

2   Heading West: Prophets of Individualism   21

3   It's a Small-Bore World after All   51

4   "A Simply Operated Machine Gun . . ."   65

5   A-Hunting We Did Go   79

6   World War II: The Game Changer   101

7   Gathering the Reins in a Runaway World   115

8   The Me Generation under Fire   167

9   Put the Gloves on the Bosses and Let 'em Duke It Out   193

Appendix A. National Shooting Sports League   239

Appendix B. Exhibition Shooters   241

Appendix C. Hitting the Target   245

Appendix D. Guns in a Big, Dark Room   253

Appendix E. Them's Fightin' Words: Video Games   261

Notes   267

Bibliography   273

About the Author   275

Foreword

Gerry Souter's *American Shooter: A Personal History of Gun Culture in America* is an informative and enjoyable excursion, both historical and personal. Souter sets out the problem of the polarization in public debate about guns. He seeks to separate "myths and truth" and "insights and blunders." This book is not about the Second Amendment controversy.[1] Yet Souter explores the nature of our gun culture and how deeply ingrained it is, both personally and individually, and broadly throughout American society.

The first chapter opens with America's colonial heritage, the regulation of firearms, smoothbore inaccuracy, the evolution of rifles, and shooting contests. Souter interjects a personal story of his father winning a turkey shoot and the beginning of a rivalry. For a shooter who got his first gun from his grandfather at age five, this chapter resonated powerfully. My son, Elwood, now the carotid specialist for his string of neck shots on deer and elk, has surpassed his father in the field. Souter then tells of the militia system and the soldiers of the American Revolution and the War of 1812. His discussion of the Battle of New Orleans echoes Robert V. Remini's telling of the question of who killed Col. Robert Rennie in the battle. A man named Withers claimed the kill, declaring, "If he isn't hit above the eyebrows, it wasn't my shot." They rolled the body over and "sure enough the fatal shot had caught the officer just over the eyebrows."[2] Accurate rifle fire carried the day.

As Americans moved west, manufacturers and shade-tree mechanics were improving weapons. Pistols designed for specific uses, and for specific clients, appeared. Souter debunks the "myth of the gunfighters." We were not a "gunfighter nation."[3] In fact, many of the cow towns in the American West

ix

restricted the carrying of weapons in the city limits. Souter maintains the reality was that "the handgun became the trademark of individualism, self-reliance, dim-witted bravado, crutches for low esteem, and a status symbol with little justification. Nothing much has changed."

Souter also explores the rise of marksmanship and the development of competition. The 1874 Creedmoor competition revealed that the U.S. team only won on the last shot against an Irish team. On the frontier, Billy Dixon made a 1,538-yard shot at the Second Battle of Adobe Walls.[4] Yet in the American military, marksmanship declined with military appropriations after the Civil War. By World War I, Souter correctly observes, "Only the U.S. Marines were combat-ready marksmen."

The 1920s were a golden age for rifle clubs, with the advent of Camp Perry, Ohio, and shooting competitions. This was also a time of small-bore competitions with .22 caliber weapons. America also witnessed the development of the submachine gun in the form of the Thompson and the BAR (Browning Automatic Rifle). German handguns now entered the American market, and Luger, Mauser, and Walther models competed for sales. John Moses Browning—the father of the BAR, Colt 1911 .45 ACP pistol, and numerous machine guns—developed the 1935 FN Browning with a thirteen-round double-stacked grip magazine using the 9mm Parabellum cartridge popularized by Germany. The 1935 morphed into the Browning Hi-Power with a fifteen-shot capacity.

Souter's explanation of the relationship between hunting and guns quickened my pulse. He moves from hunting for survival to hunting and conservation. Hunting was a wilderness experience for many Americans. He even includes a personal story about a charging squirrel, which he finished off with a headshot. My experience was not so elegant. At East High School in Madison, Wisconsin, James Richard Beckman, Herschel Lloyd Weber, and I discovered the joys of squirrel hunting. We ventured out to unposted farmland near Cross Plains in search of squirrels and ruffed grouse. To have a chance at both, we took our 12-gauge shotguns into the field. When we found squirrels in trees, we frequently let loose with all we had and created the ten-shot squirrel. On one occasion, I saw a gray squirrel running from tree to tree about forty-five to fifty yards out and ventured a shot from my brother's 20-gauge double barrel. The squirrel immediately charged us with the ferocity of a wounded rhino. I declared, "Here he comes!" I fired the modified choke barrel to no avail. Weber opened up with his J. C. Higgins 12-gauge pump shotgun. One shot . . . two . . . three . . . four . . . five blasts, and on the squirrel came. Beckman, a budding chemical engineer, fired two at long range and then waited. When the squirrel was about six feet way, Beckman hit it square and cut it in half. Weber unloaded his weapon on the two parts left in the autumn leaves. We did not bag the remains.

World War II put the M1 Garand into the hands of the infantry, U.S. Marine Corps excepted. Souter writes that the infantry "sprayed as many bullets as possible where they thought the enemy could be found." He also notes, "The U.S. Marines operating in the Pacific were a different breed of cat." The Marines went ashore in August 1942 with 1903 Springfield .30-06 rifles, not M1s. The Marines stopped the Japanese with John Moses Browning–designed 1917 water-cooled machine guns.[5] Just ask a Marine about John Basilone and Mitchell Paige. You will find that machine guns and guts were the keys to victory.

The 1950s brought change. The National Rifle Association grew stronger. Women were far more visible using guns, although they were armed and proficient long before the Cold War.[6] Most Americans knew of the prowess of Annie Oakley.[7] Now more women were armed and competing. Pistol manufacturers expanded and met new competition from Sturm, Ruger. Eugene Stoner's M16 replaced the M14, and the military had a new weapon that in this century enabled women to enter combat effectively.

Souter's seventh chapter about the "me generation" resonated with my experiences in California, where social reformers tried to right every wrong by writing legislation, product liability litigation spilled over into guns. Overreacting to the Black Panthers, antigun legislators took guns out of the hands of citizens on the street. Antigun activists used statistics to "prove" their points, and citizens afraid of crime dove for cover despite all the statistics and reason to the contrary. As Harvard law professor Mark Tushnet has demonstrated, putting people in jail in Richmond, Virginia, cut homicide rates by one-third.[8] Tushnet also cited a 2003 Wisconsin Supreme Court decision reversing the conviction of Munir Hamdan for carrying a concealed weapon in his Milwaukee liquor store that had been robbed four times between 1993 and 1999. In 1997 Hamdan killed one robber in self-defense and killed another in 1999. The Milwaukee police enforcing the city's concealed weapon law arrested Hamdan. He was convicted, but "the Wisconsin

Supreme Court reversed Hamdan's conviction because prosecuting him for having a concealed weapon amounted to 'practically nullifying the right' to self-defense."[9]

Souter's chapter 8 continues his observations of guns and the people who would ban them. In the recent past, pistol bore diameter has expanded, and we have witnessed a revolution in shotguns and "muzzle-loaders," whose projectiles are now accurate at over one hundred yards. In the long-range category, .50 caliber Barretts and .338 Lapuas are now available to snipers in the military and civilians except in California because legislators banned them. In Montana antelope hunters now can reach out and touch their quarry at over one mile. Billy Dixon lives!

Souter concludes on a personal note: "Going out the door every day with a handgun on your hip or in your purse means we have failed our children and our schools and softened our moral backbone." 'Nuff said. Enjoy the read and think about the issues.

Gordon Morris Bakken
California State University
Fullerton

Introduction

This book needs an introduction to explain what it is not, and then we can get on with what it is. *American Shooter* is not a harangue about the Second Amendment and who can or can't own a gun. The Supreme Court finally settled that question on June 28, 2010. Besides, there are enough books on that subject to fill a long shelf at the library.

Our gun culture has grown from hunting for survival. It expanded with Manifest Destiny, it has defended and avoided law and order, it prosecuted the wars that have marked our political history, and it has responded to the lure of sporting competition. Guns have become a part of the social context within our growing population. Their importance has depended upon the distribution of that population, its education, racial composition, and deeply rooted traditions. Guns have also migrated into our political dialogue. This migration has included the bellowing finger pointers on both sides of the gun ownership issue who have managed to deconstruct our traditions for their own agendas and who claim to know what is good for us. They have created a steadily widening gap obscured by a heady mix of personal ambition, misdirected passion, and economic breakdown, resulting in total polarization. Both sides have failed to look hard at history, our development as a country, and their own goals.

The antigun crowd can look for validation of their position in the Volstead Act passed in 1919, which attempted to make the United States an alcohol-free country. This worked so well that it was repealed thirteen years later. On the other side, the progun advocates still suffer from the woof, huff, and stomp oversell that put them in an untenable box so often during their long and, for the most part, distinguished representation of the sport. Currently, and with increasing fervor, they espouse the position that whoever disagrees with pro-gun advocates is not a patriot.

Our gun culture is a rich heritage, shaped by the curious twists and turns of our country's growth. What has affected the current regard for gun ownership issues is the recurring unsettled nature of our immediate financial situation (shaky), political demands (unrealistic), terrorist concerns (overkill), and diminished living standards (self-inflicted). Through our carelessness, all of these elements have once again erupted. Too many people believe they are entitled to a quick fix. Gun ownership has always soared during stressful times whenever the power we want over our lives seems to be slipping away. This revisited perception is fortified by whichever self-serving pundit shouts the loudest.

I am the American Shooter in the title. My memories will pop up throughout this narrative and deliver the occasional, hopefully witty story, confession, embarrassing tidbit, or learning experience—most of it dealing with guns, but not all. Every person I meet starts out as a potential friend. The sport was the salvation of my youth. Its challenges gave me a sense of pride and accomplishment later on, and it has always been there, allowing me to resume my lessons (between bouts of making a living). I even earned a paycheck carrying a gun for a while. What really rings my bell is precision target shooting—paper punching—which continues today about five decades after I first squinted down a barrel at a black bull's-eye. I shoot rifles, smallbore and centerfire pistols, and shotguns on a trap range. My scores have been posted on the board in many rifle and pistol tournaments, and the first shotgun competition I fired in, I won. I've even won Thanksgiving turkeys by toeing the line and shooting at the mark like our colonial forbearers. The fast-draw fad of the 1950s and 1960s got my attention, slapping leather with a single-action Colt, thumb-cocking for each shot cowboy style. My hunting days ended when my dad passed away. They were more of an excuse to walk through the woods with him than to shoot any critter.

I am an average shot. I've lost a lot more brass than I've won, and a lot of clays have sailed away untouched. But I've always figured that I'll do better the next time, with practice.

I also managed to translate the shooting skills I learned into supporting myself and, with the help of Janet, my wife and colleague, taking care of our three kids until they had careers of their own. I traded a gunsight for a camera viewfinder. As a photojournalist, commonly called a shooter in the trade, I've followed my cameras all over the world to both beautiful and dangerous places. Hold, breathe, and squeeze. The skills remain the same, except the subject of my aim always walks out of the camera frame after the shutter clicks.

Curiously, my life has found parallels to the development of our gun culture, which I only recognized when I examined endless journals I've kept over the decades. During my travels across the United States, I have been lucky to walk where history was made. From Boston Harbor and the East Coast to Kings Mountain, I saw in my mind that desperate Revolutionary firefight and held in my hands von Steuben's original drill manual, which taught our colonials how to fight with a military musket. I've walked the Custer Battlefield at sundown and recently climbed among the rocks of Monument Valley, looking out across the rutted roads made by settlers' wagons. I've ridden a stagecoach out of Deadwood, South Dakota; prowled through what remains of Virginia City, Nevada; and contemplated an old-line shack that was once a Montana home. Buffalo grass grew in neat rows on what had been a garden, and field mice lived in a rusted Kalamazoo woodburning stove.

I was tear-gassed in Chicago in 1968 and dodged behind parked cars as bullets and bricks rained down on the city near the West Side. In downtown Belfast, Northern Ireland, machine gun bunkers laced over with barbed wire squatted on side streets where Saracen armored cars hunkered with their engines running. The dead, black eyes of gutted shops looked out beneath signs on plywood reading "Bomb Damage Sale." Everyone watched for snipers.

I've been a member of the National Rifle Association (NRA) since I was fifteen years old. Off and on, I've had to step away when food and rent took precedence over guns and bullets. I always came back when able. *American Rifleman* magazine is welcome in my house except for its editorial pages, which I tear out and file along with the antigun crowd's loopy studies and sweaty prognostications. That's why I needed to write this book.

The more I studied the journey of American firearms and their heritage as they have been part of our society, the more I thought about a third path based on coexistence. This solution has been in front of us for decades but has never been pursued on a scale that can challenge dusty, shopworn, and failed dogmas on both sides of the firearms controversy. Successful models exist that require only some guts and American entrepreneurial spirit to adapt and adopt. It's worth a shot.

Looking at our fractured gun culture since that first matchlock musket came ashore in the New World reveals a tapestry made of myth and truth, of insights and blunders that we accept as a piece of our wider culture. If I can tag along as a guy who was born into this rewarding sport and stayed the course, then that's what you have here. If somewhere between the "long-range shooting matches of the 1880s" and "an AR-15 rifle under your pillow" you have a laugh or two or learn something new, then cheers to you, friend.

1

A NEW CULTURE SHAPED BY OLD FEARS

My first gun, the one that reached beyond the imagination required by my previous battery of toy weapons, was my Hopalong Cassidy six-gun, ripped free of its wrapping paper at the foot of my tenth Christmas tree. It was silver and black and came in a black holster accompanied by a package of six cartridges. The revolver had a revolving six-shot cylinder and a loading gate on the right side of the frame that flipped open to reveal the chambers for the cartridges. Each cartridge was about .38 caliber in diameter and had a brass case that slid off the end of the zamac-cast bullet, allowing a green circular paper cap to be placed on the end of the bullet, which took up the entire interior of the case when the brass was slipped back on. Reassembled, the cartridge slid into a chamber in the cylinder. I had six shots—just like a real revolver—that exploded with satisfactory bangs at each squeeze of the trigger and drop of the hammer.

At ten years old, I was on the cusp of imaginary play with my pals in the old neighborhood on Chicago's South Side. The rigors of discipline required for grammar school, stamp collecting, model airplane building, and my Lionel electric train crowded out cowboy role-play games. Our bicycles had become passports to exploration, speed, and rushing in packs over the paths that crisscrossed the park next to Lake Michigan at Rainbow Beach.

The clumsy reality of having to take apart each cartridge, scrape off the crushed cap, replace it, and then reassemble the package to stuff it back into the cylinder after only six shots slowed our game. The cowboy stars in the movies and on my family's twelve-inch Zenith round-screen TV never reloaded. For us, roll caps snaked through our less-real cap pistols, with fifty shots coiling

1

up one at a time at each hammer fall, like a black-spattered ribbon as we fired. But the loud bang was only half of the event. Nothing came out of the muzzle. At least with my trusty pea-shooter (conceal-carried in my sock), I could blow a pea smack at the back of a girl's neck and make her jump with a yipe.

That Hopalong Cassidy cap pistol—my last toy pistol—failed to bridge the slippery ease of imagination and the messy clutter of reality. The shiny half weapon eventually joined my toy soldiers, toy automobiles, and hand puppets in the toy box at the foot of my day bed in the dining room of our one-bedroom apartment, and I got on with growing up.

How do I remember this epiphany-in-progress? I have a photo taken on that Christmas morning with me surrounded by my unwrapped treasures. The pistol in its handsome holster rests in the background with my model gas station, a football helmet (my dad never stopped hoping), and a set of intricate British cavalry soldiers in Horse Guards' bearskins and cuirasses. I'm smiling and about to throw a dart at an off-camera target. The sharp steel-pointed dart was my first missile of risky consequence. Still no gunpowder in sight, but it was a start. I began with small steps toward a path that eventually took me to a life of adventures and the four corners of the world.

Before the first European immigrants packed their bags and shipped out to the New World, marksmanship—propelling a missile at a target (animal, vegetable, or mineral)—had evolved from a survival skill to a warrior's weapon to a recreational sport. By the tenth century, the bow and arrow and the spear and sling earned bragging rights for individuals, communities, and whole nations as the skills evolved from military tactics to competitive tests, ending with a laurel wreath on the victor's brow instead of the loser's head on a spearpoint.

By the fourteenth century, the Germans' obsession with organization had gathered the most skilled of these sportsmen into social clubs—no ladies, please—for the purpose of handing out prizes to the top guns. And by this time, the "propelling" had reached the stage where gunpowder—offered in a recipe from Wu Ching Tsao in 1044—replaced muscle power. The Chinese had their "fire lance" launching balls from a bamboo barrel. Big guns first were used in the Battle of Metz in 1324 and were fired from iron slabs held together with iron barrel hoops like a rolled-up picket fence. Cast bronze barrels pumping out six-hundred-pound granite balls came along in the fifteenth century. Eventually, these big "bombards" shrank to become more personal missile launchers. Christopher Columbus carried one on the Santa Maria—an iron tube at the end of a long stick whose smoky boom told the official greeters on San Salvador that the neighborhood was about to change. Therein began the "culture" developed from the constant interplay between survival tool, military weapon, and sport that eventually swept across the ocean to the North American continent.

The shoulder-fired "gun" was at best a rip-roaring blaster that was as much a danger to the shooter as the selected target. The harquebus, or matchlock weapon, was little more than a pipe packed with gunpowder behind a stone or lead (or gold, if you were aiming at a king or prince) ball, crammed down into the barrel's breech to be touched off with a smoldering match. "Breech" came from twelfth century Middle English meaning the lower part of the human trunk, the rump, or the buttocks, and later resulting in numerous Freudian inferences—especially with the invention of the "breechloader" rifle. This blaster required the shooter to stuff the hot match into a touchhole while the long barrel up front was supported by a shoulder-high notched stick jammed into the ground.[1] The resulting blast from a squad of German *lands knechts* (mercenaries) clouded the battlefield in smoke long enough for pike and sword infantry to rush the enemy lines undetected for the close work.

By the time this weapon and the brave soul who manned it reached the shores of America—specifically Jamestown, Virginia, in 1604—the gun had been refined, had been tarted up with carved decoration, and had a "tricker," or trigger, attached to a spring to snap the lit match gripped in a "serpentine" into the waiting touchhole.[2] For a long time, however, its demonstrated flash and boom was enough to keep the Native Americans at bay. Besides devastating the occasional turkey or dropping a startled deer, it was the first military-type one-man missile launcher (save for the odd crossbow) to arrive on the Atlantic shore. A description of the matchlock and the man who carried it to guard a Virginia fort was penned in 1611: "He shall shoulder his piece, both ends of his match alight, and his piece charged, and primed, and bullets in his mouth, there to stand with a careful and waking eye, until such time as his Corporall shall relieve him."[3]

Or until he dozes off and chokes on one of those bullets. Admittedly, by the seventeenth century, the matchlock was old technology, but it was simple, relatively reliable, and could be repaired with basic hand tools of the time.

Precision shooting, as developed in Europe, was the domain of the wheel lock coupled with the rifled barrel. The wheel lock was a clockwork, wind-up motor that made one revolution when the trigger was tripped. This revolution caused a piece of iron pyrite clamped in a vise-like doghead to strike against a rotating wheel's serrated surface, sending a shower of sparks down into the gunpowder and firing the ball. Because wheel locks required between thirty-five and fifty separate handmade parts, it was a very expensive gun. Only the best gunsmiths knew how to build such a weapon, and only the richest landowners could afford to own one.

Paired with the wheel lock's precise mechanism was a barrel grooved along its interior length in a shallow spiral to impart a spin to the exiting ball. This rifling (from the Old High German *riffilōn*, meaning to saw or cut[4]) added a gyroscopic center to the ball's rotation, keeping the spinning projectile's path straight for a greater distance than tumbling down a smooth bore. The rifling concept was refined, as was the ball, over the next two hundred years until today's super-accurate rifles and pistols.

In America, the wheel lock was out of its depth. Humidity rusted its parts. Mud and dust clogged its mechanism, and the wheel's spindle was too frail for heavy use. If the shooter lost the spanner, which he carried on a thin chain or leather thong around his neck and which was needed to wind its spring-powered wheel, he was unarmed. Fortunately, another invention arrived during the late 1600s and early 1700s that made shooting practical for everyone and flooded across Europe and into the New World. The flintlock musket revolutionized the fighting army, the sport of shooting, and the work of putting food on the table.

Its works could not be simpler. A spring-held cocking piece gripped a flint. When the trigger released the spring and caused the cocking piece to snap forward, the flint stuck a concave strip of steel called a "frizzen." This collision produced the requisite shower of sparks that ignited a finely ground gunpowder in the priming pan and erupted a flame through a touchhole into the breech of the barrel where coarse gunpowder exploded, propelling the ball down the tube and out the muzzle. A good man with a smoothbore musket could get off three shots in a minute. Besides being more efficient, the flintlock was cheaper to make and easier to shoot. When coupled with a long-rifled barrel, the gun's accuracy trebled over the musket's smoothbore tube.

The infant gun culture in America then revolved around two considerations: the need for a gun and the ability to buy one. Anyone with a pulse could legally own one, but society was already establishing certain restrictions. First of all, citizens were subject to British laws written for their protection. Soldiers acted as city police and also manned forts in the wilderness recently seized from the French in 1763. In the cities along the Atlantic coast, colonials had lived elbow to elbow with the British courts, "lobsterback" soldiers, and "Friends of the King" (Tories) for years. The privates and corporals who patrolled the streets in pairs and squads often took part-time civilian jobs as laborers or as artisans' assistants to supplement their pay. When the red coats were hung on a peg, the soldiers were indistinguishable from the civilian population.

Everything hummed along until the mother country decided her colonies had to pay their fair share of taxes to relieve the huge debt caused by the Seven Years' War. In the American coastal cities, where the new taxes bit down hardest on trade while local appointed governments sought representation in the British Parliament to argue their case, the soldiers' armed presence suddenly became a threat.

The king's garrison troops marched about with "Brown Bess" muskets slung over their shoulders or carried openly with bayonets affixed when confronted with unhappy colonists. For civilians, to carry long-barreled flintlock rifles or muskets, funnel-muzzled blunderbusses (from the Dutch word meaning "thunderpipe") favored by coachmen to defend against highway thieves, or outrageously expensive pistols was awkward in polite urban society. Gunpowder leaked from priming pans and stained expensive waistcoats, and pockets stuffed with lead ball cartridges spoiled the line of a gentleman's suit.

The dueling code had become frowned upon in the northeastern communities, though in the South a man's honor against insult was defensible by blazing away at each other on some early morning dewy field. Laws were enacted. For example, the Colony of Massachusetts passed An Act for the Punishing and Preventing of Duelling in 1719,[5] but still, old habits among gentlemen were hard to break.

Heavy shoulder arms were a clumsy package to tote around during a shopping trip or on social calls. They also had a bad habit of going off half-cocked. It was against the law to discharge a gun in many colonial towns.

There was passed An Act to Prevent the Firing of Guns Charged with Shot or Ball in the Town of Boston. The Massachusetts legislature also banned hunting on Boston Neck, as "the limbs and lives of several persons have been greatly endangered in riding over Boston Neck, by their horses throwing of [sic] them, being affrighted and starting at the firing of guns by gunners that frequent there after game" in An Act to Prohibit Shooting or Firing Off Guns Near the Road or High-way on Boston Neck.[6]

Immediately outside the colonial cities, wilderness still ruled, but similar restrictions prevailed as farmland and town sites cleared away the shaggy forest. Hunting laws became necessary to preserve wildlife, as demonstrated in An Act for the Preservation of Deer, and to Prevent the Mischiefs Arising from Hunting at Unseasonable Times and An Act for the Better Regulation of Fowling.[7]

Reining a stubborn mule or ox towing a single-bottom plow down a furrow is hard enough without dealing with a firearm as well. Rifles and shotguns stayed in the farmhouse. The economics of firearms ownership dictated who could even afford such an expensive accessory. Hard money was difficult to come by, the Spanish real being the most valuable currency, and the guns were built one at a time, as was the English and continental custom. Parts from one rifle did not always interchange with another by the same maker without filing and tweaking the hand-fashioned piece. Gunsmithing was artisan's work. Barter and trade were the more common methods of exchange in the countryside, so considerable collateral was required for a fair deal.

A smoothbore musket was the favorite firearm of choice. It could double as a hard-ball-firing gun for bringing down deer, and when loaded with small shot, it became a turkey, duck, or goose gun. These muskets were inaccurate due to the smooth tube barrel and the need for the ramrod to easily seat the somewhat smaller diameter ball over the powder for a quick reload. Ease of loading meant that the ball rattled around on its way out to emerge from the muzzle. A buck deer standing a hundred yards from the shooter might be struck anywhere on his body by a musket-discharged ball.

Farther beyond the cities' suburban farms, where the Vast Unknown of forests, mountains, and rivers lured adventurous explorers and vagabond trappers and hunters called mountain men, shooting became a survival skill. Where bears, cougars, and wolves could kill or cripple a man hundreds of miles from civilization, a keen eye, cool head, and a Pennsylvania long rifle were necessary. German gunsmiths who settled in that state and in Virginia around 1710 built these lightweight, smaller-caliber flintlocks. Whether you were bagging a deer across a broad meadow or discouraging a Native American raiding party, the spiraling grooves cut into the rifle's barrel allowed the tight-fitting ball to be on target at three hundred yards from discharge. If this firearm had any faults, its cumbersome length was one of them. German gunsmiths began producing rifles with barrels no longer than 30 inches. Measured from the ground to the owner's chin, the Pennsylvania rifle used a long barrel for good reasons: the extra barrel length gave the powder a longer time to burn, thereby increasing muzzle velocity. This added speed and imparted greater stopping power to the smaller-caliber ball out at three hundred yards. On the other hand, it might take a rifleman a full minute to load, ram, prime, and cock his weapon, while a musket could fire three shots in that time. The saving grace was that a line of ten men with aimed rifles could consistently hit ten targets at a hundred yards or more, while ten men with muskets could only hope for half as many hits on a good day.

Familiarity with firearms and owning personal weapons for self-defense had a long, uneven history in Britain and transferred to her American colonies. The British never had a standing army until the seventeenth century or a professional police force until the nineteenth century. The king or queen was always dependent on titled peers to raise troops to fend off invasions or invade when required. As authority rolls downhill, the landholding peers kept a ready militia made up of able-bodied men who actually worked the land. According to English law, these men were required to own a weapon and marching kit and to be ready to muster at the lord's command. There was a great distrust of a standing army under sole control of the monarch. Rulers had a nasty habit of invoking their divine right through force of arms at the drop of a gauntlet.

When weapon technology moved beyond the efforts of the local smithy to create a pike, an ax, a halberd, or arrowheads for a yew longbow, the expense of arming a militia went up. Firearms required straight tubes, slow-burning matches, lead shot, and gunpowder, not to mention casting cannon-size artillery that fired iron and stone balls. The monarchy feared armories of weapons that could be used in a popular uprising, which might spread around the kingdom. The crown did attempt to hold down the number of gunpowder and match producers. However, any neighborhood alchemist knew that brewing gunpowder and impregnating slow matches with saltpeter was hardly rocket science; it was saltpeter (potassium nitrate) that contributed oxygen to the burning process. The chemical was reduced from animal urine into a crystalline substance. A better source was donated by a local wino after stumbling out of the corner public house. With an ample supply of wine imbibers and many domestic animals about, available stocks continued to grow.[8] In 1553 Edward VI tried to account for "all persons who shoot guns," registering their names with local law enforcement. Unregistered firearms disappeared into corncribs, under floorboards, and down dry wells. Elizabeth I suggested that the government would be happy to store the militias' firearm caches and powder supplies. That ploy also failed, bringing forth suggestions for less government control rather than more. One law did stick: only the gentry could own handguns, meaning any firearm with a barrel shorter than one yard in length.

By the time of Charles I, unrest over the king's policies was verging on uprising. To remove the problem of well-armed, grouchy peasants on the march, new laws stated that owning arms had always been a conferred duty, not a right. All guns were ordered removed from every Englishman except those landholders who owed their fealty to the king. This seizure was enacted ostensibly to reduce the loss of wild game by restricting all hunting only to the landed gentry.[9] The rising became a civil war, and Charles I lost his crown and his head.

Eleven years later, Charles Stuart returned from exile to become Charles II, following the grumpy Cromwell and reopening the saloons and dance halls. Called the Merry King, Charles II proceeded to whip together a strong central army on the sly. He managed to create militias within the crown's authority with the help of a servile Parliament, and he carefully weeded out enemies within the court and purged disloyal sheriffs and justices who might cause trouble from their towns. While accomplishing this political cleansing, homes were canvassed, and hundreds of muskets seized. Then troops of the new Crown Militia marched in and tore down the town halls. They kept weapons collected by the touchy peasants, returned privately owned weapons to the gentry with apologies, and settled into local barracks.[10] With the establishment of the Game Act and the Militia Act, Englishmen were essentially stripped of firearms. Subsequent monarchies continually fiddled with strengthening this status quo.

Eventually, the Declaration of Rights presented to William and Mary in 1689 gave firearms back to the people—if they were Protestants. Catholics

("Papists") continued to be hounded from pillar to post. By the time the matter came to America's Constitutional Convention, the right to bear arms was so circumspect in the English Declaration model as to be useless.

In the colonies, all was not struggle and strife. The immigrants arriving daily from the continent brought their shooting clubs with them. Landed gentry who could afford the clockworks rifles used in wheel-lock accuracy contests adapted well to the new flintlocks. These rifle matches and clubs accommodated the colonial upwardly mobile middle class as well as the British conservative elite.

Shooting contests—usually one-shot affairs—were cobbled together, and colonials banged away at elaborately decorated targets during celebration of holidays and other festivities. Men—once again no ladies, please—gathered to admire and test the latest in firearm technology. While most of the guns were British, Dutch, or French, a few American models of the Pennsylvania or Virginia design were building a reputation.

Among the less well-heeled farmer and landowner class, marksmanship contests consisted of shooting at the mark. An *X* or *V* would be painted on a slab of wood, and each shooter would toe a line and fire to hit the center of the *X* or notch the crotch of the *V*. Instead of sherry, tea, and cakes served by the town ladies, the rustics favored corn whiskey, applejack, and a steer slowly turned over a pit fire, along with a slice of pandowdy.

As a young man of sixteen, I had the opportunity in 1965 to attend a turkey shoot held in a field in Palos Heights, Illinois, just before Thanksgiving. What was interesting was the chance to experience the gulf between riflemen and shooters using the equivalent of a musket. My dad and I thought it would be fun to try to fetch our traditional bird the old-fashioned way. The morning air was chilly and fall leaves crisp under foot when we crunched into the gravel parking area behind the firing lines and unloaded our rifles from the trunk.

Sharing anything with my dad was a rare event in my life, because the nature of his work as an electrical engineer and troubleshooter kept him always on call. He wore a brown fedora hat with a rakish snap-brim and had been a handsome young sailor when he married my mother, just out of her teens, in the 1930s. He was still slender during most of my childhood, with a cigarette constantly tucked into the corner of his mouth that caused his right eye to squint from the curling smoke. He had small hands and smaller feet, like miniature skis sheathed in size eight triple-A shoes. I inherited his whip-crack temper and the "Souter nose." The rest of me followed my mother's model: short, impatient, and inclined to stockiness, with soft teeth and weak eyes. Half of me was a mystery, because my mother had been adopted as an infant. Whenever I walked or talked with Dad, I felt I was being measured. I think most boys are lumbered with that critical examination and pass the flinty eye on to their sons.

As we sorted out where to go to sign in and learn the rules, the constant "snap!" of .22 caliber rifles firing toward distant targets caused a shiver of excitement. At one firing line, ten shooters lined up for each shoot-off, and each competitor paid $2 per shot to try to hit closest to the center of the round bull's-eye (about the size of a quarter) fifty feet downrange. The winner of the shoot-off received a frozen fifteen-pound turkey from a parked refrigerator truck. The shooters were a mix of teenagers and adults dressed in farm and hunting clothes, and there was a lot of good-natured trash talk. "Don't you go an' shoot yourself in the foot now, Donald." "The other end goes against your shoulder, Bob." They all carried their hunting rifles, a motley collection of lever-action, bolt-action, pump, and semiautomatic squirrel and rabbit guns.

Dad bought a cup of coffee, and I got cocoa from a table tended by some wives with baked goods for sale and freshly made cider poured from big plastic jugs. We watched a couple of firing lines step up, shoot, and produce a winner. Gun smoke and winter breath were caught up and snatched away by a light breeze across a prairie scoured of corn shucks. Finally, with my $2 paid, I took my place facing the target frames. I was last to shoot.

Each shooter was handed one bullet to be loaded only on command. One by one the shooters fired, with only one or two nicking the black circle. My turn came, and I hefted my rifle—a Remington Model 37 Rangemaster borrowed from my rifle club's rack. The same make of rifle had just swept most of the first place medals at the NRA National Rifle & Pistol Championships in Camp Perry, Ohio. I fired, and the range officer announced that I had missed the paper entirely. There was a pause, and then his voice barked over the public address system, "No, wait, the last shot was dead center. We have a winner."

My target was stamped, and I took it to the refrigerated truck to collect our bird. Dad decided to try his luck with our stubby Mossberg .22 carbine on the other firing line, where more distant cardboard turkey heads were mounted on a fence and each shooter got three shots to hit one. He nicked one, but it wasn't good enough to win us a second bird.

I felt a little guilty going home with that big frozen turkey in the car trunk. My club's rifle—Remington's best model at that time—so outclassed all the other firepower on that firing line that I felt a bit like a cheat. But Thanksgiving dinner still tasted sweeter. The following year, the Palos Heights folks set up a separate shooting category for "special target" rifles, and I got shaded by a fifteen-year-old girl with a bull-barrel Winchester wrapped in a custom stock. She smiled at me, and I am sure I turned the color of a watermelon slice. Dad took a turn in the three-shot turkey-head class with our Mossberg carbine again, and he won the bird, which he never let me forget. Nor did he ever let me forget that he could have lit his cigarette off any patch of my flaming face after that girl bathed me with her triumphant grin.

While a tradition of keen marksmanship developed in the states of Virginia, North Carolina, and Pennsylvania, the majority of the country relied on scatterguns and cheaply built trade muskets for hunting, which became more sport than necessity as domestic farm animals proliferated and the Native Americans were driven further west. When friction between the colonies and King George III flamed into a shooting war, it was the farmers, storekeepers, and hired hands who first confronted the British as the regulars marched on Lexington and Concord in 1775.

The express purpose of the seven hundred royal grenadiers and light infantry commanded by Lt. Col. Francis Smith of the 10th Lincolnshires and Maj. John Pitcairn of the Royal Marines was to confiscate muskets, powder, and a pair of brass cannon stored at Concord. They were also directed to arrest Samuel Adams and John Hancock, who were staying at the Reverend Jonas Clarke's parsonage in Lexington. Thanks to the hard riding of patriot-propagandist-silversmith Paul Revere and other riders galloping out from Boston, the countryside was alerted that "the regulars are out!"

This first confrontation between the British and the colonies' loosely conceived militias proved one thing: the Americans were in no state to conduct a proper war. According to minuteman Amos Barrett, "a veritable furnass [*sic*] of musquetry" rained down on the British troops retreating back along the road to Boston and pausing to set fire to homes and roust villagers.[11] During the retreat, the numbers of colonial militiamen doubled and trebled, reaching two thousand at one point. At least eight times, mobs of farmers fired in ragged musket volleys at the retreating British. According to contemporary accounts, no one in the various militias fired a weapon.

If the myth of flinty-eyed marksmen was true, then not a redcoat should have been on his feet from that "furnass of musquetry" when Lt. Gen. Hugh Percy, 2nd Duke of Northumberland, arrived from Boston with his rescue force of one thousand British regulars and pumped cannon fire into the retreating colonists. By the time militias from nearby communities arrived, a force of four thousand colonists was blazing away. The British suffered about 270 killed and wounded in the encounter. The only real redeeming quality that kept future battles close to evenly matched was the minimal musket training given to the conscripted British troops. Their officers came to rely on the shock of the bayonet charge rather than marksmanship with the Long Land Pattern musket, commonly known as Brown Bess.

In truth the American War for Independence did rely on militias between 1775 and the surrender of Cornwallis at Yorktown in 1781, but their performance was uneven and too often sadly predictable. Until the men were put under the command of good officers, learned to deal with the military muskets, and mastered the disciplined fire of continental warfare, they could only strike and run from the rigorous combat formations of British regulars.

In Boston, when Gen. George Washington took command of the mass of men who were to become his army, he was shocked. In his writings, he disparages Bostonians as a grubby, uncouth lot not acquainted with the rudiments of good hygiene; the volunteers from the South as undisciplined; and only the citizen-soldiers from Rhode Island turned out in uniforms and with proper tents. Eventually, he had a chance to observe his strung-together collection of armed civilians on the firing line, letting fly at the enemy. He discovered to his horror that the average American soldier hefting a smoothbore musket could not hit the ground with his hat. They were wretched shots. Many turned their face away from the enemy as they squeezed the trigger, letting God direct the path of their ball and absolving themselves of the taking of another man's life. Others hung good luck charms from their trigger guards to guide their launched missiles.

Ineffective gunfire had a double curse for the colonials. Gunpowder could not be wasted, because powder mills that churned out any quantity of consistent explosive quality were few and far between. Loose powder was easily spoiled by wet weather, scattered by wind, and detonated by careless handling. Only gunpowder shipments from France totaling hundreds of thousands of pounds, along with crates of French Pattern 1728 muskets, kept the Continental Army in the field.

Desperate to stop the rank-on-rank advance of British fire and bayonets into his lines with the resources he had available, Washington signed off on the use of "buck and ball" for his men. Ammunition for the troops was supplied as cartridges—cylinders about the length and thickness of an index finger, made of paper or linen and twisted closed at each end. They were carried in a belt-hung leather box fitted around a block of wood drilled with holes for the cartridges and protected by a leather flap. The shooter removed the cartridge, tore off the end with his teeth, and dumped the gunpowder and ball down his barrel, followed by the wadded-up paper or linen container—all thrust down with the ramrod carried beneath the barrel. He either poured a bit of the cartridge powder into the priming pan beneath the steel frizzen or used a finer ground powder carried in a horn on a leather thong around his neck.

The American buck-and-ball load dumped down the barrel contained one .69 caliber lead ball about the diameter of a nickel, plus three .30 caliber buckshot. This shotgun spray of lethal projectiles ripped into the advancing British with such violence that survivors of an American volley often bayoneted wounded American soldiers as war criminals. Use of the buck-and-ball cartridge was strictly against the "rules" for civilized warfare in Europe. Those rules also prohibited the use of snipers, considering such long-range marksmen to be skulking murderers. At the Battle of Saratoga in 1777, American long-rifle militiamen were used specifically to pick off British officers and noncommissioned officers to disrupt the battlefield chain of command. Captured long-rifle sharpshooters were also bayoneted as a matter of course, befitting a cold-blooded, stalking killer.

Even the term "militia" took on a different meaning as greater numbers of crack shot "longshirts" came down from the mountains and returned from distant prairies with their rifles. Organized under American generals such as Daniel Morgan, who knew the militia's strengths and weaknesses—the long rifle could not mount a bayonet and was slow to load, so retreating after firing on an advancing line was prudent—the militiamen savaged the British at

Saratoga. In South Carolina, they were victorious at Cowpens and were the sole American force of mountain men at the slaughter of a mixed regular and Loyalist army atop Kings Mountain.

As can be seen, the concept of a militia was flexible from colony to colony, but one fact appears to be common to all: not having the cash or the trading power to obtain a decent musket was no obstacle to serving. Even though the Revolutionary government was constantly scrambling to obtain weapons from France and the Netherlands through dummy trading companies, armed militias managed to fill gaps in the line until the Continental Army was equipped to meet the British on level footing. Following the English model described earlier, armories were created in many villages before 1775 to provide muskets, powder, and shot to local lads who had no such resources. A typical instance of such foresight is noted in the Public Records of the Colony of Connecticut:

> That each inhabitant so enlisted shall be furnished with good fire-arms, and that the fire-arms belonging to this Colony, wherever they are, shall be collected and put into the hands of such enlisted inhabitants as have not arms of their own; and that each enlisted inhabitant that shall provide arms for himself, well fixed with a good bayonet and cartouch box, shall be paid a premium of ten shillings; and in case such arms are lost by inevitable casualty, such inhabitant providing himself as aforesaid shall be allowed and paid the just value of such arms and implements so lost, deducting only said sum of ten shillings allowed as aforesaid.[12]

As the war dragged on, the signers of the Declaration of Independence galloped from town to town ahead of the British forces—and the hangman's noose—while Washington managed one "fighting retreat" after another. While these first lawmakers of the not-yet-independent country bundled their baggage and reams of documents into coaches and stuffed saddlebags with their shaving kits and spare wigs, they found time to draft the Articles of Confederation that shaped our first government. When Parliament ran out of patience, money, and public support for the war, Cornwallis's defeat at Yorktown in 1781 seemed a good time to pull out. The 1783 Treaty of Paris closed the book on the thirteen colonies and opened the first chapter of the United States of America.

Establishing a two-hundred-year tradition, the U.S. Army was disbanded down to a token force, as the Articles of Confederation required each state to create its own army. The fear of a strong central government led to the creation of thirteen virtually independent states, each controlling its own trade, politics, monetary systems, and self-determination. The Articles proved to be a disaster, and the United States became the sick sister of the world's governments. Thanks to the hard work, deft arguments, and devious machinations of Alexander Hamilton and James Madison, a uniting constitution was created and finally signed on September 17, 1787. This powerful document included a Bill of Rights made up of the first ten amendments to the universal provisions. The first of these amendments guaranteed, "Congress shall make no law respecting an establishment of religion, or prohibiting the free exercise thereof; or abridging the freedom of speech, or of the press; or the right of the people peaceably to assemble, and to petition the Government for a redress of grievances."

The Second Amendment, born of the possible future need to once again to call upon an armed citizenry for the defense of our hard-won liberties, read, "A well regulated Militia, being necessary to the security of a free State, the right of the people to keep and bear Arms, shall not be infringed."

Some state constitutions considered a full-time standing army to be an uneasy threat. The following text appeared in the declarations of New York, Virginia, Vermont, and Pennsylvania: "That Standing Armies in time of Peace are dangerous to Liberty, and ought not to be kept up, except in Cases of necessity; and that at all times, the Military should be under strict Subordination to the civil Power."

That the Second Amendment's language appeared on the heels of the guarantees of freedom of religion, speech, assembly, and a free press cited in the First Amendment signifies how important a future call to arms figured in the priorities of the founders. The United States had reinvented itself from a jumble of sodbusters, herders, shopkeepers, ditch diggers, artisans, scholars, and bureaucrats into a force that fought the greatest land army in the world to a frustrated standstill. Then everyone shed their uniforms, stacked their muskets, and went away, back to their families, fields, shops, and offices.

But the founders wanted to be sure, if need be, that the citizens could do it again. So the federal government guaranteed the "right to keep and bear arms" in writing. As with the English Bill of Rights drawn up in 1689, the authors of the American version realized the importance of creating an unambiguous and unqualified statement of that right. Unlike the English version one hundred years earlier, the "right" extended to all American citizens (which did not include women, slaves, tenant farmers, and indentured servants—all of whom were property to varying degrees). The authors also had a much closer relationship to the history of their mother country and the consequences of stripping the means of self-defense from the people. In 1789 that means was as important when it was brought to the village green at the ringing of the church bell as it was in the hands of the householder at his own doorstep.

With the states' jaundiced eyes still fixed upon sweeping federal pronouncements, that amendment would be subject to a variety of interpretations by elected and appointed voting bodies over the next two-hundred-plus years. Its implications also advanced from sober judgments considered with the civility of intelligent men and women to the passionate bellows of overwrought apostles of doom using fear to sway mobs of labeled "liberals" and "patriots"—on both sides of the question.

It did not take long to realize the fallacy of a weak standing army when in 1812 President James Madison listened to the war hawks in Congress and declared war on Great Britain once again. During the Napoleonic Wars, British ships had intercepted American trading vessels and pressed American sailors into the Royal Navy. To punish the British for interfering with U.S. trade and citizens, an expeditionary force was assembled to head north and invade Canada while a seaboard "navy" of a few heavy frigates engaged the Royal Fleet on the seas and another freshwater navy was built on the shores of the Great Lakes. That the United States survived the conflict as a free nation and not a reunited British colony was a matter of luck, a few courageous individuals, and slow communications.

The Canadian adventure was a disaster fueled by poor leadership. The land war was punctuated by massacres of civilians by Native American allies of the British, such as the Fort Dearborn tragedy in Illinois, and embarrassing defeats as troops tried in vain to cross the Niagara River in New York. Only the dogged persistence of Adm. Oliver Hazard Perry and his home-built gunboats during the battle on Lake Erie scored a victory for U.S. arms. Perry's famous 1813 declaration, "We have met the enemy and he is ours," made up for the burning of Washington by a British raiding force in 1812, which had sent President Madison and his wife, Dolley, fleeing into

Maryland to set up a government in a tavern. While the land war was going badly, the frigate *Constitution* carved a swath though the Royal Navy, either sinking or outrunning everything under sail until she was bottled up in a foreign port.

The British siege of Baltimore's Fort McHenry was a failure and inspired our national anthem from the pen of Francis Scott Key and the stitching together of one really big flag. But, once again, the British could not deliver the killing stroke, and everyone backed away a step until the Treaty of Ghent was signed in Belgium at Christmastime in 1814.

Sadly, slow communications did not get the word of peace to Andrew Jackson down in New Orleans in January 1815. Another British raiding party landed at the edge of a swamp below the city. Ranks of regulars and Highlanders marched toward the American redoubts and trenches manned by a motley collection of soldiers and civilians, including freedmen, Cajuns, and bayou pirates—essentially a ragtag militia. The British advanced with drums, guts, bayonets, the skirl of bagpipes, and the snap of battle flags. Secure behind prepared earthworks and cotton-bale defensive positions, American marksmanship—improved by men who had much practice with their personal arms—and Jackson's imposed discipline shredded the invader's ranks and soaked the swamp in British blood. When the dense clouds of gunpowder smoke drifted away, the British were allowed to collect their dead and wounded and sail home, leaving behind the legend of Old Hickory's great battle, won after the war had ended.

In 1798 Eli Whitney signed a contract to produce ten thousand "stands of arms" for the U.S. government in two years. He wrote: "A good musket is a complicated engine and difficult to make—difficult of execution because the conformation of most of its parts correspond with no regular geometrical figure."[13]

A completed stand of arms includes the musket, its bayonet, and its ramrod. The fifty separate pieces that make up this package had to be created from raw metals and woods by a series of "engines" designed by the water-powered Whitney Armory located on the Mill River in Hamden, a suburb of New Haven, Connecticut. This brilliant feat of combining the machine's ability to perform repetitive tasks over and over again with precisely the same outcome, a knowledge of metallurgy to maintain consistency of production quality, and a superior organizational ability helped introduce mass production to the manufacturing process in the United States. As it was, Whitney decided to experiment with this process after creating the cotton gin, which changed the economy of the southern states, and chose firearms for his product.

Until mass production became practical, every firearm was made one at a time by hand, and the parts were individually formed to fit a specific gun. Thomas Jefferson had heard of Honoré Blanc, who had developed a method for producing interchangeable parts in France. Jefferson was not unaccustomed to risk, a trait demonstrated later when he defied Congress to send Meriwether Lewis and William Clark west to explore his Louisiana Purchase. He was also an inventor and saw in Whitney a kindred spirit who had already shown his ability to find solutions.

In the eighteenth and early nineteenth centuries, the art of gunsmithing required a long apprenticeship, learning how to wrap or draw steel to become a barrel, forge each metal part from the serpentine cocking arm to the concave steel frizzen, and handle the many springs and screws. The stock was a complex carving from buttplate to bayonet lock. Since Europe held a monopoly on fine gunsmiths, they were careful not to let these artisans immigrate to other countries. The shortage of gunsmiths in the United States forced Whitney to think of processes where men could be trained to operate a machine that would use jigs and cams to precisely regulate its cutting and shaping pattern.

Whitney's ability to produce a musket had not been tested by January 1801. He had not produced a single musket, and the government's patience had run out. Here, the story gets a bit murky. Allegedly Whitney took some of the gun parts that his company had produced and brought them to Washington, D.C. There, in front of an august body of judges, including President John Adams, future president Thomas Jefferson, the secretaries of war and treasury, and leading congressmen and military officers, Whitney waded into the boxes of parts and, with only a screwdriver, began assembling muskets. Minimum hand filing was required for final fits, but his machine tool–produced parts had been turned out to tolerances of 1/30th of an inch, which was exceptional for the early nineteenth century. This is the legend.[14]

In more recent times, historians secured a few surviving Whitney muskets from this period and stripped them down to test their parts' interchangeability. It seems, according to Merritt Roe Smith, one of the foremost authorities on the history of arms manufacture, that Mr. Whitney had fudged the 1801 test, supplying previously mated (and marked) parts to give the appearance of being randomly selected. This rigged demonstration bought Whitney a new contract and additional funding to allow him to finish building the machine tools and eventually supply the muskets.[15]

Ultimately, though it took him ten years to complete the two-year contract, he built a complex, handcrafted musket and made it affordable. This application of machine-made parts assembled by professionals helped spread the concept to other industries and specifically to the firearms makers. These tool operators and machine designers, in turn, formed the firearms industry, and their products became available to a much larger buying public.

From the introduction of the flintlock trade musket and handmade rifle in the early 1700s to the last Whitney musket that rolled off his assembly line in 1808, the firearm in America evolved from an expensive military tool and one-of-a-kind sporting toy for the rich to a mass-produced commodity. The firearms manufacturers, with their ability to supply hunting rifles and fowling pieces for working-class Americans, as well as muskets for war, became a factor in American society, which brushed against the morality of expediting control over life and death. This spread of guns was questioned from more than a few pulpits, both religious and political.

Whether we liked it or not, the intellectual creation of our republic and the practical needs of its inhabitants created the all-pervasive "gun culture." The available gun became a tool desirable for many different applications, from survival and sport to defense and attack. What had to be asked was, how much of this freshly planted and rooted gun culture could we afford to accept?

2

HEADING WEST: PROPHETS OF INDIVIDUALISM

The nineteenth century was a time of migration, innovation, and calculated extermination. Innovation brought civilization and all its encumbrances to the western wilderness, and invention perfected technologies of communication, transportation, and—since our subject is gun culture—the firearm mechanism. The spreading capabilities of mass production brought down the cost of clothing, feeding, transporting, and arming Americans.

The U.S. government was virtually powerless to protect American pioneers, merchants, explorers, and speculators once they crossed the Missouri River and the Kansas-Missouri plains. Americans became "Texicans" as they built ranches and towns in Mexico territory, and settlers arrived by wagon and by ship in the bays along the California coast. And everywhere, Native Americans and Spanish grandees watched the flood first with curiosity, later with suspicion, and finally with loathing as they realized the objectives of western expansion. Guns were everywhere.

From the boom of a Hawken flintlock rifle taking down an antelope in the Dakotas to the sharp bark of a gambler's derringer in a riverboat's saloon, firearms were part of life's texture in the West. Vast herds of bison flowed over the landscape, and rivers curved snakelike in mountain-fed rushes across the trails. Above, the pioneers' roof was the huge sky until the crags of the Rockies and Sierra Nevada marched into view like an opposing army.

In the summers of 1969 and '71, we headed west with our two daughters and three cats, packed into a Volkswagen minibus with tents, a stove, provisions, and our cameras, to find stories contracted for magazines. We went out of our way to drive the back roads, ending up in one wilderness KOA (Kampgrounds of America) where the owner offered us rifles to shoot at prairie dogs. Why would anyone shoot a prairie dog except to look at something that was alive a second before you pulled the trigger and dead a second after? We also rented some horses and rode out among the coulees and ridges of the country until Janet's nag trotted her into a fly-infested bush and refused to back out.

With the girls bundled in life preservers, we shot rapids down the Yellowstone River in rubber rafts, watching the naked rock and gravel banks rush past and getting soaked when bow waves slapped over the sides. On the next day we discovered bison at a ranch and looked into their red eyes, smelled their dusty musk, and watched in horror as one charged Allison, age four, with his huge horned head. It slammed into the wire fence a foot from her, and she sat down hard on the ground, looking insulted and fingering the blob of hot bison snot on her pink jacket.

Not wanting my children to go to their graves with a fear of buffalo, we bought a Jeep tour of the herds, and our guide drove us out into the plains, bumping along until we were in the middle of a dozen or so animals. They munched, pooped, grunted, rolled in the dust, farted, and went about their buffalo business and considered us just another buffalo—maybe a rather ugly one—who had joined their group. We returned from the adventure brimming with new buffalo knowledge, and on exiting the Jeep, I stepped into a fresh buffalo chip. While standing there, I explained to my brood how the pioneers used a dried version of this plentiful commodity in place of firewood. As I scraped off my boot before heading back to camp, my daughters became fixated on buffalo chip questions—for the next five hundred miles.

After the rodeo in White Sulfur Springs, Montana, we camped in a big silence that stretched for miles in all directions, hung a hose in a tree notch, and washed the arena dust from our hair. The next morning we rode in a battered pickup truck to a very old log-line shack that had been a settler's cabin. Inside was a magnificent Kalamazoo cast-iron, wood-burning stove that over time had become a home for various critters. It had been freighted from Michigan in the 1850s and was the pride of the family that had planted the garden out back and built the watering trough out front. In the quiet heat of midday, it seemed as if the people were still out there, hoeing the garden rows. They stacked greasy sagebrush for stove kindling, sharpened an ax blade, and lifted a pan of corn dodgers from the oven all the while dressed in homespun and denim beneath sweat-stained straw hats. Another family was there, too—the ones from the 1920s who had driven the rusted-out Ford, now without doors or windows, sitting on cinder blocks in the side yard like something ancient and prehistoric. When we got back to camp, Janet and I broke out our revolvers, and as we talked about what we had seen, we popped away at some salvaged fruit juice cans. The flat bang of each shot violated the quiet and reminded us we were just guests.

That time of hopeful exploration also produced frightful slaughter both military and civilian, as thousands of dead littered Civil War battlefields and thousands more lay butchered on the western prairies. Slow, single-shot long guns had given way to magazine-fed, lever-action Sharps and Spencer cartridge rifles. Volcanic pistols, Henry rifles, and Winchester lever-action carbines provided increased firepower. Colt and Remington perfected their cap-and-ball revolvers and, following Smith & Wesson's introduction of cartridges, moved on to bored-through-cylinder revolvers capable of pounding out six shots in half as many seconds. Following the Civil War, the land west of the Missouri River appeared to be one big armed camp.

The conclusion of that four-year slaughter in 1865 drove many more men and families west—anywhere to leave behind the devastation and rubble in the defeated South, where 60 percent of the population lived in poverty, and anywhere to leave behind the septic, toxic, industrial anthills that had been created among the crowded urban enclaves of the North. The end of hostilities freed up three million guns in the hands of men—and women with grit—who knew how to use them. The transcontinental railroad threaded its way from both coasts to meet in Utah, and surveyors scrambled across the Rocky Mountains and the Southwest, hammering home the stakes that equally ambitious rail projects would follow. Guns in the hands of hunters devastated the buffalo herds to feed the railroad workers rather than the Native Americans. Sharing the vast grasslands of the West with the bison and other grazers were roughly six million wild cattle in Texas alone. The longhorn steer was a hybrid of feral Mexican cattle that had bred with domestic stock. The open range provided free fodder to grow beef, and all that was needed were hands to round them up into herds. To meet this demand, about 35,000 cowboys showed up for on-the-job training. Many had been in army cavalry or horse-drawn artillery units or were born to the saddle as Hispanic vaqueros and had learned the peculiarities of the horse and life in the field.

At end-of-track railroad towns—usually built every eight miles—gandy dancers (Gandy was a company that made shovels) put down roots or just spent their pay and moved on to the next raw town site. Rows of tents became cattle towns as the great herds began moving by the thousands to these hardscrabble terminals. Long strings of cattle cars streamed into Dodge City, Ellsworth, Abilene, Wichita, Nebraska City, and other towns that erupted like saddle sores across the prairie. And there the cowboys arrived after months on the trail moving along thousands of really stupid cattle that thought of only three things: grass, water, and sex. The cowboy thought about food, whiskey, and sex—possibly leavened with a soft bed, a bath, and new clothes. He looked forward to a good meal after months of beefsteak, ground beef, jerked beef, beef stew, beef ribs, beef potpie, salt beef, and beans. And there, in a smelly dump of a cow town, the Great Cowboy and Six-gun Myth began.

Although the romantic West has been debunked in enough books to fill many library shelves, it is almost impossible to overstate the toxic pestholes these cowboys and citizens called home.

As a young boy, I grew up during the final years of the Chicago stock yards. On days when the wind blew down from the northwest—across the blocks and blocks of cattle, pig, and sheep pens; the tanneries and meatpacking houses; the large killing sheds with their churning ceiling fans; and the great mounds of dung mucked up to dry and make fertilizer—stomachs turned over in homes along Chicago's South Shore, and lunches went cold on the table. Windows slammed shut. All outdoor play stopped. Like a great rolling plague, the insidious, invisible stink settled around us, an odiferous hiss of doom, once smelled, never forgotten.

Multiply that wretched experience, which lasted maybe a day until the fickle Chicago wind shifted again, by a factor of proximity and a length of time in months. Besides bad food and the companionship of cattle, cowboys faced a career aboard a series of horses only a little brighter than those cattle and whose every instinct focused on fear and flight to survive. Everything a cowboy owned traveled in his saddlebags and maybe packed into a wagon bed. He had no health care plan and no pension or 401K. There were only so many jobs back at the ranch house for busted, arthritic, consumptive wranglers used up by their forties. He lived from payday to payday. And yet he was the symbol of freedom and individualism to the continuing flow of easterners seeking a new start. Cattle towns, mining towns, and towns that grew up around army forts were islands in the wilderness where these hopeful transients could rest, learn, and weigh their options.

In my middle years, my daughter Allison fell in love with the idea of horses. When she reached age twelve, I made the tactical error of putting her up on the back of a roan gelding with the cantering gait of an old rocking chair. I still have the photo of her aboard Big Red at the end of the trainer's lunge line, circling in the corral, leathers and irons trimmed high up the horse's withers to accommodate her short legs. Allison's joy and the romance of the mounted cowboy picked away at me until I succumbed a few years later and joined her at a riding school.

Week after week I led whichever school horse was assigned to me out into the barn's tacking hall, brushed the animal's coat, bent down, lifted each of the horse's legs, and used a hoof pick to clean muck (manure and mud mixed with straw) from around the inside of the horseshoes. (Note: a horse fart can blow your hat off and drain away your will to live for the rest of the day.) Next, the bridle was fitted over his head and the bit crammed into his drooly, toothy mouth. Buckles were adjusted from throatlatch to noseband and reins. Finally, the small leather patch that is the Hunter seat English saddle used in arena jumping competitions—no easy-chair, box-stirrup Western rig—was slapped on and the stirrup leathers notched up so you rode with a bent leg.

And then I, resplendent in leather chaps over high smooth boots, with hammerhead spurs, leather gloves, and hard shell helmet with chinstrap, mounted the beast. I did this virtually every week for two years. And then, when Caesar, a particularly recalcitrant brute with a Roman nose and nanosecond attention span, refused a low double-bar oxer fence, deciding instead to run out at the last moment and sending me over the fence sans horse, the time came to pack up my illusions. For a week, I seated myself with great care and walked gingerly, cursing the Purple Bruise of Caesar where the tobacco pipe in my back pocket had broken my fall. Never again would I be stepped on, crushed between stall wall and horse flank, drooled upon, farted at, nipped, or face-painted with a wet snort. The joys of the full gallop, canter, and trot; the clearing of a double oxer fence in a clean round; the ribbons I won—none of it was worth the servitude I lavished upon the ungrateful beasts.

My daughter still competes, riding her own horse now. He is a purebred Swedish Warmblood born Jet Light and now named Erik who has all the attributes of a large, silly dog bound up with a regal bloodline that transforms him into a champion when he enters the paddock, shivering with anticipation under the command of my lovely equestrian. My lessons taught me great respect for the cowboy and great sympathy for him as well. After months of viewing the world over the top of a nodding pair of hairy ears, I might also pull a cork on a bottle of Bust-head and hoorah down Main Street astride my cow pony with my Colt booming. Sounds like a great stress reliever.

From spring to fall when the Texas herds arrived, cow towns of the West shimmered beneath a miasma of secondhand cattle and horse feed, which was only somewhat less odorous than the big city slaughterhouses because every critter was still on the hoof. Steers panic at the slightest noise. Cowboys herded the cattle into the slatted rail cars by shouting, snapping whips, and beating on tin cans. Ramps into the cars became slippery slides as the frightened animals voided their bowels. For the townsfolk whose stores, businesses, saloons, and hotels were near the ramps and the pens, the prosperity of town life demanded a terrible price.

For the people's bowels, there were only outhouses offering gunnysacks of corncobs or the thin pages torn from an old Sears, Roebuck catalog hanging on a nail. Hygiene was marginal, since wash water was usually in scarce supply except from hand-dug wells or communal bathhouses. Indoor plumbing was a rare luxury, and water had to be heated on a wood-burning or coal-oil stove. Besides mercantile stores selling hardware and provisions, saloons provided the primary economic base, and their wares were notoriously second-rate. The beer was warm and the whiskey sudden and lasting in its esophagus-cooking effect.

Food came in a surprising variety depending on freight service, local hunters, availability of canned vegetables, and use of chili peppers where salt was too expensive or when saved for the cattle to force them to drink and increase their weight. Sugar was worth its weight in gold. Whiskey and beer were safer than the water, because of seepage from animal pens, drippage off tarpaper roofs, and outdoor toilets near the wells. Typhoid fever and smallpox were more dangerous killers than gunplay, and children were at great risk of a variety of poxes and fevers. Infant mortality rates were high, and married women aged rapidly as they bore large families to spread out the house or farm chores and to replace those who died.

Cowboys' trail clothes were virtually ready for burning by the time they reached trail's end. Their greasy leather chaps—stiff with cattle dung, cow snot, and powdered with calèche dust—stayed in camp or were tied behind their saddles. Tailors were often available at cow town terminals and ready for custom cutting or stocked with a small supply of ready-to-wear that required only alterations. Buying new boots was a traditional expense, so bootmakers employed large numbers of leatherworkers in their shops to cut custom lasts; they also hand-tooled gun belts, saddles, saddlebags, and gauntlets.

A tannery once crossed my path when I was assigned to photograph a middlin'-to-small town that was on a downhill slide. The chamber of commerce needed industries to move onto open tracts of land that bordered the central business district. The town into which I rode in my red rental Ford had two going concerns that generated revenue, but at a soul-sucking cost.

One was a tannery, and the other was a hog-rendering plant. I learned that there are experiences in life that defeat the English language. My first clue came when hotel management told me that under no circumstances was I to return through the front door when I finished my day's documentary work. The rear basement entrance was for me, as was the shower in this subterranean airlock, this bulwark between my post-livestock world and civilized society.

Cows do not smell good when they are walking around. Curing their hides in brine for twenty-four hours did not improve their olfactory impact. Photographing the huge sloshing vats from high beneath the ceiling of the beam house—where lime is added and chemicals remove the hair to produce nude, rubbery skins ready to become leather—shrivels the memory of duck-walking, wrapped in a yellow hooded slicker, beneath dripping, chain-hung, throat-slit pig corpses into a stroll through a dew-damp rose garden.

Sitting in the hotel dining room that evening, scrubbed pink and in fresh clothes, and contemplating a plate of gray stew, boiled potatoes, cauliflower, and a splash of red wine was like anticipating slippery labor at an autopsy table. So much for the romantic myth of the globe-trotting photojournalist, the vagabond man of mystery.

These freshened herders were the cowboys seen by most newcomers as six-shooter–toting cavaliers, trimmed in leather and silver conchos, rowdy and ready for a good time. These free spirits also became the characters written into pulp fiction that was devoured in the East. Engravings from tintypes, sketches, and talbotypes (early photos printed on paper) accompanied these stories as their authors plucked out specific gunfighters to mythologize. Wyatt Earp would have passed unnoticed as just another opportunistic thug without Ned Buntline's romantic tales in "penny dreadfuls" and Stuart N. Lake's semifictional *Wyatt Earp, Frontier Marshall*, written from Earp's dictation and published in 1931.

Duded up in new clothes and boots, bathed, and barbered, the cowboy faced the delicious prospect of a town built entirely for his needs and pleasures—and prepared to strip every hard-earned dime and peso from his jingling pockets. For instance, the town of Livingston, Montana, had only three thousand residents but boasted thirty-three saloons. In this atmosphere of cowboys with cash and proprietors who wanted it, a "them against us" sentiment prevailed, creating situations that could rapidly escalate from sarcasm to ancestral imprecations to threats and end with a cracked head or a bullet in the spleen. While gunplay was a last resort, improved technology since the Civil War had made reaching for a firearm an easier solution to settle grievances. An interpretation of the Second Amendment was not an issue when a fifth ace landed on the table.

Patented in 1835 in England and then in the United States in 1836, Samuel Colt's Paterson five-shot revolver trumped the single-shot and patented repeater firearms currently available. The revolving cylinder that lined up with a single barrel at each cocking of the hammer gave Texas Rangers fighting Native Americans and Mexicans near the border a decided edge. Ten years later, Capt. Samuel Walker of the regiment of Mounted Rifles fighting in the Mexican War suggested improvements. The Paterson design was enlarged and modified to produce the huge Walker Colt .44 caliber cap-and-ball weapon that established the basic revolver we use today.

These heavy guns that had to be carried in saddle holsters used percussion caps, loose powder, and ball loaded into each chamber of the five-shot cylinder. They were self-contained and, unlike the more basic Paterson model, did not require taking apart to be reloaded. A steel guard protected the Walker Colt trigger rather than the odd and fragile pop-up trigger of the Paterson Colt that appeared when the gun was cocked. The smooth curve of the grip allowed for natural aiming, and when out of ammunition, it was heavy enough to serve as a handy club.

From the Walker Colt came subsequent downsizings, such as the Dragoon, Army Model, and Navy Model designs, which adapted to personal belt holsters. Well-practiced shootist James Butler "Wild Bill" Hickock wore a brace of Colt revolvers during his careers as army scout, gambler, town lawman, stage actor, and professional drunk. The Colt Pocket Model of 1849 in .36 caliber was a particular favorite with town businessmen, who preferred its minimum bulk even if they sacrificed a man-stopping, heavy lead ball.

While walking about the cow town wearing a pistol was commonplace, especially for strangers who received a flinty eye from local law officers, some towns had their limits. The *Ellsworth Reporter* editorialized in 1873, "We protest against so much arming by our police. It may be well enough for our marshal and his assistants to go armed, but one six-shooter is enough. It is too much to see double armed men walking our peaceful streets. . . . One pistol is enough."

The breakthrough revolver design of this period was the small 1857 Smith & Wesson .22 caliber cartridge revolver that used a bored-through cylinder and copper-cased cartridges that loaded into the chambers. While the Smith & Wesson was little more than a toy, it became popular with Civil War officers as a last-ditch holdout weapon and threw open the door for the final addition to our present revolver design: self-contained ammunition. Following the Civil War, where the percussion-cap, loose-powder, and ball revolvers were popular on both sides, all subsequent designs used self-contained cartridges.

The old revolvers were converted to rimfire and centerfire cartridges by swapping out the percussion cylinders and adding some form of empty-case extraction. Rifles such as the Henry, Spencer, Burnside, Sharps, and Remington all used fixed ammunition. Brass shells that fit the new breech-loading shotguns also became available. Though the rifle and the shotgun were useful to bring down game for the campfire and cook stove, revolvers had only a narrow selection of uses: as a weapon of last resort in a life-or-death situation on the trail or to shoot people.

Eastern writers and journalists largely created the myth of the gunfighter in the middle of a dusty street, facing an opponent, both with hands twitching above the grips of their holstered six-guns. The reality was too mundane by far. Though the American gun culture had settled over the western states and territories like a well-fitting boot, it was largely utilitarian. Shotguns were the gun of choice for upland bird shooting, stagecoach strongbox guarding, small game hunting, and desperado threatening. Sodbusters and small ranch owners relied on shotguns or war-surplus rifles bought cheap. Native Americans prized anything that would shoot. They kept rifles repaired with rawhide and decorated them with brass tacks and beadwork.

Rarely did a pistol-packing hard case wish to try his luck against an 8-gauge sawed-off shotgun held steady at belt level. But the rifle was the true self-defense champion. A Winchester or Sharps rifle could drop a man at two hundred yards. At one hundred yards, a charging grizzly bear could be brought down with a blizzard of lever-fed .44-40s or the .50 caliber Sharps slug ahead of a handful of black powder. Who in their right mind, if given a choice, would select a revolver?

Most revolver action happened (and still does) at ranges of fifteen to thirty feet. In an enclosed space, after the first two or three shots, the billow of lingering black powder smoke was so thick that locating a target for follow-up shots was strictly guesswork. Speed in getting a revolver into action was less important than "getting the drop," according to lawman, gunfighter, gambler, and sportswriter Bat Masterson. Many potential gunfights ended when one opponent was still fishing for his weapon and looked up at the muzzle of his intended victim's cocked Colt.

While living in Arizona, I succumbed to romantic tradition and bought a replica of a Colt Single Action Army revolver and a "quick-draw" belt and holster of the style created by trainer of movie and TV cowboys Arvo Ojala. The belt's drop loop put the gun's grip on a level with my palm. Sweeping back my hand, my thumb brought the hammer to full cock as the barrel cleared the holster's lip. A small upward tilt of the grip, and I fired. Everything was a matter of triangulation, timing, and muscle memory. I spent way too much time practicing this skill that I most likely would never use.

During the night as an officer of the Arizona State Guard and Detective Agency, I carried a loaded .38 S&W Chiefs Airweight revolver while defending power tools, electric generators, tires, and piles of construction bricks against the depredations of evildoers. During the day, except when I was teaching fourth graders the mysteries of watercolors, crayons, and papier-mâché, I practiced holding a quarter on the back of my outstretched hand. I'd drop the hand, draw the single-action Colt replica, and try to time hitting the dropping quarter with the muzzle of the revolver as the hammer clicked on an empty chamber. "Click, clink" meant success within the duration of a half-second. "Click, clunk" meant failure. I listened to a lot of clunks.

On TV the cowboys were helped by editors, stunt gun handlers who replaced the movie's star's gun hand and holster at the edge of the frame, and actors who played the bad guys and got no help at all. Actor Glenn Ford was the fastest movie star gunslinger. Hugh O'Brian as marshal, town policeman, gambler, brothel owner, killer, and boxing referee Wyatt Earp was television's top gun. O'Brian fired so many "four-in-one" blank shells on and off camera that he eventually went deaf. I watched all the Westerns of the 1960s, from *Sugarfoot* and *Maverick* to *Have Gun—Will Travel* and *Yancy Derringer*. Facing an Arizona desert sand dune studded with empty bleach-bottle bad guys, I created in my head my own dusty streets and pungent saloons and prayed I wouldn't shoot my toe off.

Cowboys, for the most part, have received a bum rap when it comes to their reputations as troublemakers in the western towns. Life on the trail was hard, working in all weather and sleeping on the ground—under a tarp if they were lucky. They ate the same boring food (and not enough of it) and learned to sew and patch their gear as it wore out. Snakes, saw grass, Gila monsters, quicksand, fire ants, wolves, coyotes, prowling Indian bands, and a dozen other ways to be injured and face infection one hundred miles from any doctor added misery to the need for covering ground with a few thousand head of—as mentioned earlier—really stupid cattle.

The other wranglers you rode with were from all strata of western life. One in four was Hispanic or African American. They had their own agendas, personal habits, tics, prejudices, hygienic peculiarities, modes of expression, dress, and boiling points. Over a three- to four-month drive, the new man had to learn his place.

To earn money for school, I sailed in the U.S. Merchant Marine aboard the Great Lakes ore boat fleet as an ordinary deckhand, although my work card said I could also work as an oiler, coal passer, or food handler—all on the lowest rung of the ladder. To the crew I was the smartass college kid trying his hand at a man's job. Not unlike the dude easterner turning up at a cattle camp under the critical and bemused gaze of seasoned trail waddies, I was the new squeaky toy to play with while they tended to their repetitive tasks. I don't know which is the most unsatisfying: babysitting a few thousand head of dimwitted cattle bred to feed people, or transporting tons and tons of dirt used to make steel. I knew nothing except that I had spent years helping my dad lug his tools for the Sperry Gyroscope Corporation onto the big ore boats to repair their gyrocompasses and radar sets. It was different being under the command of the entire thirty-man crew, including the mates and skipper. They made sure I worked at every dirty job, from chipping rust to greasing the steering gear bearings in the hull channel to dangling over the side in a bosun's chair above the hissing, freezing lake with a long brush and bucket of trisodium to swab the red ore off the bow's whiteworks and the boat's painted name.

At the end of each trip up and down the Great Lakes, either with an empty hold or a load of red ore or gray taconite marbles, at some point after docking and being relieved of my watch, I got to go "up the street" with a few of the crew members. Pushing through the doors of a dockside slop chute like Peckerhead Kate's was as comforting as coming home. The click of the pool table balls, stink of cheap cigars, reek of stale beer, stench of stale seamen, and bite of that first shot of Old Overholt rye whiskey with a beer back was all a nineteen-year-old freshwater sailor could ask for. Some men I worked with were barely literate, and their families sent them gifts through the mail like mason jars filled with white lightning corn whiskey that were waiting for them when we went through the Sault Ste. Marie locks. Others owned dairy farms where they worked during the winter season after the boats laid up and waited for the lake ice to melt in the spring. A few were gripers, whiners, and complainers, but all of them knew their jobs and were content looking out at the lake's empty horizon, or maybe what was just beyond it.

As young cowboys learned skills like braiding their own lariats from strips of rawhide, I learned how to use a chipping iron and properly coil cables.

While a cowboy rode night herd, keeping the steers calm under the cold blanket of stars, I hauled one hundred pounds of cable down the dock as the boat was shifted beneath the Hulett gantry cranes, scooping iron ore from our holds. Gripping the steel loop palm down, I lifted the hawser's cable, thick as my forearm, from one spile, dragged it to the next one fifty feet down the dock—or the next one after that—and waited for the donkey engine to take up the slack, pulling forward the boat's six-hundred-foot hull, all under the scalding gaze of orange sodium vapor lamps. I could not let my mind wander, because like the night herd rider fearing a stampede in the dark, there were ten ways I could be killed doing that job. Cables under tension had skidded off spiles, snapping through the air like a bullwhip and shearing off the heads, arms, and legs of daydreaming deckhands. The great lakes and great seas, like the vast prairies and mountain ranges, are unforgiving teachers.

Once those bawling, shit-smeared cows were herded into cattle cars and the lanterns on the end of the train's caboose became diminishing red dots in the twilight, the quality of cowboy life began to improve. True, a few glasses full of Who-Hit-John made that life a happy blur, but the great majority of cowboys were not man-killers. Some had their photos taken while in their new clothes, and they sported all manner of firearms and knives draped about their person. Smart photographers kept a ready supply of weaponry as props for these photos.

It is also true that many cowboys wrapped their best leather around heavy-caliber six-guns to hoorah or "run" a town on horseback, shooting holes in the sky. A .45 caliber Colt Peacemaker sold new for $17. A day's pay could buy six cartridges over the counter, so a holstered Colt with its gun-belt bullet loops filled with a couple dozen shots represented a considerable investment. The gun store proprietor ordered the same ammunition from Sears, Roebuck at $1.57 for a box of one hundred .45 Long Colt cartridges or $1.38 per one hundred for .44-40 Winchester cartridges plus shipping weight of about one-and-a-half pounds.[1] In Western movies, every cowboy seems to have a Winchester rifle in a saddle scabbard. A Winchester Model 1866 ("Yellow Boy")—a popular model with brass side plates—cost $40 new, or more than a month's pay. A cartridge-firing 1865 Spencer repeater was a better deal at half the price with seven shots loaded through a tube in the shoulder stock. The Colt's competitors also offered up six shots and for less money. Remington, Starr, Whitney, and the elegant Smith & Wesson Model 3 Schofield revolver were all popular substitutes. When the Winchester Model 1873 came out in .44-40 caliber, the cowboy only had to carry one cartridge for his six-gun and saddle gun. Between 1873 and 1919, Winchester sold 720,000 Model '73 rifles.[2]

While the cowboys were considered a major source of income to local businesses, the social status of the saddle tramps, working for about a dollar a day on the trail, was that of unskilled labor. They were one jump up from ditch diggers and the swampers who cleaned out the spittoons and mopped the floors of the saloons.

Many towns did not appreciate troublemakers and hired enough police or constables to keep the peace. Wyatt Earp was a man-killer who knew how to work a town both for a salary as a policeman (as in Ellsworth, Kansas) and also for a piece of the action—like owning a faro bank at a table, called "bucking the tiger" by the players—in one of the local gambling saloons (as in Dodge City, Ellsworth, and Tombstone). Most towns had ordinances on the books against carrying firearms within the city limits, though the degree to which they were enforced depended on the grit of the lawmen. Explaining rationally to a psychopathic dentist named Dr. John Henry Holliday that he had to shed his revolvers before he could enjoy a drink in the saloon required more sand than most peace officers possessed. Of course, real hardcase lawmen such as Bill Tilghman would have just thrown the skinny, consumptive alcoholic into a cell to cool off. Rules of conduct posted by known lawmen who did not hesitate to "drop the hammer" were treated with respect. The *Abilene Chronicle* alerted the town in an 1873 editorial: "Fire Arms – The Chief of Police (James B. Hickok) has posted up printed notices informing all persons that the ordinance against carrying fire arms or other weapons in Abilene will be enforced. That's right. There's no bravery in carrying revolvers in a civilized community. Such a practice is well enough and perhaps necessary when among Indians or other barbarians, but among white people it ought to be discountenanced."[3]

A Colt, Smith & Wesson, or Remington revolver was a prized possession and usually rode in a cowboy's saddlebag along with his best and second-best shirt, shaving kit, extra canvas pants, and father's old Elgin watch and fob. Revolvers were too heavy to wear hanging from a cartridge belt every day on the trail. The holster was designed to protect the gun from the elements, not to act as a slippery pocket for a quick draw. Fine dust worked into the mechanism, and damp leather turned the metalwork green. Brass bullet cases moldered in leather belt loops. Revolvers were used to twist-tighten strands of barbed wire fencing and hammer staples into posts, and they had a bad habit of going off when dropped if the hammer rested on a live cartridge primer in the cylinder.

Regardless of the inconvenience of dealing with the clumsy weapon, many westerners felt obligated to live up to the stories and legends they read and heard, which were concocted by visiting scribes. In all, Colt built about thirty million guns. The handgun became the trademark of individualism, self-reliance, and dim-witted bravado, as well as a crutch for low self-esteem and a status symbol with little justification. Nothing much has changed.

If the actual need for a handgun in the Wild West was less than exaggerated in the eastern press, then Texas cattle owners would seem to have the last word. In 1888 the management of a famous ranch on the Panhandle published the "General Rules of the XIT Ranch." These twenty-three rules of operation and conduct of XIT Ranch cowboys and other employees were writ in stone and spelled out exactly what was expected on the property or on the trail. Rule number 11 stated:

No employee of the Company, or any contractor doing work for the Company, is permitted to carry on or about his person or his saddle bags any pistol, dirk, dagger, sling shot, knuckles, bowie knife or any other similar instruments for the purpose of offense or defense. Guests of the Company, and persons not employees of the ranch temporarily staying at any of the camps are expected to comply with this rule, which is also a State law.[4]

Inexorably, the business of the West overtook the romance of the West. The cowboy era lasted roughly twenty years. Eastern investors created cattle and mining companies that gobbled up the small holdings, ran rails to terminals near their properties, turned many small towns into important distribution centers, and killed other communities located off the beaten track without a backward glance. Assassinations took place in boardrooms with fountain pens rather than across poker tables with a derringer bullet.

The federal government moved west, along with judges and courts, and while some states like Arizona permitted open display of holstered handguns on city streets, many others forbade handguns from the city limits. But the American tradition of dealing with problems head on and maintaining skills handed down from our forefathers—that tradition stubbornly held its ground. Whether it was a repeating rifle in a saddle scabbard, a side-by-side shotgun primed with double-ought buckshot in the back of a Ford flivver, or a cheap "Patriot" .32 caliber rimfire "Suicide Special" in a waistcoat pocket, the West accepted its heritage.

During the late nineteenth century, railroads carried crates of handguns, rifles, and shotguns to western gun distributors from eastern factories to meet a demand largely created by eastern writers in magazines, pulp novels, and "authoritative" guides to western fortune seekers. Sears, Roebuck and Montgomery Ward catalogs offered a variety of revolvers and long guns through the mail, and even popular weekly magazines included firearm ads. *Harper's Weekly* of 1885 offered "Good pocket plated revolvers for home defense – Cash with order – Small, $1.00, medium $2.00, celebrated Bulldog, $3.00. . . . H&D Folsom, 15 Murray Street, New York."[5]

The Sears, Roebuck catalog offered twenty-two pages of guns and ammunition, everything from Parker or Greener Damascus double-barreled, self-ejecting, 10-gauge shotguns for $64 to a Forehand & Wadsworth new double-action, self-cocking revolver in .38 caliber with a two-and-a-half-inch barrel for $1.45, "For Home or Pocket." In Chicago during the late nineteenth century, it was possible to rent a gun for an hour and return it to get your deposit back.

In those eastern and midwestern cities that cranked out both the Western mystique and the means to its fulfillment, quite another phenomenon took hold following the Civil War. Among its many results emerged the seed of today's National Rifle Association. The war had caused a considerable improvement in firearms technology, adding cartridge repeaters to the arsenal as well as improved metallurgy and ballistics. More effective and accurate ammunition was produced, and gun clubs began opening across the East and Midwest. These clubs were largely the preserves of well-heeled businessmen and enthusiasts who could afford the latest custom rifles. Shooting clubs had existed in Great Britain, and German *schützenverein*, with their meticulous organizations, were models for the American counterparts.

The major difference between the European and American approach to marksmanship was that the Europeans shot for the highest score on the paper target. Of greater concern to American enthusiasts was the size of a group of shots subject to "string measure." The tighter the cluster of holes in the target depended to a large part on a micrometer to determine consistency of bullet diameters, scales for bullet weights and powder charges, barrel lengths, rifling twists—all the elements that affect flight and accuracy.

Many club members were also officers serving part time in National Guard units, and others had served in the army during the Civil War. If anything, the war had proved that the level of marksmanship among recruits was very low, training was insufficient and unrealistic, and the weapons were far more capable than were the men who used them. Tactics handed down from the Napoleonic Wars were still taught at West Point and practiced in the field. Even the roughly trained recruits prized self-preservation above military dogma, so the military tried variations on the volley-fire theme to suppress enemy positions.

In volume one of Silas Casey's infantry textbook *Infantry Tactics, for the Instruction, Exercise, and Maneuvers of the Soldier, a Company, Line of Skirmishers, Battalion, Brigade, or Corps d'Armée*, one such variation, the "Short Rush" by successive ranks loading and firing as they moved forward, discovered the following:

> The technique had two problems. First, it failed when defenders refused to cooperate by firing volleys. Skirmishers could not effectively suppress aimed fire by people who outnumbered them. Trying to solve this by deploying more skirmishers, even to the point of comprising the entire assaulting force, sacrificed cohesion and momentum, reverting to the deadly but static firefight. . . . Second, the high degree of command control demanded more training and rehearsal time than volunteers were given.[6]

The longer-range capabilities of the soldiers' rifled muskets and the ability to reload more rapidly after each shot, using the percussion cap and fixed ammunition in a paper cartridge, shredded advancing lines before they reached their objective.

In 1871 a colonel in the New York National Guard, William C. Church, saw the need for some sort of organization not unlike Britain's National Rifle

Association to bring together the best marksmen in that state. He was editor of the *Army and Navy Journal* and wrote in an editorial, "An association should be organized in this city to promote and encourage rifle shooting on a scientific basis. The National Guard is today too slow in getting about this reform. Private enterprise must take up the matter and push it into life."

Following a meeting of National Guard officers to debate the proposal, the secretary of state of New York approved the charter of the NRA. In that same year, the New York state legislature authorized an appropriation of $25,000 to purchase land for a rifle range—on the proviso that the new NRA pony up $5,000 in matching funds. A total of $10,000 was also contributed by the cities of New York and Brooklyn.

Fortunately, the Long Island Rail Road was being built, and its investors were in search of both freight and passenger revenues to justify its trackage. A particularly well-sighted seventy-acre strip of land along its right-of-way was not suitable for major construction due to the peaty nature of the soil, but a rifle range made no great architectural demands. This stretch of acreage that had been part of the Creed Farm was sold to the NRA and its partner. Col. Henry G. Shaw named it the Creedmoor Range, because of its resemblance to English moorland.[7]

By 1873 Creedmoor had become host to many local clubs and regimental long-range rifle matches as well as the testing ground for the latest crop of American single-shot rifles. These guns were unique brutes firing large-caliber bullets at targets out to one thousand yards. To brace the thirty-two-inch barrels, the shooter most often lay on his back with his legs crossed and supporting the long-rifled tube. The buttplate of the stock was back near the shooter's ear, held in place by his left hand (if he was a right-handed rifleman). His crossed legs had the effect of propping the barrel up on a shooting stick for maximum steadiness. The rifles were single-shot breechloaders and required a swabbing of the bore after each shot to remove black-powder residue buildup. This "fouling" could affect the flight of subsequent shots once the sights were finally set for the target's range by firing "aimer" shots and adjusting the rear aperture for windage and elevation.

Across the Atlantic, an Irish team had just won the Elcho Shield trophy from England and Scotland and was the hot team on the long-range competition circuit. Searching for other teams to conquer and unaware of the small and new NRA, they sent a letter to the *New York Herald* challenging the

Americans to a match involving fifteen shots per man at ranges of eight hundred, nine hundred, and one thousand yards. They would bet $500 against the same amount from the Americans. Put off by the Irishmen who had bypassed their association, the NRA dismissed the challenge. However, Capt. George Wingate, secretary of the association, was also president of the New York Amateur Rifle Club and accepted on their behalf. He took up the challenge knowing that no member of the amateurs' sixty-two-man roster had ever fired a shot beyond six hundred yards.[8]

On September 20, 1874, the match commenced. Following a big buildup by the local newspapers, spectators streamed out on the LIRR, which continually upgraded its service with extra trains. High-stepping matched horses in polished harnesses drew carriages of gentlemen to Creedmoor accompanied by ladies with parasols and picnic baskets for a day's outing. Every shooter relied on a spotter with a long brass telescope on a tripod to call to the scorekeepers the position of each shot's hit on the target. Tension was keen, especially as it became apparent that the Americans had a chance to post good scores against the crack-shot Irish.

The match came down to the final shot by Col. John Bodine. The previous Irish shooter, J. K. Milner, had fired his first shot at nine hundred yards on the wrong target. All Bodine had to do was hit the target anywhere and the Americans would win. With his hand sliced open by a tin-can lid and oozing blood, Bodine sighted his Sharps Creedmoor rifle, firing a .44 caliber cartridge packed with sevety-five grains of Fg black powder behind a five-hundred-grain paper-patched bullet. On his forty-fifth shot of the match, once again facing the punishing recoil of that long-range rifle, he touched off the trigger, and five thousand people leaned forward to listen for the strike of the big slug against the cast iron target one thousand yards distant. "Wang!" The American team won with a score of 935 points against Ireland's 931.[9] A hurrah went up that caused horses to rear at their hitching posts.

The Americans had gone high-tech, using large-caliber cartridges rigorously tested for bullet weight and powder charge to obtain optimum and consistent scores. The rifles were the finest ever built by American manufacturers, who had learned from designing long-range guns for buffalo hunters and commercial meat shooters on the Great Plains.

A practical—and lethal—example of the capability of this new generation of long-range sporting rifles is the shot taken by buffalo hunter Billy Dixon at the Second Battle of Adobe Walls fought in the Texas Panhandle in June 1874. The community of Adobe Walls was a collection of stores and establishments created to support the local buffalo hunters. It was built on the ruins of a fort from which Kit Carson had waged a successful campaign against the Native Americans. On the night of June 27, the lodgepole that supported the roof of Jim Hanrahan's saloon and trading post cracked and roused the hunters sheltered there. Consequently, when a force of seven hundred Comanches, Kiowas, and Cheyennes led by Quanah Parker and Isa-tai attacked the town, the residents were already up and about. The swift raid turned into a four-day siege with casualties on both sides.

After fending off the initial charge with revolvers and repeating Henry and Winchester .44 rimfire rifles, the hunters reached for their long-range Sharps buffalo guns. Called Big Fifties, these rifles were the most accurate firearms on the Great Plains. The Native Americans retreated to a distant ridge to consider their options against the well-armed hunters. On the second day, young Billy Dixon crouched by a bullet-scarred saloon window that faced the ridge and saw a Native American warrior seated on his horse. The other hunters cajoled him to take the shot. Four of their fellow hunters already lay dead under blankets.

He shouldered an 1872 Sharps .50-90 cartridge rifle borrowed from Hanrahan, adjusted its tang sight to the top of its scale, and laid the barrel on the windowsill. The boom was loud in the morning stillness, and time passed as the heavy slug arced toward its distant target. Then the overconfident Native American jerked and silently tumbled from his horse. The Comanches packed up and left. When the army arrived, a surveyor measured the shot's distance at 1,538 yards[10]—the longest recorded sniper kill until the reintroduction of .50 caliber rifles in the Iraq War.

A world away from Dixon's famous shot, the Irish team had stayed with its Rigby muzzle-loader percussion cap-and-ball rifles, the finest of their kind. Until that time, no cartridge rifle had ever beaten a carefully prepared muzzle-loader. Times were changing, and that winning 1874 match at Creedmoor ignited a fierce public interest in rifle matches and shooting sports that lasted until the 1890s, inspiring a new generation of marksmen.

Other than the Irish team, the only people not cheering as the whooping 1874 victors celebrated were the officials of the NRA who had disregarded the Irish challenge. To regain their place as the official New York State shooting authority, the NRA went to their strength. Being largely made up of military representatives, in 1882 they decided to stage an international military match with England. They saw it as a win-win situation, since a loss to the English would force the military to recognize the sorry state of American armed forces marksmanship and training. A win would prove the value of long-range shooting skills and advance more marksmanship training for the line soldier.

Military marksmanship training had slipped badly after the Civil War, mostly due to cutbacks and lack of funds. Army recruits, such as the lads who rode off with Lt. Col. George Armstrong Custer in 1876, fired as few as seven rounds a year on a rifle range. Depth of training was dependent on the commanding officer's commitment to sharpshooting. Cartridge weapons had replaced muzzle-loaders, adding the .45-70 rifle bullet and the .45 caliber Long Colt revolver round to the soldier's field kit. If a trooper in the Western Department had concerns about the security of his scalp patrolling among the Sioux, Comanches, and Apaches, he bought ammunition with his own money and practiced on his own time.[11]

On September 14 the English showed up at Creedmoor with their .450 caliber Martini-Henry falling-block, self-cocking, lever-operated, single-shot infantry rifles. The Americans fielded a very competent team but were equipped with the Model 1873 Springfield "trap-door," single-shot rifle with a thirty-two-inch barrel firing a .45 caliber, five-hundred-grain bullet wrapped in two layers of cotton paper and propelled by seventy grains of black powder for optimum ballistics. The .45-70 was no Sharps-, Remington-, Ballard-, or Wesson-grade rifle. On its best day it had what was called a high-arcing "rainbow" bullet trajectory to reach out to the long ranges.

The Americans were not expected to win, and they lived up to expectations. Their highest scores at all ranges were lower than the lowest English scores. The old Springfield remained in service until 1892 and even saw service in the Spanish-American War of 1898 in Cuba. The horrific Creedmoor loss jolted the military, and they began improvements in rifle training.

Petty jealousies and infighting among the military and civilian shooters caused logistical problems with the Creedmoor facilities. In 1891 the NRA, frustrated and feeling underappreciated for their efforts, gave the Creedmoor property back to New York State. The following year New Jersey opened its own rifle range at Sea Girt, an undeveloped, unincorporated area on the coast. National Guard captain Bird W. Spencer offered the facilities to the

NRA if the association would include its sponsored matches together with the New Jersey competitions.

Colonel Wingate, however, saw no future for the NRA now that Creedmoor was gone, and he threw in his cards. The NRA New York offices were closed, and everyone went away. While the new disciples of rifle marksmanship were scattered back to their respective states, the Spanish-American War proved how American troops were still tragically unprepared to fight a modern war, lugging about antique equipment, poorly trained, and led by officers with political agendas rather than military objectives.

One of the biggest problems was the internecine warfare between states. What was needed was a comprehensive training regimen in small-arms marksmanship for military regulars, National Guard members, and civilians of a military age. The only way that was going to happen was to involve the federal government, and that is what these disciples set out to accomplish.

With the adoption of cartridge ammunition, the quality of revolvers and the new semiautomatic Colt pistols allowed precision marksmanship competitions to be held under NRA auspices beginning in 1900. That same year marked the organization of the American Trapshooting Association and its matches. Trapshooting involves a single tosser flinging clay targets (pigeons) away from the shotgun shooter at a variety of angles, simulating upland bird shooting.

In 1910 C. E. Davies of Andover, Massachusetts, created skeet shooting, first called "around the clock shooting." This test of shotgun skills is named after the Scandinavian form of the word and uses two target tossers that hurl clay pigeons as the shooter advances from one station to another to achieve different shooting angle combinations. This sport offers the challenges of duck and goose wing shooting.

The revival of the Summer Olympics in 1896 was held in Greece, and America's shooting hopes were centered on brothers John and Sumner Paine, who participated in pistol events. John won the military pistol event, and to keep from embarrassing their Greek hosts, only Sumner agreed to compete in the thirty-meter free pistol competition. He won it and became the first relative of an Olympic champion to also win Olympic gold.

In 1901 Congress directed the secretary of war to create a National Board for the Promotion of Rifle Practice (NBPRP). This board was served by the regular military, National Guard, and the NRA, representing civilian marksmen and clubs. Competitions and trophy events combined the NBPRP matches with the NRA events and finally gave recognition to the NRA as a national organization. President Theodore Roosevelt became a lifetime member, as did William Howard Taft, further legitimizing the NRA's status. Intercollegiate competitions were begun under NRA auspices in 1905, as were interscholastic competitions with .22 rimfire rifles, and Washington, D.C., high school cadets began training and competing with war-surplus Krag-Jørgensen .30-40 caliber infantry rifles.

By 1903, after trying to modernize the Krag infantry rifle to match the excellence of the German Mauser design, the government finally created the Springfield Model 1903 rifle firing a hot new .30 caliber cartridge. The new Mauser-type, bolt-action rifle used stripper clips to speed-load the five-round magazine. The NRA condemned that practice, as opposed to single loading, as wasting ammunition and approved of the idea of a "cut-off" added to allow single-cartridge loading and keeping the magazine for emergencies only. The army tried to beat the 1903 Springfield back into the nineteenth century with a switch on the left side of the action for having the magazine "on" or "off." They ended up stuck with what is considered today to be one of the finest pieces of military-designed ordnance ever created.

In the face of the European war, Congress broadened the scope of the NBPRP in the National Defense Act of 1916 by creating the position of director of civilian marksmanship (DCM) at the War Department. The DCM was directed to provide organized civilian clubs with arms, ammunition, and targets as were available to help stiffen the quality of experienced shooters ready to transition into the armed forces.

Unfortunately, this act came too late for effective application when the U.S. Army shipped troops to France in World War I. Because of the need for rapid deployment of new soldiers to support the fading and ragged Allies, too many half-trained men were sent to the trenches. Sergeants had to show men how to load their rifles, while other green troops considered the rifle just a long handle for their bayonet. Gen. John Pershing sent back seething reports on the lack of training that turned soldiers into cannon fodder. Only the U.S. Marines were combat-ready marksmen. As the saying went, "The most dangerous weapon in the world is a Marine and his rifle."

There were exceptions in the army ranks. Sgt. Alvin York grew up in Pall Mall, Tennessee, in the Valley of the Three Forks of the Wolf River where, like his colonial ancestors, a long rifle was a tool you used to put meat in the pot. He was a crack shot but had biblical objections to killing other men, even in a war. But after some soul searching, he wrote in his diary, "My religion and my experience . . . told me not to go to war, and the memory of my ancestors . . . told me to get my gun and go fight. I didn't know what to do. I'm telling you there was a war going on inside me, and I didn't know which side to lean to. I wanted to be a good Christian and a good American too."

He became a member of Company G, 328th Infantry Regiment, 82nd Division, called the All-American Division, with soldiers in it from every state in the Union. His skill with a rifle had made him an instructor at Georgia's Camp Gordon, but now, on October 8, 1918, his unit was wading through death and carnage in the Battle of the Argonne Forest, facing hill 223, which had to be occupied.

With seventeen men York set out to flank some German machine gun nests that were chewing up his company. He suddenly found himself ambushed by dozens of German soldiers and machine gunners who killed half his squad. He took cover, aimed his Springfield Model 1903 rifle, and began to shoot. When he ran out of ammunition, he drew his .45 caliber Colt pistol and kept firing.

The officers of the 82nd Division reported the aftermath of his action to general headquarters:

The part which Corporal York individually played in the attack (the capture of the Decauville Railroad) is difficult to estimate. Practically unassisted he captured 132 Germans (three of whom were officers), took about thirty-five machine guns, and killed no less than twenty-five of the enemy, later found by others on the scene of York's extraordinary exploit.

The story has been carefully checked in every possible detail from headquarters of this division and is entirely substantiated. Although York's statement tends to underestimate the desperate odds, which he overcame, it has been decided to forward to higher authorities the account given in his own name. The success of this assault had a far-reaching effect in relieving the enemy pressure against American forces in the heart of the Argonne Forest.

For his work that day, he received the Medal of Honor, Croix de Guerre, Distinguished Service Cross, the French Legion of Honor, the Croce di

Guerra of Italy, and the War Medal of Montenegro, and finally was able to return to his home in Tennessee.

———————————————————◆◆◆———————————————————

When I was seventeen and living large as a company commander in the ROTC, shooting as cocaptain of the high school rifle team, winning qualification medals for the American Legion post's junior rifle team, and actually getting good grades while dating my new girlfriend, Suzanne, everything got even better. M. Sgt. Henry Harpel, the regular army noncom who commanded our ROTC battalion, called me into his office. The National Guard unit in our South Shore neighborhood had a problem. They were a logistical support company and had let their rifle requalification regulations get behind. The guardsmen were truck drivers, typists, load handlers, clerks, and some Korean War shipovers who were working off their military obligation on the weekends. Their main problem was their inability to "hit a bull in the butt with a bass fiddle," according to their commander. The Guard needed instructors to teach this mob how to shoot and was not too proud to ask the local high school ROTC units.

I had just received my NRA instructor certificate. Harpel knew I had my expert rating with the M1 rifle over the army's "C" Course, and when he learned I was also a certified instructor, he smiled his Cheshire Cat recruiting sergeant grin and stuck out his big hand. "Welcome to detached duty, Captain."

The range used by the National Guard was a bleak stretch of dirt outside the city that lay between the firing line and the concrete trench target butts two hundred yards distant. The troops had arrived in deuce-and-a-half (two-and-a-half ton) trucks, while I rode in a dark green station wagon with some officers—all of whom regarded me as an amusing, temporary aberration. The soldiers were broken down into training platoons, one of which was mine, and my job was to demonstrate and individually teach the four shooting positions they had to master in order to qualify. Again, these were hardly 82nd Airborne paratroopers. Mostly they were guys who had learned how to game the military system to make their hitch pass with as little friction as possible. Also, virtually none of them had ever fired a rifle. Now, here was this short high school kid with glasses telling these grown men how to shoot. I needed an edge.

When I arrived, I had asked the range officer—a balding career soldier who had landed at Inchon with Gen. Douglas MacArthur and had a hard, lean look that went with the long row of hash marks running down his sleeve—if a target could be manned in the butts so I could demonstrate the M1 rifle for my assembled platoon. He agreed and sent word to his assistants down at the butts to raise a target frame up into view from the trench. The platoon, numbering six squads of nine men each, was assembled, and I walked out in front and got their attention with a shouted "Listen up!" My voice cracked.

As the smirks and behind-the-hand chuckles caused my sweating under the summer sun to assume tsunami proportions, I lifted the rifle at my side to port arms and called out, "This is the U.S. rifle, caliber .30 M1, an air-cooled, clip-fed, gas-operated, semiautomatic, shoulder-type weapon. It weighs 9.56 pounds without the bayonet. You are going to qualify with this rifle over the next two weeks. Let me show you how it works."

My knees were jelly as I walked over to the firing line shooting mat. When I was facing at right angles to the lone target raised above the butts, the range officer (RO) barked, "Load and lock!" I removed a metal clip loaded with eight cartridges from the ammo pouch on the web belt I had scrounged, thrust it into the rifle's magazine, eased back the bolt with the edge of my hand, and let it go, clearing my thumb from the forward-slamming bolt just in time as a cartridge was cammed off the top of the clip and seated in the breech. I clicked on the trigger guard safety.

The RO continued, "Ready on the firing line!" He paused. "Take your position and await my command to fire!" I dropped down into prone, adjusted the sling, wiped a trickle of sweat from my eyes, and waited.

A glance through the rear peep sight revealed a shimmering blur where the target's black circle should have been. The shimmer was a sea of eyestrain, with wriggling snakes and heartbeat silver spots firing off like Fourth of July fireworks. An attack of nerves that would follow me for all my competitive shooting days ambushed me. I couldn't see. I couldn't breathe. My face was on fire and my hands had no feeling in them.

"Fire when ready!" the RO concluded. I fumbled off the safety, shut my eyes, and took a deep breath. I knew how to do this. I felt the RO look over at me. I opened my eyes and the sight picture looked better—not perfect, but good enough to squeeze off one of three sight adjustment shots before I fired for score. The rifle bucked against my shoulder, and the empty cartridge case sailed behind me. The RO, watching through binoculars, called out "Seven at three o'clock!"

The range was dead on, but the wind, which I now felt on my cheek and saw stroking the range flag, had pushed the shot to the right. I also felt the wiseass smiles behind me anticipating failure. It was as if the entire Illinois National Guard had paused in their daily tasks to stare at me. I gave the micrometer peep sight some left windage correction clicks, settled in, and fired again.

"Nine at three o'clock!" the RO shouted.

Almost there. The sun had become a warm blanket and evaporated the sweat. My eyes cleared as I concentrated on adding more left windage correction. The third and last aiming shot drilled the bull's-eye, and the RO commanded, "Pinwheel! Dead center of the bull! Fire for record!"

I locked into what I knew best. Automatic pilot took over, and I inserted a fresh clip. The next outside-world event I was aware of beyond the view through my sights was that empty metal clip ejecting with a "ping" from the rifle's breech as the last of eight rapid fire shots buzzed downrange.

The target descended into the trench to be scored with circular white cardboard markers. My stomach became uneasy as I waited, rising to one knee next to my grounded empty rifle. The target rose into view. Only one marker was showing. Oh, shit. It was in the center of the bull but where? Then, the wood wand with a marker affixed to its end rose from the trench in the hands of the RO's assistant and tapped the center marker eight times. I had shot a perfect score with six of the eight shots in the "X" ring within the bull's-eye—a circle the size of a beer coaster. When I turned to face the troops, a smattering of grudging applause greeted my equally grudging deep bow from the waist, and after that the training began.

I was still deep in the woods with these guys. Demonstrating how to shoot was not hard. Contorting the trainees into the shooting positions was straight body mechanics. Firing the rifle was always the big problem. The noise, the recoil, the clatter of the mechanism—all that happened in a fraction of a second, and it was startling. Anticipating this slam-bang of activity causes many new shooters to flinch—an involuntary jerk of the body, a blink of the eyes, a twitch in the trigger finger, a "Maggie's drawers" (miss) downrange.

I had brought a paper sack of .30-06 caliber bullets with me to the National Guard range. They looked like the standard M2 ball ammunition, except there was no powder in the shell, and the primers had been neutralized. They were dummies. I prowled behind my group of shooters, straightening an arm here, spreading legs there, watching the score sheets as the qualifiers fired for record. I noticed a lot of red flag waving across a target face downrange. Nine out of ten times, the red Maggie's drawers was caused by a flinch.

Sitting cross-legged next to the sweating, eye-blinking shooter whose mug was also red from embarrassment at having this high-school kid in his face, I watched him fire, single-loading each round. The noise and recoil masked some of the flinch, but I could see it as he nerved himself up to pull the trigger. After the shot, I reached over and single-loaded a round into his rifle. I was regarded with a baleful eye. He went into his routine white-knuckled, squinted through the sights, blinked, and fired. Click. His entire body twitched. He dropped the rifle butt from his shoulder and stared at the closed breech, then at me, and then back to the breech.

I ejected the dummy round and inserted a live round, slamming the breech closed. He was not stupid and expected another dummy. The bang and shoulder punch surprised him. Downrange, he had put the round into the black. We went through this routine for ten shots, with him never knowing whether the round was live or a dummy. By the end he was consistently hitting the black circle two hundred yards distant. He had forgotten about the noise and recoil. I didn't realize it right away because I was seventeen years old and had about six-dozen things clanging around in my noggin, but later the accumulation of those show-and-tell experiences demonstrated to me how much I enjoyed teaching people to do stuff, whatever the subject. That enjoyment stayed with me, but it started with curing a flinch.

On the last qualifying day, my work was done, so I went over to the M1 carbine range where the officers were shooting, helped a couple of them, and then, after receiving permission from the RO, shot the carbine course of fire. While I qualified expert, the unit's commanding officer had been in the butts. His Jeep came bounding back to the firing line, and he climbed out enthusiastically with a big grin.

"Which of my officers was shooting on Number Six?" he called out, extending his hand. The officers all looked at me. I shrugged. He sagged but shook my hand anyway.

With passage of the Volstead Act in 1919, the prohibition of alcohol sales in the United States opened a new door to opportunity for gunmen who had vanished with the taming of the West. From appreciation of elegant shooting sports drawing the gentry to suburban meadows, the gun once again became the devil's disciple. Genteel target-, skeet-, and trapshooting events faded from notice, replaced by bootleggers, bank robbers, and union busters blazing away with the best new technologies gunmakers could provide.

3

IT'S A SMALL-BORE
WORLD AFTER ALL

During the time between the end of World War I and World War II, civilization overtook the Wild West, and America's gun culture became institutionalized. Failing to learn the war's bloody lessons, the military downsized mentally and physically, falling back into the prewar horse cavalry garrison force as its roles were reduced in peacetime by a traumatized civilian government and populace. Following President Warren Harding's "Return to Normalcy" speech and President Calvin Coolidge's declaration that "the business of America is business," the country put death and destruction behind it, sang, danced, and swigged bootleg liquor into the Great Depression. President Herbert Hoover's administration allegedly promised "a chicken in every pot," but a great number of people ended up without a pot to put it in.

Besides Prohibition, the year 1919 also focused public attention on what had been referred to as the Great Migration. Unrest among African Americans, caused by the white society in southern states still smarting after the end of the Civil War, manifested itself in a northern migration. Roughly one-and-a-half million black citizens streamed toward the large northern population centers where jobs, housing, and greater equality waited. The jobs were readily available in the giant Carnegie steelworks, factory assembly lines, and in Chicago's slaughterhouses. The housing was poor and crowded, and the equality was heavily laced with segregation. Northern whites feared job loss and a slide down the social ladder as many factories paid African Americans the same wages as Irish and Slav immigrants and second-generation whites who worked at the same low-skilled occupations.

On July 27, 1919, the tension boiled over. A group of white men were hanging out on a Chicago beach when some blacks swam close to the shore. The white men challenged the blacks' need to be on that particular stretch of beach. A shoving match broke out. One of the white men tossed a rock at the swimmers. A young man was struck and sank into the water. He was carried to the beach but was dead. The police were called, and the responding officer arrested one of the African American men. This set off an escalated situation on the beach, and word spread back into the South Side neighborhoods. A full-scale race riot developed and spread to cities across the country, creating the "Red Summer" of 1919.

Soldiers returning to job shortages, labor riots, race riots, and a general recession on top of Prohibition's ratification in 1919 had the lower classes in the country on edge. Middle-class people tended to thumb their noses at the reformers and do-gooders who preached thrift and abstinence. There was money to be made in the stock market and booze to be made in the bathtub. Even President Harding had his own bootlegger to keep his White House bar stocked.

During the 1920s and 1930s, the civilian gun culture declined as beans won out over bullets in the family shopping list. Unemployment hit the cities hard, and crime went up. There was little public money for more police or better police weapons, so what money there was went into communications, outfitting squad cars with two-way radios that stretched out the thin blue line. Graft in police departments became all too common as liquor, gambling, prostitution, and drug money tempted cops who had families to feed and other lawmen who just saw the opportunities. Wounded civic budgets cut law enforcement training, and both federal and state officers found themselves outgunned, outshot, and outmaneuvered by the 1930s crime wave that filled newspaper headlines across the country. What saved most law enforcement agencies was that the bad guys, with all their firepower, were not the brightest candles on the cake.

The pinch in the economy also had another effect on our patchwork gun culture. The cheap .22 rimfire cartridge came into its own. So far, from the days of black powder, the march of ammunition technology had been focused on bigger, faster, and more powerful missiles. More powerful cartridges required stronger rifles and pistols to handle the increased pressures at ignition. Eventually, during the nineteenth century, smaller-bore guns working down from .58 caliber to .45-70, .44 Henry rimfire, .38-40, and .30-40 Krag replaced the heavy slugs. The military finally lit on the .30-06 caliber ball cartridge for its Springfield Model 1903 rifle. For civilians, the .30-30 Winchester was—and still is—considered a good deer-hunting cartridge.

Independent hand loaders and experimenters such as Elmer Keith cooked up many hot derivations, necking down larger cases to smaller bullets called "wildcat" loads. The .219 Zipper was made in 1937 from a necked-down .25-35 Winchester centerfire cartridge case to hold a forty-five- or forty-six-grain hollow-point bullet. It had a flat point so the Winchester Model 64 lever-action rifle could load them in its tubular magazine beneath the barrel. Nobody wanted sharp-pointed spitzer-type bullets bumping against center-fire primers in cartridges stacked end to end. This flat-pointed design limited the slug's ballistics to short-range shooting, before it began to tumble.[1]

Another wildcat of that era was the .218 Bee, designed in 1938 for the Winchester Model 65 carbine. Its claim to fame was its superior performance to the then-popular .22 Hornet. The Bee, however, suffered from the same flat-nose limitations of the Zipper.[2] Many backroom chemists cooked up new hot loads during the period's search for the next super-round. All the time, it was developing just beneath their radar.

The homely little .22 rimfire was a nineteenth-century round that began with the BB cap that was fired only with the power of the priming compound that was spun into the inside rim of the cartridge case. The hammer crushed this rim on impact, triggering the explosion. The BB cap was replaced by the CB cap, which fired a twenty-nine-grain conical bullet but added a dab of powder into the case to give more push. These were anemic rounds, usable only for indoor target or gallery shooting. The early cases were copper due to the light loads. In 1857 Smith & Wesson introduced the .22 Short as the first American metallic cartridge for their break-open, hide-out revolver. The small pocket pistol became popular during the Civil War, where it became a "last ditch" gun for officers on both sides. The bullet used a twenty-nine-grain lead slug over four grains of finely ground FFFFg black powder. It remained in production loaded with smokeless powder and is used in Olympic rapid-fire target competitions today.

In 1871 the twenty-nine-grain bullet was pushed into a longer brass case that was packed with five grains of fine black powder, which doubled the velocity of the Short round, creating the .22 Long. The ultimate result of this rimfire progression was the .22 Long Rifle created by the Stevens Arms Company in 1887. The .22 LR abandoned the twenty-nine-grain Short bullet for a forty-grain slug ahead of a still heavier powder charge. In ballistic terms, this combination shot flat, accurately, and with a copper-jacketed or hollow-point slug, hit harder than previous iterations.

What made the .22 LR catch on with target shooters, besides its inherent accuracy and cheap price, was that the range for competitive matches could drop in yardage from two hundred and one thousand yards, back to one hundred yards, fifty yards, and the gallery distance of fifty feet. The entire physical aspect of a shooting match changed. Paper targets were only a short stroll from the firing line. Backstops could be a simple graded hill of dirt or an inexpensive bullet trap. The great boom of the heavy-caliber long-range rifles had been reduced to a barely audible snap under the big sky. Matches were held indoors year-round using bullet traps and official NRA concentric-circle fifty-foot targets, one-and-a-half inches in diameter. Rifle and pistol competitions shared range facilities.

However, with army ranks being divided into factions by progressives such as Billy Mitchell, who demanded a better Army Air Service, and George S. Patton Jr., who showboated for more and better-armored tanks, the military brass would have none of it. It was not the job of the military to provide facilities for civilians or teach them to shoot. The army and navy had to use frayed budgets to keep a reduced force of soldiers and sailors under arms. At military schools, mossbacked officers—sadly with logic on their side— taught the value of "volley fire" as an effective way to make use of a body of soldiers with minimum rifle training. In their reports, they still referred to rifles as "muskets."

In 1919 Winchester Repeating Arms Company was on the horns of a dilemma. They wanted to introduce a new rifle design but were stymied by the success of their older model. When match shooting had become popular back in 1871 with the Creedmoor International Matches and created a following much like golf today, Winchester saw a ready market. By 1885 they developed a series of single-shot, long-range rifles based around the "rolling block" breech system. This simple mechanism had a cocking hammer that was pulled back and an under-lever trigger guard that swung down, pivoting the breechblock that contained the firing pin clear of the breech so a cartridge could be loaded. With the bullet poked into the backside of the barrel, the lever was raised to become the trigger guard again, the breech swung up into place, and the hammer was drawn back from half cock to full cock, ready for firing.

Fold-up peep sights were mounted on top of the barrel, or onto the "tang" of the shoulder stock's grip just behind the hammer. This rifle was available in a variety of calibers, including the .50-70 Government and .45 caliber ammunition fired by Sharps, Remington, Stevens, Maynard, Ballard, and Wesson in the long-range match rifles. The Winchester became a hit offered in "High Wall" and lighter version "Low Wall" designs, referring to the height of the side walls reinforcing the breech for heavy and light cartridge loads. At the same time, these heavy guns were lobbing their big slugs one thousand yards at Creedmoor and the U.S. Navy Rifle Range at Caldwell, New Jersey. Winchester also produced a model shooting the .22 Short cartridge called the Springfield practice musket, or the Winder musket, specifically for target shooting at short ranges. The army snapped it up. More than 140,000 Winders were produced between 1885 and 1920. The army version was also fitted with a detachable sword bayonet.

By 1919 Winchester had made it known to the army through its Washington agent, Thomas A. Davis, that a new bolt-action, small-bore rifle was in the prototype stage. This rifle had a box magazine for rapid fire. Some urgency was needed, as the Savage Arms Company had also designed their Model 19 bolt-action rifle in musket form—wood stock to the muzzle and a bayonet lug—called the Experimental Design Number 111 that was the equal of Winchester's offering. Davis wrote Vice President Henry Brewer at Winchester in New Haven:

> While in the offices of the National Rifle Association this morning, [I] heard that the Savage Arms Co. were ready to make delivery of their new .22 cal Bolt Action Rifle.
>
> Colonel [Townsend] Whelan told me at lunch with him today that the Savage Co. expected to have their .22 cal Bolt Action Rifle ready about April.
>
> The Ordnance Department will want a rifle that will permit the use of the rear sight now in the course of construction by the Engineering Department. This cannot be done on the Savage Rifle. The construction of the .22 cal Bolt Action Rifle will have to be made so as to be able to attach the sight on the receiver.

The War Department has decided to discontinue manufacture of the .22 cal Springfield Armory Practice Rifle.

Even though a Bolt action Rifie is accepted by the Ordnance Department, the Winchester [bolt action] Single Shot Musket will be the rifle recommended by the National Rifle Association, and the Director of Civilian Marksmanship as the most practical Rifle for indoor rifle shooting and rifle club work.[3]

With the Savage rifle at their heels, Winchester also heard rumors that the army was seriously considering abandoning the .22 Short cartridge for the more powerful and accurate .22 Long Rifle. Knowing they could make a nice dollar converting the Model 1885 single-shot muskets for .22 Long Rifle ammunition, they would also be snuffing the demand for their bolt-action design. Fortunately, tests made at Winchester firing the .22 Long Rifle–converted 1885 muskets showed that the bullets were tumbling and "keyholing" into the target. Even using lighter powder loads produced the same accuracy-ruining effect. With this evidence in hand, they dissuaded the army's conversion plan for the existing rifles.

Meanwhile prototypes of the Number 111 bolt-action rifle were rushed to Washington for demonstration in mid-April 1919. Lt. Col. Townsend Whelan of the Army General Staff, the DCM, and the secretary of the NRA joined Kendrick Scofield, editor of the magazine *Arms and the Man*, to test the Winchester entry. The rifle received rave reviews for accuracy and handling, with only one army comment that the rifle should be wood-stocked clear to the muzzle because military men are used to seeing that kind of weapon.[4]

Winchester suggested that handmade samples of their new rifle—now called the G22—be given to the American international rifle team for the upcoming Caldwell Matches in August 1919. Pursued by the specter of the Savage Model 19 stealing their thunder, Winchester made every effort to keep tabs on their opponent's performance at Caldwell. To their collective relief, the Model 19 suffered from a common fault of box magazines that fed rimmed ammunition straight up into the breech. The cartridge rim forces the bullet into a nose-down attitude as it slides off the top of the spring-fed stack. This causes bullet shaving as the soft lead is tipped up and thrust into the steel barrel's breech. Lead shaved from each bullet builds up at the breech, causing shell casings to eventually jam, and alters the weight of the bullet, affecting accuracy. The Winchester rifle used a curved magazine that delivered the cartridge easily up and into the breech unshaved.

"Tom Davis reports the new Savage gun is making a very poor record," wrote Henry Brewer. "One of the Brooklyn Rifle clubs . . . was obliged to discontinue using it almost immediately, because [shaved lead] accumulated as to render the rifle unserviceable."[5]

Following the rifle's big success, the G22 was designated the Model 52 on September 11, 1919. If life was simple, that would be the end of the story, but military requirements have little to do with real life, and the DCM, Maj. R. D. LaGarde, who was in charge of providing military firearms to civilian clubs, had a problem. He had three thousand of the 1885 .22 Short muskets cluttering up his supply depot and was in favor of fobbing off those guns to ROTC units and civilian clubs (who didn't want them) and ordering a token few of the Winchester Model 52 for "special shooters" who had marksmanship aptitude. It was the old "volley fire" for the lowest-common-denominator thinking again. To make Winchester really sweat, the army had purchased hand-loading equipment and considered producing "reduced load" ammuntion for the Springfield and Enfield service rifles in .30-06 caliber. This would allow the regular service cartridges to be fired on the short ranges reserved for .22 caliber rifles.

Winchester had seen sales plummet following the wartime contracts and was spending big money to create the tooling for this new precision Model 52 rifle. Because civilian clubs that used the .22 caliber rifles were just beginning to form, achieving success with the new rifle depended upon military acceptance to fuel advertising. Savage had corrected its bullet-shaving problem and was climbing back up from its Caldwell Match embarrassment. After many delays, the Model 52 was finally advertised to the general public on May 15, 1920.[6] American marksmen firing the new Winchester Model 52 rifle began sweeping trophies off the shelves wherever their clubs appeared.

The Golden Age of rifle clubs was in the 1920s. The upsurge in popularity of the .22 rimfire cartridge seemed less threatening than the heavy-caliber, long-range guns or the high-velocity ammo fed into military weapons. The small, deadly accurate cartridge democratized the sport of shooting. What had been a casual pastime of backyard plinking and rural squirrel hunting became a recognized, institutionalized sport. High schools, American Legion posts, colleges, ROTC programs, Boy Scouts, police departments, and summer camps cobbled together shooting programs.

Sadly, what suffered was spectator interest. Rifle and pistol matches allowed spectators behind the firing line, but their entertainment value diminished to zero. The sport boiled down to competition between participants, and because showmanship was nowhere on the NRA radar, the only big winners were the award manufacturers. Top shooters lined their walls with plaques and glass cabinets sparkled with gold and silver trophies and medals that virtually no one saw them win. Only the NRA and its affiliates kept alive any sense of accomplishment, plastering the pages of *American Rifleman* magazine with lines of agate type and a few stuffy grip-and-grin photos. The lack of public recognition for accomplished shooters and creative spectator-friendly contests has dogged the sport until today.

Driven originally by the 1903 establishment of the NBPRP and the army's DCM and following the Caldwell matches in 1919 that gave legitimacy to the .22 rimfire, civilian clubs sought affiliation with the DCM to receive the smaller-caliber rifles for their own interclub matches and range practice. The DCM and the NRA also assembled necessary qualifications required to teach marksmanship safety and range practices. What was needed was a range for target shooting that had the prestige of the old Creedmoor and Sea Girt ranges to bring more shooters into the sport.

About forty miles east of Toledo, Ohio, is the community of Port Clinton. Ohio's National Guard adjutant general, Ammon B. Critchfield, saw the need for a new rifle-training center based on the lessons learned in the Spanish-American War. The United States had won the land war by the narrowest of margins, and only the grit and initiative of the troops against the poor organization of the Spanish served them well. The firepower and audacity of the American navy had denied the Spanish use of the sea while poor training, poor leadership, and worse weapons almost lost Americans the victory on land.

While the exploits of Col. Theodore Roosevelt and his recruited Rough Riders stole the headlines with their capture of Kettle and San Juan hills, both they and the army regulars were badly served by their rifles. The volunteers relied on the .45-70 "trapdoor," single-shot Springfields dating back to the 1876 Custer massacre, while the regular army troops and Roosevelt's Rough Riders carried the new .30-40 Krag rotary-magazine infantry rifles and carbines. The .45-70 fired an antique black powder cartridge that released a plume of smoke, immediately revealing the positions of the soldiers who had fired. The five-shot, bolt-action Krag fired a .30 caliber (7.62 millimeter), rimmed, round-nose bullet in front of forty grains of smokeless powder, which gave it a muzzle velocity of two thousand feet per second for the thirty-inch barrel rifle and 1,960 fps for the twenty-two-inch carbine.

The Spanish M93 Mauser, a five-shot bolt-action rifle fired a 7.57 mm rimless cartridge with a pointed spitzer-type bullet with superior ballistics pushed along at 2,203 fps.[7] The hotter Mauser round's powder blast was almost invisible on firing, and the slug had more punch when it arrived. The Model 1893 rifle's internal magazine accepted stripper clips of 7x57mm ammunition five rounds at a time for speedy loading. The Krag's slow-loading, one-shot-at-a-time rotary magazine doomed it for rapid-fire combat purposes. This performance led directly to the adoption of the Mauser-action Springfield Model 1903 .30-06 caliber rifle, which required a safer range for training because of its more powerful cartridge. The "06" stood for 1906, the year the .30 caliber cartridge was adopted, and was added to differentiate the new hot ammunition from the frumpy Krag ammo.[8]

Critchfield selected a bleak Ohio swampland that faced out onto Lake Erie for the new training ground. With a little work and some humble plank and tarpaper buildings for storage and barracks, the range could service Ohio's needs as well as offer a variety of setups for national matches. One of our great naval victories had occurred on Lake Erie during the War of 1812 when Oliver Hazard Perry built a jury-rigged fleet of small boats to fight the larger British sailing ships cobbled together in Canada. Critchfield named the new rifle range Camp Perry. It would go on to become a regular mecca for precision rifle and pistol target shooters until this day.

Complying with Title 10 of the U.S. Code that stated in 1903 that "an annual competition called the 'National Matches' and consisting of rifle and pistol matches for a National Trophy, medals and other prizes shall be held," these competitions were held at Sea Girt for three years. The more powerful new Springfield rifle and the Jersey Shore weather caused the matches to be moved to Camp Perry in 1907.

One of the interesting points of Camp Perry is that the backstop for the .30 caliber matches is Lake Erie. During July and August when various matches are held, the water is patrolled by the Ohio Naval Militia out to a

thirty-two-mile exclusion zone prohibiting watercraft from sailing into the
bullet impact area.

———————————————◆◆◆◆————————————————

During my years learning to shoot the M1 Garand .30 caliber infantry rifle,
most of our qualification rounds were fired at the Fox Valley Rifle Range
near Algonquin, Illinois. They had a two-hundred-yard facility complete with
Aiken target butts. Col. Robert Aiken developed that target system in the
late 1890s. Housed in a below-ground level trench with a berm of earth in
front and a higher berm to the rear, the target frames could be raised and
lowered like a double-hung window by "butt-boys" (or girls) who took their
turn from the firing line. This allowed successive lines of targets at different
ranges to be set up and controlled from the firing line by hardwired telephone communications. After a hit, the targets were lowered into the trench,
six-inch circular shot markers (white for hits in the black target circle) were
inserted into the bullet holes, and the targets were raised for spotters at the
firing line to see where hits were made.[9]

Our tournaments were mostly shot at Fort Sheridan in Evanston, Illinois,
but we did fire at Camp Logan, which was made part of the Great Lakes
Naval Training Station after World War II. This range backed up against
Lake Michigan. During matches, the U.S. Coast Guard and their auxiliary
patrolled the offshore waters for wandering pleasure craft.

It was a warm July day in 1957 when my team took our turn in the butts.
The butts officer stayed by his telephone to repeat the orders of the RO in
charge of the firing line two hundred yards distant. Each of us stood by a
counterbalanced target frame with a freshly patched and pristine bulls-eye
target the size of a dinner plate stapled in place. "Ready on the right!" called
out our officer, the phone to his ear. We stood to our frames. "Ready on the
left!" came the shout. We were preparing for a nine-shot rapid-fire sequence
and bent our knees, waiting for the push. "Ready on the firing line!" Check
to make sure nothing fouled the pulley wires. "Up targets!"

At the firing line, three dozen shooters dropped from standing position to
the prone position, shouldered their rifles, pushed off their safety catches,
and took aim. As they dropped, we heaved up on the frames, hoisting the big
targets into view. One target halfway down the line jammed in its track. The
butts officer dropped his phone and ran past us toward the errant target. In

the lake behind us, coming around the point, a motor sailer pleasure boat hoisted its sail and was wafted close-hauled by the wind into our impact area. A rattle of gunfire came from the firing line. The "hizzz" of copper-jacketed bullets passed overhead.

Everyone in the butts watched the sailboat with morbid fascination, its big white sail drawing nicely. Past us pounded the butts officer, running toward his phone. We flattened against the concrete wall of the trench to let him by, but it was too late. Mixed with the rattle of gunfire to our front, we all heard the "pok . . . pok . . . pok . . . " as .30 caliber bullets smacked into the spread of canvas. Even without binoculars, we could see bits of chrome or brass spin off into the lake as slugs caromed off cleats or other pieces of brightwork. As holes magically appeared in the bull's-eye targets above our heads, the "tink" of breaking glass, "whack" of splintering wood, and "ping" of ricochets reached us on the offshore winds. The wind carried the hull in a straight line across the impact area as if on rails, and those aboard were seen diving over the far side using the boat as cover.

By the time the officer cranked the telephone to call a cease-fire, the fusillade was finished. Out in the lake, the hapless sailboat lurched out of control, bow toward the shore, its sail flapping listlessly in irons from the stern breeze as its boom, fastened to the base of the mainmast by its gooseneck, swung from port to starboard and back. A Coast Guard cutter motored toward the abandoned hull that was black with brown and yellow trim, which probably blended in with the rocky shoreline as it ran under diesel power until it unfurled its white sail. Lengths of cordage drooped over the side, giving it the look of a broadsided frigate.

The butts crew hauled down the frames and began scoring hits on the targets, but our minds were on how many riddled and bloody bodies the Coast Guard would salvage from the choppy water. Eventually, our despondent butts officer was made aware that no civilians aboard the punctured boat had been hit and all were in Coast Guard custody. It was the only rifle or pistol match I ever attended where a sailing vessel of any kind was almost sunk.

Camp Perry shut down during World War I and then blossomed again with small-bore matches in 1920. The surge of homegrown ranges that opened through the 1920s and the demands placed upon the NRA to furnish classification systems eventually brought American teams into international competition. The Pershing Trophy International Team Match was created in 1931 for the purpose of international participation in small-bore rifle matches. Only six years later, forty-one NRA-registered pistol tournaments were scheduled. By 1939 the number had climbed to sixty-one, with more anticipated by the end of that year.

Army, police, and NRA schools flourished at Camp Perry and on other ranges around the country. Only trained shooters were sanctioned by approved clubs. While blue-collar and white-collar shooters mixed comfortably, unified by the jargon, fussy technology, and comradeship of the shooting sports, spectators, who were excluded from the clubby atmosphere, went away. They gravitated to collegiate and professional football, basketball, baseball, downhill skiing, bowling, or any place where some easy-to-follow sports action provided entertainment. Watching a rifle or pistol bull's-eye target match is like watching paint dry. Great drama is occurring, but it is buried beneath layers of procedure and protocols, and only tiny holes appear on distant paper targets.

Golf draws larger crowds every year because every action of a golfer can be seen and analyzed. Commentators follow every shot. Spectators identify with each stroke as they relive the muscle memory of their own duffer's game. The golfers' personalities mirror the game's frustrations.

By the 1930s and into the 1940s and 1950s, three- and four-position rifle competitions and one-handed pistol matches became part of an inbred sport where the same winner and gun combinations dominated, but there was no action to draw the curious, let alone admission-paying crowds. Gun and gun accessory manufacturers faced a flat market composed of white, middle-aged men, some youths, and some women who used three or four types of rifles and three or four types of pistols. The Great Depression had bled out most folks' disposable income, further reducing serious competitors who could not afford the latest upgrade of Winchester, Remington, or Anschütz rifles. Pistol shooters had Smith & Wesson K-Series .38 and .22 caliber revolvers, and Colt .38 Super and .45 ACP semiautomatic pistols. The .22 caliber Colt Woodsman, the High Standard Model 10, and a smattering of expensive foreign models like the Hämmerli free pistol for Olympic-style shooting rounded out the list.

The promotion of shooting sports would have led to beneficial participation and competition for the gun manufacturers and mom-and-pop accessory makers, as well as increased NRA prestige and membership recruiting. Now that the NRA had corralled America's target shooting competition, rules, regulations, and schools, where would growth come from?

American parents clung to the "you'll shoot your eye out" fears for their sons and daughters. Shooting teams didn't sprout like youth baseball, hockey, or football, with their attendant broken bones, contusions, concussions, and abrasions. There was a primal, underlying danger that went with the loaded rifle or revolver that did not accompany the baseball bat, hockey stick, tennis racket, or golf club. If Dad was not a shooting sportsman, then rifle, pistol, or shotgun shooting was a last-ditch hope to find a sport for Junior, or even Sis. It was a haven for failed jocks, low-esteem siblings, and—though the term would not be coined for decades—nerds.

During those years between wars, *American Rifleman* became the voice of the NRA and featured pages upon pages of rifle and pistol match scores along with a growing number of hunting articles like "My Favorite Gun" and "On the Trail with Joe." The text was folksy and laced with unexplained jargon that acted as a code for the initiated: pinwheels, possibles, nippers, fliers, squibs, and Maggie's drawers.

The magazine's roots traced back to 1885 and *The Rifle* magazine, published by Arthur Corbin Gould. *The Rifle* shrewdly kept its fingers on the pulse of America's shooting culture and then established itself as the self-designated mouthpiece for everything having to do with shooting in the United States. Gould's *The Rifle* expanded its audience in 1888 by changing its scope and renaming itself *Shooting & Fishing*. On a visit to Sea Girt in 1894, Gould watched some NRA matches as a member of the Massachusetts Rifle Association. The quality of the competition impressed him. He editorialized in his magazine that American shooters would be wise to join the NRA. In a rush, membership shot up, and what had been an anemic organization blossomed, complete with a board of directors.

In 1906, with Gould dead and *Shooting & Fishing* on the rocks, James A. Drain, secretary of the NRA, purchased it and changed its name to *Arms and the Man*. As editor and eventually president of the NRA, he moved both organizations to Washington, where political decisions were made concerning American gun use and ownership. By 1916 Drain was no longer president of the NRA and decided to sell off the magazine in favor of his law practice. On July 1, 1916, he sold *Arms and the Man* to the NRA for one dollar. Once under NRA control, what had been largely a log of rifle matches and winners and articles on various rifles now included articles about hunting, ballistics, handguns, shotguns, and the growing accessories industry. In June 1923 the magazine name changed for the last time to *American Rifleman*.[10]

This expansion of shooting subject matter plus the mailing of free copies to NRA members pushed circulation of the magazine to thirty thousand copies a month. Advertisers saw a good thing, as did gun manufacturers in search of expanded civilian sales from market visibility and lucrative military contracts from favorable product reviews. As the end of the 1930s approached and the technical expertise of the German army gradually became known, it did not take a genius to look around at the sad state of the Depression-crippled American armed forces or the still-amateur status of the British military establishment facing the well-oiled, armored, and motivated Wehrmacht and see a massive economic opportunity.

Franklin Roosevelt's declaration that America would become the "arsenal of democracy" said it all. As if someone had fired a starter's pistol, the NRA designated itself as the recruiter of shooters for the armed forces. Like the minutemen of 1775, civilian hunters and target shooters today would become the rifle-trained soldiers tomorrow when needed. It almost worked out that way.

4

"A SIMPLY OPERATED MACHINE GUN . . ."

These reassuring words of advertising copy accompanied an ad showing a cowboy in wooly chaps and a sombrero gunning down a band of rustlers from his front porch with a Thompson submachine gun. In 1925 anyone with $225 could buy a Thompson and have it shipped to his local hardware store, complete with a 100-round drum magazine and many boxes of bullets. That price was off-putting for most people, since an entire Ford automobile cost about $400, but the allure was genuine if ripping off 800 rounds per minute intrigued you.

Until the end of World War I, combat had clung to the noble ideals of massed troops, glittering bayonets, charging horses, officers with sabers, and bugle calls. Americans had conveniently forgotten the butchery of the Civil War and the malarial jungles of Cuba and the Philippines, and they had woven a mythical patriotic tapestry around "our doughboys" and sang "Over There" with gusto as their half-trained sons and husbands tramped up the gangplanks onto ships bound for French ports. The blinded, shell-shocked, amputated, hobbling, and gassed detritus that shambled off those same ships only a few months later sobered more Americans than the Volstead Act. The "war to end all wars" was history, and its grim global aftermath hung over the world for decades.

As the nation's saloons closed, street corners in the cities' concrete canyons reverberated with gunfire. Illegal beer barons and bootleg whiskey mobsters fought for turf and a piece of the American dream. Much of that gunfire erupted from the muzzles of new technology that came off the boat with our boys from France or, like the Thompson, arrived at the dock just in time to miss the boat to battle-proven bragging rights earned in Flanders.

The Browning Automatic Rifle was another casualty of bad timing but found a niche with law enforcement and the motor bandits that plagued the Midwest in the 1930s. The Colt Model 1911 semiautomatic pistol was flat, held eight shots, and could be quickly reloaded with a seven-shot clip. Its .45 caliber ACP (Automatic Colt Pistol) bullet was the same round that fed the Thompson's twenty-round stick magazine or one-hundred-round drum.

"The gun that made the twenties roar" was invented by Brig. Gen. John Taliaferro Thompson, a retired Ordnance Department officer who wanted a fast-firing weapon that used pistol instead of rifle ammunition. The gun's efficiency was made possible by a delayed blowback mechanism designed by Cmdr. John Blish that figured in other weapons during World War II. Thompson collaborated with Blish to form the Auto-Ordnance Corporation. They called their brainchild a "trench broom" even though it never saw a French trench. They set out to peddle it commercially to the military and law enforcement.

Auto-Ordnance contracted with Colt to produce the gun in numbers, though Colt was hesitant to invest in a device that was so far ahead of its time. With its thirty parts and wood furniture, the gun was expensive to build, but the results of Thompson's demonstrations were electrifying. At the 1920 Camp Perry National Matches, he ran through hundred-round drums in less than six seconds, making a continuous sound not unlike "the rapid ripping of a rag." Everyone was amazed and then, for whatever reasons, walked away. The military was also full of praise but decided not to spend $225 for the Thompson and instead put its money—$650 apiece—on the old tried-and-true Lewis gun. Its flat drum on top-loaded the same .30-06 cartridge as the Springfield Model 1903 rifle, and it could be lugged around by one (relatively muscular) man.[1]

The light machine gun chosen for our boys was the French Chauchat (pronounced "show-sha"), the world's worst-designed gun for use in the mud-caked French trenches. Its only rival in the one-man carry category was the Colt/Springfield M1909 Benet-Mercie Machine Rifle. This design was a version of the Hotchkiss Model 1909 eventually accepted by the French. It used the same strip of bullets fed from the right side and incorporated a clunky bipod and buttstock monopod. Unfortunately, it broke almost every time it was fired, and the strip of .30-06 cartridges could be inserted upside down in the heat of battle. In World War II the Japanese Nambu Model 11 and

Model 96 copied much of the Benet-Mercie and Hotchkiss design elements, maintaining Japan's consistently poor weapon performance. A few M1895 Colt "potato-digger" gas-operated guns with a slow cyclic rate of 450 rounds per minute were lugged overseas after their debut in Cuba. But the automatic gun that saved many an attack was the Browning M1917A1 belt-fed, water-cooled heavy machine gun that also went on to serve in World War II.

So, for a time, the "Tommy gun" was flogged to security agencies and trigger-happy cowboys besieged by rustlers. However, it was the adoption of the weapon by what passed for organized crime in the 1920s that really drove sales. Sedan gunships loaded down with bullet-spewing hardware cruised city streets, whacking the competition at a time when agents from the new Bureau of Investigation (eventually the FBI) were not even allowed to carry a pistol. Local cops waved .38 Colt Police Positive revolvers and lever-action Winchester rifles. The Winchester Model 1907 auto-loading semiautomatic rifle was popular, with its .351 Winchester self-loading cartridge offered in a ten-round detachable box magazine. The twenty- to twenty-two-inch barrel gave the short pistol-type round a high-energy impact comparable to the game-changing .357 Magnum round offered in 1937.

Though the press often exaggerated the use of fully automatic weapons by the bootleggers and bank robbers, the stars of the criminal hierarchy swore by them, if only to cause confusion and chaos. Al Capone had an arsenal of "Chicago typewriters" for his less-than-well-trained marksmen to spray and play the odds. John Dillinger usually had at least one, with its shoulder stock removed for concealment, to pin down local lawmen. In the hands of socio-pathic killer Baby Face Nelson, the Thompson was a preferred tool. An arms race developed between the cops and the robbers.

Over the months of May and June 1934, the Bureau of Investigation was authorized to carry firearms after two of their agents were machine-gunned along with two Kansas City police officers while transporting a felon in the Kansas City Massacre of 1933. Until that time, BOI agents had to depend on local police to confront armed criminals. On July 1, 1935, the BOI was renamed the Federal Bureau of Investigation.[2]

Across the East and Midwest, gangs and police began building arsenals of heavy-duty weapons. The shootouts of the Wild West in the nineteenth century paled beside the blazing confrontations between the good, the bad, and the extremely well armed of the 1920s and 1930s.

Prohibition resulted in everyday people who never had a drink in their lives suddenly frequenting speakeasies or the lower-class "blind pigs," drinking often-lethal back-room-brewed cocktails out of coffee cups or beer that would grow hair on a bowling ball from barrels with the owner's blood still smeared on them. Out on the street, a car backfire could send a dozen people dropping to the pavement only to look up to see who did not get back on their feet.

People who had never considered needing a gun for protection witnessed bloodstained sidewalks and read of the police arriving in time to cart off the bodies and swab up the gore. Even the readers of armchair explorer publication *National Geographic* were urged in the advertisement pages of the January 1924 issue:

Sheltered behind castle walls several feet thick! Guarded further by an ancient moat and clumsy drawbridge! How primitive this protection appears today compared with the absolute security afforded millions of homes by the modern Colt—Revolver or Automatic Pistol.

Safe to handle—quick in action—always sure and accurate in fire—small wonder the Colt's fire arms are the choice of the government and its citizens.[3]

Gun manufacturers who had a relatively flat trade in long-barreled target pistols increased production of "practical" revolvers and compact semiautomatic pistols imported from Europe. These small-caliber weapons had short barrels and small grips for women as well as men. Seeking to capitalize on the exploits of lawmen punching holes in the bad guys, Colt and Smith & Wesson emphasized their more expensive and larger caliber Police Specials and Military and Police revolvers and semiautomatic pistols for home defense. With the return of so many veterans from the Great War, there were fewer Americans with scruples against dropping the hammer on a fellow human being.

My grandfathers took separate routes to the self-protection concept. Eldred V. Souter, who worked with a shovel at a crematory and then as part of the electrical gang at the Peace Bridge being built between Buffalo, New York, and Ontario, bought an Iver Johnson break-top, .32 caliber short revolver that held five cartridges. I still have that gun with a few of the original bullets. It is blued steel with grips made from black gutta-percha—a sort of molded wood product made from the sap of a tropical plant. It was the plastic of its day.

My mother's father, Earl Nye, was a railroad man who worked for the Buffalo, Rochester & Pittsburgh Railway and then the New York Central. His arsenal contained an 1890 Winchester nickel-plated, pump-action, .22 caliber rifle. He was quite cheap, and for motor trips into the countryside, he picked up a Quackenbush Herkimer Bicycle Rifle in .22 caliber that had a ten-inch barrel, and was all metal with a folding wire stock. The idea was for bicyclists to carry this lightweight gun in a canvas holster on their cycle. Its firing-pin block swung to one side, revealing the breech where one bullet was seated. The block was then swung closed and the firing pin drawn back on the side of the block against spring pressure until locked. The trigger released the lock, firing the shot. I have fired both of these with reduced loads, and neither one blew up. I feel fortunate and lucky that neither relative ever had to fall back on them in a life-saving situation. I might not be here today otherwise.

Besides shiploads of cheap Spanish semiautomatic pistols and U.S. sweatshop knockoffs of respected manufacturers' pocket pistols and revolvers, a few first-class handguns elbowed their way to acclaim. Germany already had their Luger and even the clumsy but effective Mauser Model 1896 (C-96) "Broom Handle" pistol with its wooden holster/shoulder stock and ability to be converted to full (if uncontrollable) automatic. To these classics they added the Walther PPK, the favorite sidearm of German military and police officers, and the Walther P38, a replacement for the Luger in the field. Italy's Beretta M1934, designed by Tullio Maregoni, also joined this group. Rivaled only by his own Model 1911 Colt .45 semiautomatic was John Moses Browning's 1935 FN Browning with its thirteen-round double-stack grip magazine. A variety of Browning's pistol designs, including the legendary .38 Super semiautomatic, filled holsters and pockets during the Depression years.

What made this generation of new pistols stand out was the 9mm Parabellum cartridge invented by George Luger in 1902. Its name comes from the Latin phrase "Si vis pacem, para bellum." ("If you want peace, prepare for war.") The high-velocity slug jacketed with steel or, later, copper was a man stopper in a small package, arriving at 1,017 fps. That 9mm cartridge continued as a classic rimless pistol bullet alongside the .45 caliber ACP round. In today's pistols it is still preferred to some far more ballistically perfected ammunition.

Revolver progress accelerated into the twentieth century with the development of the Smith & Wesson .38 Special cartridge. Originally this popular round descended from the .38 Short that became the round used in revolvers converted to cartridge use from percussion-cap-and-ball blackpowder guns of the Civil War era. While the bullet is actually about .357 in diameter—derived from the .35 caliber autoloader—the ".38" comes from the need for "heeled" slugs to work in the converted revolvers that required the slug to be the same diameter as the brass case to hold a seal in the 0.374 diameter chamber. Originally designed in 1899, the .38 Special was created to supplant the .38 Long Colt used in U.S. Army revolvers against the fearsome Moros in the Philippines. The Colt cartridge lacked sufficient stopping power against the adrenaline-driven Moros with their heavy wooden shields and razor-sharp *kampilan* swords.

The .38 Special round has relatively low pressure in its original powder loading, allowing for exceptional accuracy. This made it perfect for law enforcement use and centerfire target shooting, with its low recoil and less expensive cost. Eventually, a higher-pressure cartridge was created for use in heavy framed revolvers such as the 38/44—a .38 Special built on the frame of a .44 caliber gun. That development of the .38 Special High Speed led to the .357 Magnum introduced in 1935 as the high-power king and initially restricted to law enforcement sales. Revolvers chambered for the heavy-duty Magnum also worked with the .38 Special—but not the other way around, since the .357 is longer and will not chamber in the less robust gun.

Colt had a chance to upstage the .357 Magnum when, in 1932, Elmer Keith, Skeeter Skelton, and Bill Jordan built the .41 Colt Special from a trimmed .30-40 Krag-Jorgensen brass case, holding a two-hundred-grain semi-wadcutter (conical shape with a flat tip) bullet that covered ground at nine hundred to one thousand feet per second. The cartridge fit the Colt Official Police revolver as well as the Colt New Service, but the larger slug and ammunition costs made the .38 Special and its hulking interchangeable bigger brother, the .357 Magnum, the logical choice against the firepower of the 1930s motorized bandits.

The man in the gray uniform reached into a paper bag and drew out a revolver. I had arrived at the Canon Electric Company in Phoenix, Arizona, at about 9 p.m., ready to perform my first assignment as a security officer for the Arizona State Guard and Detective Agency. The officer I was relieving had worked the day shift. Slanting orange sunbeams reached ruler-straight into the building's shadowed, humming interior that smelled of packing crates and oiled machinery. His station by the main plant door was suffused with a warm animal odor that was not as offensive as it was permeating. Sitting on the cushion of his wooden armchair with caster feet was like sharing a bed with a below-decks crewman on a cattle boat. He was nice and welcoming and had been warned that I would be lacking a necessary bit of gear to do the job properly.

I had no revolver. In order to purchase the blue-gray uniform shirt and pants, the black leather belt, handcuffs, handcuff belt case, chrome whistle and chain, plain-toe black shoes, patent leather–brimmed officer's hat, and badge of authority, I had pawned my cherished Winchester Model 52C rifle, which I had brought from Chicago to Phoenix for some obscure reason. I would soon start teaching art during the day at the P. T. Coe Elementary School, but that was next month, and this was now. The guard handed me the extra revolver he had brought as a loan in the interim.

Now, I was a very good pistol shot, having been a member of a team in competition on ranges in northern Illinois. I had a couple of medals to prove it. In order to defend the property belonging to my assigned employer—and to battle any criminal element who might storm the warehouse in a rampage of looting and destruction—I was handed a British Enfield Mark II pre–World War II break-top .38 caliber revolver. The expression on my face must have been telling.

"It's real," Jeff said. "My dad brought it home as a souvenir from the war."

I hefted the matte-finished Parkerized revolver. "Which war?" I asked. I thumbed the lever that released the action lock and pulled down on the barrel to tilt up the cylinder for loading. I looked at Jeff, as I now held a gun that was in two pieces.

"It does that sometimes," he said, took the revolver pieces and reassembled the barrel and cylinder section back onto the frame and trigger at the hinge bolt. He handed it back to me. "It's hard to find parts."

Having satisfied myself it was unloaded, I aimed the gun out at the parking lot and squeezed the double-action trigger. The cylinder rotated a chamber into position under the hammer, and the hammer dropped obediently to fire the cartridge that would be aligned with the barrel. Keeping the hammer down, I grasped the cylinder and rotated it a half-chamber off center and looked at Jeff again.

His brow furrowed.

"It also does that sometimes?" I asked.

"It centers up to the barrel most of the time," he answered helpfully. "I always check it, you know, the cylinder lock."

"So, in a blazing gun battle with the forces of evil, I should check it?" This was a thought that came later, but had I said it then with just the right snide tone, I would have felt pretty clever. Having nothing else to offer, I just stared at the lump of metal in disbelief.

"Oh, you'll need these," Jeff said digging into his pants pocket. One by one he dropped five .38 Smith & Wesson Short cartridges in my palm. "They came with the gun. There were six, but I shot one, and I know the cylinder won't explode." He turned away to dump a half-dozen Genoa salami rinds into his paper lunch bag and sign out on the log sheet.

"There's three guys still in the plant doing maintenance." He handed me a floor plan map showing the guard clock stations and snagged the round Detex Guardsman watchclock that had been hanging on a peg next to his chair. It was steel, about three inches thick, wrapped in the leather with a shoulder sling and about the size of a cake plate. Its clock dial was covered with a protective cage of steel bars like a diver's helmet, and there was a slot into which a large key was inserted. Inside was a moving paper record onto which a pen registered a code. At each key insertion, the pen scribed a wiggle.

"You go to each of these stations in the order they are numbered every thirty minutes. Take the key you find there, stick it into the clock, and turn it. Put the key back and walk to the next station. You do that all night. When these three guys here leave, they have to sign out. If you're not here, they're supposed to wait."

I just stood there during this soliloquy, staring at the five bullets and the antique revolver. He gave me a manly poke on the shoulder. "Don't worry, you'll get the hang of it." He gathered his bag, a dog-eared anthology of Mickey Spillane mysteries, and left. I put the bullets in my pocket and holstered the empty revolver. Otherwise, I might have been tempted to draw it in self-defense and have to endure the hysterical laughter and guffaws of the marauding felons as they watched me hop about clutching my mangled hand and what digits remained.

Realizing that my only defense in that shadowed warehouse was to lure my attackers close enough to swat at them with the heavy Detex, I set off with the time clock slung over my shoulder and hoped for the best. By the second hour, the last employees had signed out and gone to their cars in the parking lot, accompanied by the chittering mating call of crickets and the distant whine of a climbing jet airliner. The Arizona night was balmy and dry, a relief from the 90-degree-plus day. By the fourth trip around the main floor, I had memorized all the key station locations—sort of a scavenger hunt—and dutifully inserted the large key into the time clock's side. As I did this, a gnawing dissatisfaction with my actions began to grow—along with the initial pangs of soul-sucking ennui.

My pattern of exploration was, essentially, on rails. At any moment within the half-hour trip around the deserted plant, anyone could know exactly where I was. At 3:15 a.m., I walked by a cyclone fence gate guarding shelves stacked with suspicious-looking technological gadgets. I would not walk past that door again until 4:15, according to schedule. Starting at 3:30 any thief worth his salt could clean off those shelves and be back in his pickup truck by 4:00, leaving me to blunder upon the scene at 4:15.

By the third night of lugging the clock and the empty gun around that warehouse, my hopeless situation had fused my logic circuits. I had identified most of the eerie ticking, humming, and hissing sounds, and had peered into most of the deeper shadows; now the boredom born of suffocating monotony blunted my senses. At one point I passed a machine shop that hummed ominously and smelled of warm lubrication oil and metal shavings. Its interior was pitch black except for pinpoint red and green status lights glowing and winking. Something went clank, and then a shadow moved.

My quick draw was greased lightning. If I had not tromped on the Enfield's cylinder release with my thumb and had not had the muzzle's front sight hooked on the lip of my holster, and if the hinge bolt at the front of the frame had not wrenched loose, sending the barrel, cylinder, extractor, and assorted springs twirling through the air, I'd have had the drop on the large brindled cat that fled down the aisle.

Later, as my heart slid down my throat to nestle in my chest once again, I located the scattered pieces and reassembled the revolver. I made note of the cat incident—but not the shower of gun parts on the warehouse floor—for my superiors. Seeking revenge, I did my next round in reverse, and after that, I did an every-other-clock-station round and then an odds-and-even round—anything to erase the mind-numbing predictability of my patrols. I was on to something!

The next day, I was summoned to the offices of the Arizona State Guard and Detective Agency before the start of my shift. I assumed I was to be praised for my initiative. My boss, a starched crag of a homunculus beneath an ex-Marine's crew cut, a heavy brow line, and high cheekbones, began his appraisal of my work with "What's all this happy horseshit?!" in a bellow loud enough to register on the Richter scale.

The clock codes produced during my rounds were on the desk in front of him. His eyes were hot little BBs as they scanned my good intentions. He explained, as if to a slow child how, since time immemorial, no guard had ever produced a graph like . . . this! My first two day's discs were inked with perfect code entries with a pen jiggle whenever the key was inserted—symmetrical, predictable. My third day disk looked like a plate of pasta, its pristine surface slashed to ribbons by diagonal lines, carving that ideal lockstep world into a demonic map of random chaos.

To top off my grotesque obscenity of a clock graph was my report about the cat. The heat that radiated off that man in the throes of his dyspeptic horror could have melted solder. I assumed the demeanor of the penitent, promised total fealty to the Arizona State Guard and Detective Agency, and was told I could report to my duty post. On the way out the door, I turned and asked if I could return the revolver to its owner and carry a baseball bat instead. He made an unintelligible sound in his throat, and I hurried out of the office.

Eventually I redeemed the pawn ticket on my prized Winchester rifle, and while working as a mild-mannered art teacher during the day and a gun toting champion of warehouses and construction sites at night, I was finally able to purchase a decent weapon. Having laid out my NRA qualification medals and certificates in front of the guard agency bosses, I was permitted to buy the revolver of my choice. Semiautomatics were not in fashion in 1962, so I chose a Smith & Wesson .38 Chiefs Special Airweight with a two-inch barrel. It sat lightly in my regulation holster and snug in a smaller belt holster to wear concealed when working in plain clothes as a deputy sheriff.

My dual identity was revealed to my students when I had to proceed to a work site directly from school one late afternoon. This meant I had to change into my cop suit in the teacher's lounge, a drab space filled with cheap furniture, that reeked of ancient, embedded cigarette smoke and rancid coffee. I had no classroom, only a materials cart I pushed from room to room, so I had no personal closet. The teachers loved me because my arrival at their classrooms meant they were sprung for forty-five minutes for a smoke, gossip, coffee, and marking tests.

They were also leery of me because of the days I changed clothes in the teachers' lounge bathroom, tugged my cop hat low on my forehead, buckled my gun belt, snapped down the sunglass clip-ons over my spectacles, and strode out of their sane world into the vortex of crime and vigilance. They could almost hear the "ka-ching" of invisible spurs as I sauntered into the parking lot and the hot disk of the setting sun. I never had discipline problems with my students because they knew that "Mr. Souter is a cop!"

The revolver that swept through almost 80 percent of police departments in the 1920s and 1930s was the Smith & Wesson Military and Police in .38 Special caliber. Originally designed in 1899 as the Hand Ejector Military and Police model, its swing-out cylinder with attached ejector rod that dumps all six empty brass cases at a stroke and permits rapid reloading was a big hit with law enforcement. It also featured a double lock at the front and rear of the cylinder to hold it securely in place during ignition. All the working parts were encased in the rigid K-Frame crafted of blued steel.

This security made the revolver popular with target shooters as well, finally giving them a real competition gun chambered in the latest .38 Special cartridge. In 1946 the K-Frame revolver was produced in a target version for .22 caliber, matching the large-bore gun in weight and balance in the "Masterpiece" series. This was the small-bore target gun until challenged by the second series (1947–1955) of the Colt Woodsman semiautomatic, the High Standard Model 10, and the Ruger Mark series of semiautomatic pistols.

I had a wonderful brush with history two years ago as I made my regular stop at the Maxon Shooters Supplies and Indoor Range in Des Plaines,

Illinois, near my home. Besides offering range facilities to civilian and police shooters, the owners provide gunsmith services and a wide selection of handguns and rifles for sale. They also have a few vintage weapons on consignment from owners. Usually the prize Colts, Smith & Wessons, and European museum pieces are beyond my price point. I don't collect. I shoot, and to fire some of these antiques would be a sacrilege and a risk to my health insurance coverage ("stupidity" is considered an uninsurable precondition). On that day, however, as I passed the glass cases heading for the target range desk, I stopped short.

The revolver was a gleaming, nickel-plated brute. It had adjustable sights built into the frame, not added later after the fact. The finish was immaculate, and the grips were oversize combat types, lightly stained reddish walnut and checkered. It looked both modern and antique at the same time. I asked to see it. Picking up that big revolver was like putting on an old familiar glove. The cylinder chambers had virtually no corrosion, nor did the barrel, and the cylinder lock at full cock was rock solid. The price was within my means, and the caliber was .38 Special, so I would not go broke feeding it. The sale was consummated—our old lawn mower could get along for another summer—and the background-check waiting period required in Illinois for handgun purchases commenced.

Smith & Wesson offers a verification service for a small research sum, and I sent them the gun's specs. On their embossed stationery, I discovered I had bought a ".38 Special caliber Hand Ejector Military & Police model of 1905, Third Change." That third modification was made in 1909 and remained for sale until 1915. My revolver had been shipped to the Chicago sporting goods store Von Lengerke & Antoine Co. in 1911 in blue finish, and the nickel plating was added by customer request. It is the "five-screw" target model M&P and, I discovered, a real tack driver at twenty-five yards.

I've sent boxes of bullets through it since then and, following the instruction of the late Ed McGivern, have been able to shoot five shots at double action in just under two seconds and cover the group with a playing card. It is a great satisfaction to fire a gun built in 1910 and score well with it. That is one of the lures of shooting: to be able to turn back the clock and share a moment with our peers of another age.

It wasn't until 1934, with the passage of the National Firearms Act (NFA), that machine guns and other classes of firearms—short-barreled rifles and shotguns and accessories such as suppressors (silencers)—were eventually placed under strict federal regulation. Even the NRA supported the move to take fully automatic weapons off the streets.

5

A-HUNTING WE DID GO

At two o'clock in the July morning, the Alaskan sun was still high above a horizon that stretched as far as the eye could see—until you looked to your right and there loomed the north ridges of the sawtooth Brooks Range. Straight ahead, across the rolling hummocks of tundra was our objective: a gathered herd of caribou. It was a special time in their arctic life cycle. The cows had finished calving and stood thin, damp, and exhausted with their shaky youngsters. On the outskirts of the herd, beneath magnificent racks of antlers, stood the bulls. They paced and blew and looked out for interlopers. Bears and wolves only saw easy prey in the wobbly newborn calves. None of the bulls saw us as we used the hummocks to move closer for an absolutely certain shot.

I was dressed in a vinyl jacket with the wrists taped tightly closed where they tucked into my tight leather gloves. Old jeans stiff with dirt were shoved into calf-high boots and taped to the leather. A dark green hat was pulled down tight over my head and ears. Wherever flesh was exposed, it was slathered with oily liquid mosquito repellent purchased in Deadhorse at an exorbitant $4 for a small bottle. Billions of mosquitoes milled in buzzing clouds rising from the damp permafrost and hexagonal breeding ponds— caused by the crystalline structure of the melted ground ice—that dotted the landscape.

We had been stalking the herd for almost two hours. There was no trail, just searching for dry sedge grass ahead as we hiked past clusters of lichens, moss, and fitful bunches of sturdy arctic poppies. My guide and driver, a tall, lanky kid swathed in buttoned-up denim, was an employee of Atlantic Richfield, which owned the oil drilling rights to this part of Alaska's fabled North Slope. We rarely spoke, because that meant getting a mouthful of mosquitoes to chew and spit out. Hand signals were better. He signaled a halt.

Mosquitoes had been known to spook herds of caribou into stampedes, and we were also getting close enough to no longer blend into the tundra hummocks. The cows were edgy, the bulls were nervous, and the calves bleated for an early breakfast. We stopped our crouching shuffle and dropped to our stomachs, and I took aim at a magnificent bull, head held high, edge-lit by the low but still-bright sun. Steady grip, take a breath, let out half . . . squeeze. Clackita, clackita, clack! The burst sounded loud in the deep stillness. I fired again. Clackita, clackita, clack! The magnificent caribou head turned in our direction. I moved to the cows with their calves. Their heads were also up but a few seconds too late. In less than a minute, I was empty. I let go of the 300mm lens Nikon and snapped my wide-angle Leica into place, and the panorama of caribou, blue-black sky, and orange sun poured into the eyepiece frame after frame. In less than five minutes, the two-hour crawl and duckwalk across the mosquito-infested muskeg had netted seventy-two shots, or two rolls of thirty-six-exposure Ektachrome. The herd, compressed into a more defensible ring, moved away from us as we stood up and made our way back toward the pickup truck that waited on a distant gravel road.

The only blood shed was ours, to the benefit of the mosquitoes. I was photographing oil drilling in 1972 on Alaska's North Slope for the Motorola Corporation, showing their radio communications equipment in action on the rigs and in the field. Since the end of my cushy days with the *Chicago Tribune*, I had put away my guns and used all my time to earn a living with my cameras. Janet and I had two daughters, and both of us worked for groceries and the rent. For me, that meant travel to wherever photos were needed.

When the tall kid and I got back to his truck, he reached under the seat, pulled out a plastic bag of marijuana, and rolled me a cigar-thick joint. The oil companies allowed no alcohol or firearms on the slope. As we fired up (when in Rome . . .), he unzipped his jacket and hauled a .357 Magnum Ruger single-action revolver with a 7-1/2-inch barrel onto the truck fender.

He grinned and rubbed his bruised stomach where the gun butt had rubbed the skin raw. "I wasn't goin' out there naked with big grizzly bears on the prowl."

Beneath the incredible blue-black vault above us and the reluctant-to-leave sun hovering at the horizon, peering shyly through a curtain of purple cumulus, we finished our weed stogies. My tool-pusher friend drove me back to the Atlantic Richfield camp, made of portable, single-story shelters bolted together. Still feeling buzzed and exhausted, I went to my room. Outside the chest-high sliding window, it looked like dusk at 3 a.m.

Then I saw the bear cubs. The company stored its truck fuel in large, house-size rubber bladders. The fuel was basic naphtha made from crude oil in a small jury-rigged refinery near the camp. The two cubs had discovered a game of climb-the-bladder and slide-down-the-side. I grabbed a few shots of their antics with my Nikon and was turning to take off my boots when I heard a crunching sound against my room's outward facing wall.

Looking out my window, I smelled a heavy, musky odor and then looked down at the top of a head the size of a turkey platter. Mama Grizzly Bear had parked herself beneath my window to watch her cubs play. Feeling very at peace with the world, I reached down and gave her a little knuckle noogie. She reacted like a sumo wrestler on speed. Never had I seen anything that big move that fast. A couple dozen feet from my window, she turned, stood, and regarded me through hot, squinty eyes. At that same moment, my tall guide came through the door of my room with his Ruger pistol drawn. I didn't know who I was more afraid of—a .357 Magnum-toting tool pusher with a Mary Jane buzz or a honked-off grizzly bear.

The bear stamped, woofed, pooped, and rumbled away to take her kids in tow. The oil company guys who followed my guide into my room explained that grizzly bears are dangerous and giving one a knuckle-rub is not cool. Then they took me outside to show me their former meat locker. Its very thick steel door had been peeled open like tissue paper by a hungry bear of similar size. My room's wall was made of less stern stuff. Abashed and numb, I returned to my cell and fell asleep in my clothes as the sun finally slipped below the far horizon. For the next three nights, I dreamed of large bears in close pursuit.

Hunting in the United States has had a bumpy roller-coaster ride beginning with survival, moving to unreasonable slaughter, and ending with the necessary conservation that goes along with habitat reduction and economic needs. Its perception has moved from honorable tradition to the need to feed and clothe our immigrant population since Jamestown to the flood of home-steaders westward answering the call of Manifest Destiny to wanton destruc-tion of the Native American culture for economic gain. Soaring population and development of once "barren" lands has wiped out some species and brought others to the edge of extinction. Thirty million bison were killed in a decade. Their hides with the fur on sold for three dollars as robes and coats. The bones were ground for fertilizer, and stripped hides became belt leather to drive the wheels that turned the spindles that fired the industrial revolu-tion in the East.

Today university think tanks and land-hungry developers have managed to muck up the natural balance of predators to prey, causing a real need for hunting to "thin the herds." Hunters are in the moral and necessary position of working hard to preserve the game they want to shoot. In many cases, such as with the white-tailed deer, natural predators have been so reduced that hunters keep herds from overpopulation and starvation. Songbirds have been depopulated from eastern forests, and entire species have been hunted into extinction or forced into existing only in captivity.

This is not a tirade against hunting. It is the simple reporting of a result that everyone who hunts has come to recognize. Thousands of sportsmen and women go into the fields every day stalking wild game, bringing out what they shoot, and enjoying the fellowship that goes with the experience. Our hunting tradition runs deep. The minority of trigger-happy goons who have given hunting a great deal of bad press are anomalies. But too many of the macho clowns with more money and guns than brains have caused non-hunting legislators to sponsor truly stupid restrictive regulations. How did we arrive here?

Hunting, if it is successful, results in death, and the hunter must make that moral choice at the moment of pulling the trigger. Our hunting her-itage faced similar questions the day a Pilgrim touched off his matchlock and popped a turkey at the same time, scaring the feathers off some observ-ing Native Americans (who didn't yet know they were Native Americans). Since the first English and Spanish boots touched North American soil, the gun offered a twofer: it provided food, and it cowed the neighbors who met the boat. Of course, once the Native Americans figured out that the matchlock "thundersticks" were nothing more than plumbing combined with a basic chemistry—they were already smelting copper themselves—the power base shifted.

While photographing my way across the Northwest Territories of Canada on my way to Alaska in 1972, I took some time in the village of Tuktoyaktuk on the edge of the Beaufort Sea. There I met Gordon Aluviak, an Inuit hunter. It is not easy to speak to the Inuit when you are a white man loaded down with cameras and a backpack. But as I passed through town, I saw the village men trying to pull a stump from its pit in front of the school building. I shed my gear and tailed onto the rope, and soon we had the stump out, and everyone sat on the ground huffing and puffing. From then on, the doors and windows were open in the homes as I passed them, going down to the bay where the fishing boats waited to set out each morning when the thaw was done. Children played in the yards while women chopped wood and strung dead geese up to dry on clotheslines. I had become part of the furniture of the village.

Gordon sat on the steps of his shack, combing out the pelt of a large brown bear he had shot that winter. He was forty years old but looked thirty-five with his smooth, sunburned face and wide-spaced teeth. He slouched indifferently, wrapped in the worn hang of his clothes. I paused in my walk and asked him what he had used to kill the bear. Without looking up, he said, "Bow and arrow."

"What caliber?" I asked.

He grinned. ".30-30."

I sat down on the step, went through the ritual of lighting my pipe, smoked for about five minutes in silence, and soon we were talking about guns and hunting, and then he invited me inside to see his rifles and to get away from the stares of his neighbors—all this chitchat with a white man. His three rooms were warm against the cold sweeping in off the sea across the late spring ice and up over the still-beached fishing boats and the empty net racks. Linoleum floors and prints from magazines on the walls added color to the deep shadows, and the kitchen-living room smelled of the hot wood-burning stove that rested on sheet iron in front of the outside wall blackened by soot from the burners.

We sat and smoked, and he told me about hunting over the ice and the things his father had taught him: candles are good at giving cheap light, and a reflector made of snow cuts the wind and makes the light brighter. Dogs are good, but the Ski-Doo has replaced them, though the steering skis sometimes break and the rubber track becomes stiff and must be replaced, and there is no warm belly to put your feet against in the darkness of the tundra night. Seventy miles of trap lines must be tended every winter, but the prices are good: forty-five dollars for red fox. Not many are trapping, so the prices are better than a few years ago. The trap lines are not tended consistently because jobs on construction crews are easier and welfare is easier still, but the children are schooled in the white man's hostels, learning the New Math and all about the Battle of Hastings in 1066 while the traps rust and the sledge sinews dry and crack and the home brew sputters on the wood-burning stove in dry Tuktoyaktuk. Not dry for the white man, but dry for the Inuit.

We sat at the kitchen table and talked about his father, working in the summer, loading cartridges for his old Winchester held together with moose gut, and how he taught Gordon to watch the wind blow loose snow on the slopes to test its direction and how the bullet drops more in cold weather than in hot. He showed me his rust-pitted rifles, each wrapped in hide cases, fringed, and folded carefully over the top.

"Normally, I wouldn't have killed the bear," he said. "He was small and not a very good color, but I had tracked him a long way and had been fooled by the depth of his foot in the spring melt. At best, maybe he'll bring forty-five dollars." Gordon makes about fifteen hundred dollars in a good winter. Maybe more if prices keep improving.

"I'm getting tired faster now," he went on. "Used to go forty to fifty miles a day and then pitch my tent, but now I'm getting tired." We walked outside into the cold breeze that ruffled the fur of his brown bear as clouds boiled across the sky. "I'll have to quit one day." He peered across the bay at the DEW Line radar station dome that squatted concave like a massive igloo pierced with antennas on a spit of island. "Maybe one day, I'll just stay out there." Gordon Aluviak smiled good-bye and sat down to resume brushing his bear.

The use of flintlocks on rifles, shotguns (fowling pieces), and muskets improved hunting bags, as the time between trigger pull and launched projectile was shortened. The Midwest and West were crowded with all manner of big game, small game, game birds, and game that ate all of the above, including the hearty pioneers. Wagons moved across the mountains, rivers, and prairies accompanied by the dual report, "Cha-boom!" of the muzzle-loading gun. During their exploration of the Louisiana Purchase from 1804 to 1806, Lewis and Clark chose to bring along a Staudenmayer air rifle. Realizing their gunpowder was vulnerable to rain, snow, and river water, they brought one rifle that stored air in its shoulder stock through vigorous pumping—about one hundred pumps for a full reservoir—that proved to be a stroke of good planning. Native Americans along the route were amazed at the gun that could kill game "with a breath of wind."[1]

That amazement wore off as the trickle of curious white faces became a torrent of heavily armed settlers who did not understand that they were part of the earth's life cycle and did not hold dominion over it. Wagonloads of immigrants of every possible ethnic mix followed rutted trails, hunting and defending themselves as they went and leaving thousands of their fathers, sons, daughters, and wives buried beside the trails. Following the railroads, merchants, farmers, and herders created towns, which invited industry that needed elbow room and had to feed new workers who came by train from both coasts.

Great buffalo herds, antelope, deer, and flocks of birds that could darken the sky fell to the guns of the growing population. What could not be eaten was left to rot—anything to deny subsistence to the Native Americans, driving them off valuable land. The old flintlock had been replaced by the percussion cap muzzle-loader after the Civil War. Ballistic-minded technicians such as Maj. Alfred Mordecai had made a study of every variation of the single-shot muzzle-loading musket and pronounced it the only weapon suitable for combat.

After considerable scholarly investigation, he considered that the breech - loader rifle shot too rapidly. It caused soldiers to waste ammunition. His argument was not unlike the rigid thinking of noncombat "experts" during World War II who considered the single accurate shot by a thoroughly trained soldier more valuable than "fire suppression" tactics successfully emerging on the battlefields.

The Union Army's strained logic dictated the use of volley fire, but the weight of fire depended on the number of troops each firing one shot. With the breechloaders, half the number of troops could deliver twice the volume of fire over a longer duration. Many times in the war, Union soldiers fired on the advancing lines of Confederates, only to have the howling gray lines charge with bayonets before they could reload. Union companies armed with repeaters fired their volleys and hesitated. The surging line of rebels stormed the Union position. Fifty men armed with Spencer rifles firing seven shots each rose up and sent a wall of lead downrange, shredding the surprised attackers.

If there was a single redeeming factor in the army's thinking, it was that standardizing ammunition to one rifle caliber and one pistol caliber allows greater availability of battlefield distribution. An example of this necessary consistency is the story of the Union ordnance chief who asked for a list of needed ammunition before the Second Battle of Bull Run at Manassas Junction. He received a sheet requesting eleven different calibers.[2]

Unlike the achingly glacial thinking of the Military Ordnance Department—which considered the refinement of the single-shot, muzzle-loading, percussion-cap-and-ball rifle to be their primary goal—cartridge-firing weapons began gaining favor. The army was enamored of the new conical Minié ball, while the fast-firing Spencer and Henry .44 rifles put more firepower in the hands of fewer soldiers. Even the single-shot breechloaders were both accurate and quickly ready with a second shot when needed.

Pioneers and entrepreneurs brought with them the new cartridge guns, the Sharps, Spencer, and big Winchester repeaters. Game hunters from the East joined the shoot, rolling down the rails in private cars, firing out the windows, watching pronghorn antelope tumble into heaps of flailing legs as the shooters cheered and had another round of drinks. Visiting foreigners hired famous western characters like Buffalo Bill Cody to take them on hunts. As the bison faded from the scene, and as the great migrating flocks of birds were reduced—or, like the passenger pigeon, eventually driven into extinction—the century turned over, and another voice was heard.

Theodore Roosevelt was a hunter from his childhood, when he began collecting songbirds, rodents, and small raptors with a rifle that fired tiny shot cartridges that didn't spoil the feathers or ruin the pelts for taxidermy. When he went west for his health and opened up a cattle ranch in the Dakotas, he discovered a hunting paradise and like-minded comrades he would later recruit into his Rough Riders. But it was as president of the United States that he made his greatest impact on hunting. The White House was filled with his trophies, from standing bears to lion heads on the walls. He ordered custom-made weapons from Winchester, well stocked and heavy hitting. His voluminous writing included chapters on the technology and personal motivations that contributed to his hunting trips.

The conservationist John Muir took up the need for preserving our wild spaces and the creatures that lived there. He enlisted Roosevelt's aid and prestige to begin setting aside the first national parks as sanctuaries and places where the public could visit and learn nature's lessons. The bloodyminded Roosevelt saw nature through Muir's eyes and set the pattern for conservation and preservation among hunters and outdoorsmen while selling the "vigorous life" to his fellow Americans.

Following World War I and the huge technological leaps that came from its carnage, Americans experienced a sudden rush to be "modern." After all, hadn't we saved the world from destruction? It was time to cut loose the old Victorian restraints and have some fun. We'd spend some money we didn't have on stuff we didn't know we needed using the new time-payment plans and maybe buying some stock. Everyone was in the market. Why not take a chance?

The Wild West was gone, but there was still hunting and "tin can" camping along back roads leading to the new parks and wilderness areas. For hunters, this postwar time was particularly exciting. With the adoption by the military of the .30-06 cartridge and the Mauser-type, high-pressure, bolt-action rifle, large-caliber shooting started to dry up. The next decades were devoted to the experimenters, cartridge engineers who worked with smaller bullets designed for ballistic perfection, from tapered boat-tail back to pointed spitzer tip. "Streamlining" ruled. Target shooters only cared about a bullet's ability to buck the wind, minimize drop, and not turn sideways (keyhole) at longer ranges. They didn't care a fig about impact on the target. But hunters cared very much.

Hunters turned to these ballistic experimenters, or "wildcatters," who toiled away in basements and backrooms or rustic cabins in the middle of nowhere to brew up special bullets for all kinds of game. For example, even the homely little .22 was not immune to tinkering. In the 1920s reaching way out to touch something was the goal of wildcatters who took a forty-grain .22 bullet and stuffed it into an old black-powder .22 Winchester centerfire cartridge case filled with smokeless powder. The resulting .22 Hornet was hot and shot flat out to two hundred yards. It hit hard enough to annoy woodchucks and henhouse raiders. Its success as a home brew proved commercially viable, and it became the first wildcat cartridge commercially adopted by a U.S. manufacturer. Rifles retrofitted for new, hot hunting bullets had to be carefully chosen because of the increase in chamber pressures. The .22 Hornet, for instance, found a home in the rethroated breech of the 1922 Springfield rifle that was shipped to ROTC and college rifle teams by the army. Its solid bolt action, designed to mimic the .30-06 Springfield and overengineered for the .22 rimfire, could easily back up the feisty Hornet.[3]

The nerds of the shooting sports repurposed a number of the old standby cartridges that had distinguished pedigrees, to create more modern and capable rounds that were not coming from the ammunition and gun manufacturers. One of these owed its existence to the pioneering and venerable .30-30 rifle. This round-nosed bullet had been designed for the Winchester lever-action repeating rifle as an outstanding deer combination—the perfect saddle gun of the late nineteenth century. Charles Newton thought he could do better than the .30-30—which was considered a hot cartridge for its time—and in 1915 designed the .25-3000, which had a muzzle velocity of 3,000 feet per second with an eighty-seven-grain bullet and would chamber beautifully in the rotary-magazine Savage Model 99 lever-action rifle. The upgrading to a hundred-grain slug brought the cartridge into the deer-hunting league. And the Savage rifle was a streamlined work of art, which gave it a popular cachet.

Newton went on to "neck down" the case to a .248-inch bullet diameter, which inspired wildcatters to pinch in the case shoulder to an angle of 28 degrees and stuff in a .224 caliber slug. These small-bullet/large-powder-charge combinations became the ".22 varminters," which begat the .22-250 and eventually the .222 Remington created by Mike Walker. What resulted from these hot, flat-shooting loads was a new shooting sport that became the test bed for many new technology innovations, the fine art of benchrest shooting.

These meticulous, precision target punchers strive for the goal of America's earlier long-range target shooters: the smallest possible group of five or ten shots fired from a rifle at various ranges. Instead of aiming from a body-supported shooting position, benchrest rifles are securely held in a rigid mount to remove shooter movement error from the equation.

Benchrest shooting has created many critter-hunting cartridges in many calibers. The sport's competitions have categories that include "Light Varmint," "Heavy Varmint," "Sporter," and "Unlimited" classes. Unlimited shooting uses rifle components assembled with a built-in machine rest, often called a "railgun." Because the idea of the sport is based on extreme accuracy, virtually all ammunition is hand-loaded and "tuned" to the particular hand-gunsmithed rifle.

For example, barrels rifled in the factory vary from one to the next, even though the reamer is computer driven to industry standards. The metallurgy of the tooling, gradual dulling of the cutting edges, and metallurgy of each barrel create variables that make each breech and bore unique. To the hand loader, the point at which the ogive diameter—the place on the bullet where its diameter begins to decrease just before the bullet actually jumps into the lands and grooves of the rifling when fired—is a critical measurement. To accommodate the micrometer-variable breech depths, the cartridge brass case can be stretched (sized) to place the "bullet jump" as close as .003–.005 inches from the barrel's lands. No factory load can match this precision. Finicky hand loaders understand that the brass case containing the powder and bullet stretches, or "flows," forward when fired to accommodate the breech depth. Consequently, they never use brass cases that have been fired in another gun (stretched) until each case has been resized to fit their rifle.

Longer-range contests reach into the .30 caliber class of bullets, and powerful telescopic sights are common to all ranges. While most shooters are happy to achieve minute-of-angle (MOA) accuracy (a one-inch group at one hundred yards, two-inch group at two hundred yards, etc.), benchrest shooters strive for groups measured in 1/8 MOA with their telescopic sights. However, lugging a bull-barrel, telescopic-sighted, composite-stocked bench rifle into the field to pot an inedible woodchuck at two hundred yards seems counterproductive. But every day, hunters and target shooters take advantage of the hard work these inventive wildcatters throw downrange.

I was never much of a hunter and today even less so. But when I was a young man, I discovered the only way I could find some time to be with my father was for us to drive north from our home on Chicago's South Side to the woods in the northwest suburbs and hunt squirrels, rabbits, and pheasants. Dad received service calls over the telephone and worked out of our apartment as a troubleshooter for the Sperry Gyroscope Company fixing radar, steering gear, and gyro compasses on the Great Lakes ore freighters. It was hard to find a weekend when the phone didn't ring, sending him off with his tools, so we held our breaths whenever we planned a hunting trip. But once we were out the door, there were no cell phones or even CB radio, so Mom (his live-in secretary) could not reach us, and we were gone.

Not having the spare money to join any local hunt clubs where farms were stocked with pheasants and hunters charged a fee per bird shot, we usually parked off the road and followed a railroad track. Of course, we trespassed on railroad property, and when we slanted off into a deserted cornfield with no farmhouse in sight to walk the rows, we were trespassing on private property. Nevertheless, railroad work gangs who saw us and farmers who rolled past us atop their Case and Farmall tractors just waved. On those chill November days with the last of the leaves clinging tenaciously to their branches and the rows brown and yellow with stalks, mostly we enjoyed a walk and talk through the corn shucks. Rarely were our perambulations rudely interrupted by something to shoot at.

Dad carried his father's 12-gauge, side-by-side, Ithaca shotgun, a real shoulder buster custom stocked for Grandpa Souter, who had arms like an orangutan. Usually by the end of a shooting day, under his shirt and jacket, Dad's shoulder was the color of an eggplant. I carried a bolt-action, three-shot, box-magazine Mossberg 16-gauge shotgun with an adjustable choke. It was serviceable, but the idea of taking a second shot on a winged target was a myth. By the time I finished latching open the bolt and camming another shell into the breech, I was looking at empty sky. Also, its serrated safety lever had a nasty habit of punching back against my thumb on the stock tang at each shot. By the end of my day, the tip of my thumb was also the color of an eggplant.

Late one morning, neither of us had yet achieved our eggplant colorations by the time we exited some corn rows. Ahead of us were five hunters, all wearing orange hats and spread out about twenty feet apart about to advance into the next field. Dad stopped at the edge of the grass tractor road between our field and the one they were about to assault and called out, asking if we could join their drive on the flanks. That was the least favorable spot. If any birds rose near the center of the group, we would have that last chance to shoot if no one else scored a hit. But beggars can't be choosers. One of the hunters wearing a plaid shirt and suspender overalls waved us toward each end of their line.

With Dad's Ithaca safely broken open at the breech and my Mossberg across my shoulder with its bolt open, we started across the grass verge. We were halfway there when their line moved into the tall corn. No sooner had they stepped forward then a ruckus rattled the stillness. From the center of the line came a large tan-and-white rabbit bounding clear of the cornrows and shifting into high gear straight at us. Unprepared, with our guns hors de combat, we froze. Our hosts however, were galvanized into action by a shout: "Bunny!"

All five cocked and ready shotguns swung our way. The bunny made a course correction hard-a-port and exploded past us in a thunder of hind feet. The muzzles followed Br'er Rabbit, who by now was a blur just short of a sonic boom. When the gun blast came, it was more of a rippling broadside, as if a battleship had just uncorked her sixteen-inch main battery. All the number four birdshot ripped into the grass where bunny had been. We were frozen in place, a waxworks tableau. The gunners looked our way as the gunpowder smell wafted across the cornfield.

I guess the fact that we had not been shredded down to our shoe tops by the shotgun volley was apologies enough, because our former hosts turned and sheepishly disappeared like phantoms into the corn. We wandered over to a small copse by a creek bed that bordered the field and sat beneath an apple tree. Amid its wormy refugees and heady fall fragrance of damp earth and leaves, we quietly ate the sandwiches we had carried in our pockets and savored a thermos of coffee laced with cream and sugar. That was a story we never told Mom.

The United States is blessed with a variety of geography that is home to an exceptional range of animals considered wild game. When our intrusion into this world was based on trailblazing and survival of nature's casual cruelties, hunting meant that most wild fauna went into the pot. Until domestic animals had a chance to graze, grow, and furnish our protein, the vast prairies, mountains, and forests provided our food on the hoof, paw, or wing. We were, by necessity a nation of hunters. Eastern and southern gun and ammunition manufacturers hustled to fill orders and create the desire for the latest in hunting technology.

Today hunters have become part of the campaign for conservation. Civilization has reduced the wild spaces and, accordingly, regulated hunting, with game and bag limits that have helped keep overpopulation from scouring away food sources. Predators' places in the life cycle are better understood. Release of gray wolves back into Yellowstone National Park has been a success. License fees have allowed states to improve hunting facilities and police out the knuckle-dragging poachers who are a menace to the sport.

Hunting has its rituals. For safety's sake, much hunting is a group affair. Crunching around in the wilderness while carrying a loaded gun opens the door to many emergencies, which can require the aid of a hunting partner. Back in the day, a hunt started with simply fetching the rifle from a closet or rack, dropping a handful of cartridges into your pocket, grabbing an apple off the kitchen table, and walking through the back gate. Add to that a good pair of lace-up high-top boots and maybe a Ford Flivver to transport everybody back to Jethro's north forty where the timberline started, and you had hunting in the 1920s and 1930s, right up through the 1940s.

The guns were sporter-stocked war-surplus Springfields and Enfields in .30-06, lever-action rifles such as the Winchester Model 94, Marlin, and Savage Model 99 plus a mix of foreign rifles such as Mausers and Mannlichers. Many of them had their breech throats reamed out to accept the latest hot horror cartridge guaranteed to drop an elk at two hundred yards or blow a coyote in two at a hundred. Besides their rifle and ammunition, serious hunters carried a pack frame on their backs to haul the meat from their kill back down the mountain. Ernest Hemingway once bemoaned the fact that few skiers ever walked up the mountain in order to ski down, so they didn't have the legs for the heavy planks that passed for skis back then. Today, we have four-wheel drive, gas-engine, all-terrain buggies to bring out the hunting kills. Hunters should spend their money at gyms to trim waistlines and harden up calves. (So says this 5'7", 220-pound author.)

Hunters in the prewar years had a simpler time of it than today's wilderness warriors. For an overnight, their gear amounted to a blanket parka, a plaid shirt, denim pants, long johns, good boots laced calf-high, a sharp knife, a bag of beef jerky, flapjack makings, some dried beans, a nesting cup, a bowl, cook pot, a skillet, a tent half for a ground cloth, a canteen, an old army blanket, a couple of bars of Red Man chewing tobacco or a tin of Prince Albert for the pipe, a fedora, and a pair of leather gloves. To that equipage was added a slung rifle and ammunition and possibly a .22 handgun for small game to fill the stewpot or skillet and not spook any sharp-eared game nearby.

Today the hunter looks more like a sniper trainee in camouflage or, in a ghillie suit, resembles a bush with feet. The clothes are lighter weight but more efficient, keeping out cold and damp. Gun-spooked game must be closely approached, so hunters now blend with the woods rather than warn other shooters of their presence with bright colors. The guns are different, too. Shotguns firing solid slugs and black-powder retro rifles ignited by percussion caps are popular.

The latest sporting gun is a single-shot weapon that exchanges barrels to fire a variety of ammunition from .17 HMR to a 12-gauge shotgun shell, with a bunch of rimfire and centerfire cartridges in between, plus a muzzle-loader barrel in .45 or .50 caliber using a percussion cap. Imagine heading into the field with a golf bag holding barrels instead of clubs. The Rossi Wizard is truly a gun for all seasons and takes us back to the day when one shot had to do it all in the hands of a real hunter.

The retro craze has opened new markets for Italian manufacturers who have shipped replicas of Colt Single Action Army revolvers, percussion revolvers and rifles, and the latest from Uberti, a modernized replica of the famous 1885 Winchester/Browning High Wall single-shot long-range rifle with a thirty-two-inch-barrel version. To continue the authenticity, the 5X telescopic sight is a long-tube replica designed by William Malcolm, and the drop-block-action chambers the venerable .45-70, .45-90, and .45-120 caliber cartridges. On this side of the pond, the Henry rifle is alive and well in a variety of calibers and looking like the brassbound lever action that paved the way for the legendary Winchester.

On the other side of the coin, the quasi-military, AR-style, modular semi-automatic rifles are tricked out with muzzle brakes, optical sights, night-vision scopes, collapsible stocks, Picatinny rails (named for the army research arsenal in New Jersey) for handgrips, flashlights, lasers, and bayonets for if that white-tailed deer becomes obstreperous and charges. Manufacturers and the gun magazines make bags of money off convincing hunters they need all this gear and a thirty-round, double-stacked-magazine, SWAT team/special ops rifle with added Egoboost to bring home the beastie. But if your pockets are deep enough, it's all good fun with no lasting scars—except to your wallet, especially if you come back with an empty sack and out of ammo.

The slopes of the Mauna Loa volcanic crater are steep and, fortunately, laced with scruffy trails. These trails, however, receive the occasional river of red-hot lava hissing and flaming down through the vegetation. On a warm tropical morning, I found myself as a kibitzer to a three-man hunting party in search of *Sus scrofa*, the Hawaiian feral pig. I was on assignment in the Hawaiian Islands for a couple of weeks, blazing away at tourist attractions with my Nikon cameras for a series of travel poster images. Some businesses on the islands had purchased advertising space on the posters, and I had been dispatched to the Big Island of Hawaii to photograph and be a guest at this plush resort tucked into the Pacific shore. One of the guest perks happened to be a guided wild pig hunt.

These feral pigs are not native to the islands but arrived with the early Polynesian explorers about 1,500 years ago and then again with Captain Cook. They have no natural predators and do considerable damage to local flora, noshing on native plants, trampling soils, creating wallows, scattering pig poop about, and making lots of baby pigs. They are unwanted, unloved, and quite ugly, with nasty little tusks and a disposition only another pig could love. Hunting is one form of population control. Unlike the ubiquitous prairie dog in the western United States, the pig is edible and quite tasty if properly prepared using caution to look for parasites in the guts and muscle tissue.

The two hunters footing the bill for the day trip were a dentist and a stockbroker in their late thirties dressed in polo shirts, slacks, and computer-designed sneakers. Each carried a rifle supplied by the outfitter, a Savage Model 99 lever action in .300 Savage caliber. Our guide was a short, stocky native Hawaiian wearing a broad-brimmed hat with chinstrap, khaki shirt, and shorts with calf-high leather boots. He carried a small backpack and a wide, twelve-inch-long bowie knife in a leather sheath.

After a brief demonstration and orientation with the Savage rifle, we took a ride in a Land Rover to the resort's hunting preserve. The dentist let me hold his borrowed rifle and work the lever action. I liked the Savage immediately. Firing the Winchester lever action requires the shooter to extend his index finger clear of the trigger as he throws down the lever to extract the spent cartridge case and cam a fresh bullet into the breech. If you don't, you risk getting your digit skewered on the protruding, unguarded trigger on the lever's upswing. After a while it becomes an automatic reflex, but it is one more thing to think about until you become familiar. Not so the Savage. On this rifle, the entire trigger assembly levers down as the rotary magazine advances and empty cartridge cases are swapped for loads in the breech. You can blaze away from the get-go.

The guide and I, with my cameras poised, discovered early on that the two gentlemen were truly neophytes to hunting fundamentals. As we skidded on the trails' rocky soil and groped our way around snake dens and dangerous-looking outcroppings, they never shut up their nervous banter. It was as if they were calling out, "Run, pigs, run! We're coming!" The guide kept a professional smile in place, but in his bones, I'm sure he knew it was going to be a long hunt.

By the middle of the day, we had seen a half-dozen wild pigs whom we must have surprised from their mid-afternoon naps. They scattered ahead of us, their bristly tails erect, snorting as they trotted. The two hunters loosed volleys but could not grasp the concept of leading the running pigs and shooting where they would be, not where they had been. We took a break for lunch.

Since I had not been expected to share the resort-packed lunch, I gnawed on a Three Musketeers bar and chomped down a small box of raisins. In an act of noblesse oblige, the stockbroker asked if I wanted to take a couple of shots from his rifle just to see how it feels, for my article. I accepted, and the guide threw a couple of empty tinned fruit cans down the slope, and they stopped bouncing at about fifty yards distant.

Shooting uphill or downhill is tricky. If a rifle is sighted in at three hundred yards on level ground but the angle of the hill is 30 degrees, then the cosine of 30 is .087, leaving the actual range of the downhill target at 261 yards (300 x .087), so the sight must be held lower to hit the target. That is the mathematical theory behind squinting at the hill and taking a good guess based on all your previous misses. Knowing that gravity affects the bullet travel perpendicular to its horizontal path also helps. Anyway, the open iron sights on the rifle were sharp and clear, and I sent the first can spinning up into the air. The second can was five feet to the right, and I popped that one. What I had not seen was the guide pick up the second rifle, and as the can twanged into the air, he fired and hit the airborne can, kicking it higher and to my left. By that time I had reloaded, and as the can froze in its apogee, I holed it with the luckiest shot I ever made in my life.

I handed back the rifle with thanks while the guide tidied up camp, and we scrambled down to retrieve the blasted tin cans, which went into the backpack. Neither the guide nor I could make eye contact. I imagine it was like making a hole-in-one in a golf tournament—being both pleased and embarrassed at the same time. The silly chatter stopped, and after lunch the silence on the trail was total. At three o'clock, an hour before we were due back at the parked Range Rover, a middling-size porker zagged when it should have zigged and ran into a blizzard of .300 caliber bullets. The guide probably said a silent Hawaiian prayer as he drew his skinning knife. My Nikon's motor drive had caught the action. I made a trophy shot of the proud hunters and sent a copy to their offices on the mainland. Nobody had photographed my tin can wing shot, so, like the hole-in-one sunk with no one else on the course, I must enjoy the memory in solitude.

Hunting offers what no other shooting sport can approach: the chance to experience the wilderness, elbow to elbow with nature. The sport gives the hunter a chance to learn woodcraft and test instincts that are part of our DNA but rarely get exercised. A hunter has to have a stoic streak, an ability to go all day without getting a shot and still be able to enjoy the experience. The hunter has to calm the adrenaline surge when his game is finally in range and hours of practice have to be tested. For the enthusiast, the justification for all that equipment and the cost of the trip to the hunting grounds—the approbation of your hunting partners—often comes down to one shot. Choice of rifle, choice of ammunition, where's the wind? Your glasses are fogging, and your mouth is dry. What's the actual range compared to the sighted-in range? Should I hold off? Can't feel the trigger. Can't feel my feet. Exhale and start over.

No matter the size of the game, the moment is always dramatic, always personal. The hunter experiences the transitional moment between life and death, ending everything that sustains cognition. The target is life, whether it is a squirrel flattened on a tree branch or a bull elk crossing a meadow at a high lope. Hunters must distill all the joys of the discovery, the stalk, and the skill of the clean kill, and touch what is now, remembering what once was. For many, it is a restorative moment. For others, not so much, and they hang up their hunting guns and go back to the range to kill paper.

After World War II, the NRA looked around for new areas where education and training were needed. It settled on the hunting community. In 1949 the NRA partnered with the state of New York to establish the first hunter education program. From that beginning, hunter education courses are now taught by state fish and game departments across the country and Canada and have helped make hunting one of the safest sports in existence. Due to increasing interest in hunting, the NRA launched a new magazine in 1973, *American Hunter*, dedicated solely to hunting topics year round.

The hunting gear flogged in the pages of *American Hunter* include much exotica, which always keeps the subject fresh. Gone are the days when the only choices were lever-action or bolt-action rifles. Today, the retro-minded are catered to by manufacturers with accessories such as the TAC-15 cross-bow, which validates the purchase of an assault rifle ("AR-type" in NRA lingo) for hunting. Clap it on the TAC-15, and you've converted your AR-15 into a crossbow firing one arrow at a time. In the not-too-distant past, Wham-O offered a pistol crossbow on the back pages of *Popular Mechanics* magazine. Today, though the weapon is no longer made, you can buy one for less than $50 on eBay.

Unless you plan to take out enemy perimeter guards silently with this gizmo or train for the International Crossbow Union matches held every two years, the TAC-15 joins the "Olde Curiosity Shoppe" collection including: the bolt-action, percussion muzzle-loader (oxymoron?), the giant heavy-frame revolver lumbered with large telescopic sights, and the retro double-barreled rifle firing a brutish .50 caliber load. The snap-together, double thirty-round magazines for the AR-15-type rifles give the hunter the look of an al Qaeda terrorist. Hunters embrace all the trappings and novelty items just as car customizers champion chromed valve head covers. No fault, no foul if the shooter's pockets are deep enough. There will always be an entrepreneur with a garage, a lathe, and a vacuum press out there to create and fill the need.

My last hunt with my dad also included my then-girlfriend, Janet, and another school friend, tall, gangly Gerry Cole. It was the start of squirrel season, and we drove out to a wood in a northern county that bordered a large cornfield. It was a brilliant sunny fall day, and many leaves were still in the trees giving the squirrels shadowy places to hide. After an hour, we decided we made too large a group and split into pairs. Dad bit the bullet and took Gerry. I took Janet, who was along just for the walk, not the shooting. Now, Gerry was a swell guy—attended all the best prep schools and was kicked out of all the best colleges. He was also a Gilbert and Sullivan savant. He knew all the words to all their operettas. As he and Dad disappeared into the trees, Janet and I heard the first sotto voce bars from *The Pirates of Penzance*.

Normally for squirrels, I took my Ruger .22 rimfire target pistol that I used to shoot in tournaments when I was a member of the 53rd Street YMCA team. This time, however, because of the heavy leaf cover, I brought my Model 1890 nickel-plated Winchester .22 rimfire, pump-action rifle. It was a beautiful antique gun with 85 percent of its plating intact, a fine wood stock with a crescent steel buttplate, and a fold-up marble peep sight on the tang behind the exposed hammer spur. The tang sight gave me an instant look at the rifle's open sights at the muzzle and was perfectly aligned above the breech. The old Winchester's only shortcoming was that the magazine-loading arm was worn from use and would only transfer .22 Long cartridges from the tubular magazine to the breech—a little under-powered, but a tack driver just the same.

Janet was also perfectly aligned, slender with soft blue eyes and a thick mane of rich red hair. I was still a goon around girls, not yet twenty-one, and realizing every day that she was way out of my league, but I hoped it would get better. The woods rattled above our heads and crunched beneath our feet as sunbeams edge-lit the tree trunks and mottled the fading gold of the fallen. I scanned the treetops, and she occasionally stopped and picked up a multi-hued leaf to add to the collection building in her coat pocket. Finally, I called for a break and plopped down on a particularly dense pile of leaves, and she neatly settled down beside me and we lay looking up at the sky and towering woods.

I had to admit, hunting with Dad was fun, but this had it beat all to hell. I rolled onto my side facing her, propped up on my elbow. She flicked a glance in my direction and smiled. I was trying to remember a line Jimmy Stewart had used in a movie when I saw the squirrel.

Looking across Janet's . . . torso . . . I saw the critter frozen to the side of a tree about sixty yards away, give or take. She noticed my shift in attention and started to speak. I raised my finger to my lips. Her eyebrows came down.

I mouthed the word "squirrel." Her eyebrows shot up. I reached behind me and groped around until I found my rifle in the leaves. As I snaked it up, her eyes got wider and then followed the muzzle past her nose as I brought the nickel-plated octagon barrel across her.

"Shh," I said and reached up to cock the hammer. A .22 Long cartridge was already in the chamber. With the barrel just above her . . . torso . . . I squinted through the tang peep sight, and the squirrel was still there. If she had not been slender, I would have been aimed too, well, high. She closed her eyes. I squeezed the trigger and bap! The rifle snapped out its small bullet.

I rose from the leaves and walked to the base of the distant tree, still carrying my rifle in case he was only wounded and I had to defend myself. No problem. I had made a clean head shot and held up the big cat squirrel by his tail. Janet smiled but not with her eyes. She was happy for me but not so happy for the squirrel. When we met back up with Dad and Gerry, we kept the circumstances of the shot to ourselves. As Gerry hummed, "He was the perfect model of a modern major general . . . " we field dressed Mr. Squirrel, and on the following weekend, Janet came over for dinner and had squirrel stew, ears of corn, and mashed potatoes. We were married two years later. Gerry and Dad have since gone to their reward, and she still has that thick mane of beautiful red hair.

6

WORLD WAR II:
THE GAME CHANGER

In September 1941, *American Rifleman* magazine published a star-studded, eagle-and-shield-headed combination essay for preparedness and hyperbolic call to arms by associate editor Raymond J. Stan that obviously had the imprimatur of the NRA governors. By this time, the newsreels and press had been full of Hitler's henchmen posturing, marching, saluting, and finally rushing across the Polish border in a "preemptive" attack, bombing the daylights out of Great Britain, rolling up France, and invading Russia. Germany's naked aggression and offensive military machine was galloping across Europe. America's "Sleeping Giant" had snoozed its way to a ranking of seventeenth most powerful army in the world, though signs of stirring were evident.

Two years earlier, fifty old destroyers had been leased to the British, and President Roosevelt signed the Selective Training and Service Act of 1940. In October of that year, the first peacetime military draft in American history began gathering civilians. The Japanese diplomatic and naval codes were broken, and all shipments of U.S. scrap steel and iron to Japan were stopped. While the upper echelons of government began rumbling into action on rusty treads, the stupendous job of converting sixteen million civilians already registered for military service—and more still jobless because of the lingering effects of the Depression—got under way.

Long-dormant forts and rows of cobwebby 1917–1918 barracks became crowded training centers. Acres of uniform khaki, cotton drill, and denim began flying through mills and garment manufacturers. Automobile manufacturing pitched in with enthusiasm, as Chrysler recorded in a company newsletter interview of a gushing "ranking employee" on June 7, 1940:

Chrysler Corporation is cooperating whole heartedly with the United States Government in the steps it is taking in the interest of national defense. In recent weeks we have accelerated our contacts with the government on important phases of this program.

Besides the thousands of Dodge trucks and reconnaissance cars which we have already made and are now making for the Army, our corporation has been selected to handle several important educational orders in munitions products.

These orders include almost $500,000 worth of work on such items as fuse bomb noses, forging and machining shells, and the making of cartridge cases. A special ordnance manufacturing division of the corporation has been formed to handle this type of work. We are also working very diligently on preparations for other major equipment for the Army which I do not feel at liberty to discuss at this time.[1]

Training men to operate those tanks, fire those shells, and drop those bombs was the big problem. As with World War I, the military was once again having to do a rush job to create a professional army. It was as if all the wars in our past had not taught us a single lesson. The anathema of funding and maintaining a standing army of any effective size was still a non-starter in Congress, and the Depression had even further reduced appropriations. States could not afford adequate National Guard regiments, let alone modern weapons. Yet again, the downsizing of the military had left us vulnerable. Now we faced the Axis powers threatening both coasts, and we did not have the tools or the training to defend our shores or strike back if attacked.

The brand-new M1 Garand rifle had been introduced in 1937, won praise at Camp Perry, and was in production, but the rifle on most shoulders was still the Springfield Model 1903. When there were not enough real weapons, trainees drilled with sticks, fired mailing tube mortars, and lobbed flour-sack grenades at old trucks with "tank" painted on the side. Men shouted "rat-a-tat-tat" and aimed wooden machine guns at imagined enemy troops charging en masse from trenches. In this chaos the NRA saw an opportunity to raise its profile in the national community and wrap their motives in the American flag. In Stan's *American Rifleman* editorial, titled "The NRA and National Defense," he states:

It might be said here in behalf of the NRA participation in the defense move that the shooting sport is offered not only as an opportunity to serve the country but a chance to firmly establish the sport and the clubs as an integral part of our democratic form of government in the eyes of the authorities. It has a chance to build up a community leadership that will carry over even when security is again established. There is no reason why the rifle clubs should not be called upon and available in any emergency in peace or war. There is more than one reason why they are better suited than other civic organization, for instance, for auxiliary police duty in maintaining order, preventing looting and re-establishing public morale following fire, flood, explosions or tornado.

Operating as a unit, the coordination, enthusiasm, morale and discipline of a band of civilian riflemen would be of the highest order. . . . The coolness of an experienced rifle or pistol shooter under heat of excitement and his confidence to do the right thing at the right time is obvious. . . . [2]

While this appears to be a simple updating of the minuteman concept of armed citizens ready to defend their communities against the overbearing British in 1775, in the 1940s there were other models with more sinister motives to consider. The Prussian Landsturm had been created as a guerrilla force to combat Napoleon in 1813–1815. The concept was revived on paper in 1925, but the Soviet advances on the eastern front during World War II rekindled the civilian paramilitary force by panzer pioneer Heinz Guderian in 1944. The Volkssturm comprised Hitler Youth, the elderly, and the previously unfit for service. Their morale and fanaticism was guaranteed by placing Volkssturm forces under the commands of local mayors and governors (*gauleiters* and *kreisleiters*) who were under the thumbs of Joseph Goebbels and Martin Bormann, among other shining stars of the Third Reich. The Volkssturm's weapons were crude but included the Panzerfaust, a one-shot grenade launcher that fired a shaped charge that could take out an Allied Sherman tank.[3]

In Japan, as the Allied noose tightened around the home islands, the Japanese cabinet turned the transportation and construction auxiliary, the Kokumin Giyūtai, into an armed civilian militia. All males between fifteen and sixty years of age and females between seventeen and forty were conscripted. Retired military officers and civilians with weapon experience were assigned as commanders. The forces were ordered to practice guerrilla warfare in their home cities, towns, and in mountain redoubts while continuing to remove rubble and help fight fires.[4]

In Italy the National Security Volunteer Militia was formed following World War I and was known as the Blackshirts. Operating as the military arm of Benito Mussolini's fascist government, the groups were nationalist intellectuals, retired army officers, and young landowners who opposed peasants and labor unions. As Mussolini consolidated his power, their tactics against opposition became more brutal until many Blackshirt units were incorporated into combat organizations to fight in Italy's various theaters.[5]

No one should infer that the NRA had any fascist intent in proposing that armed members of the NRA were the best arbiters of law and order because they could (A) follow a range officer's orders at the firing line and (B) shoot the eye out some annoying, lawbreaking snot at two hundred yards. However, putting forward the concept of "Rely on Your Local Gunman" to enforce civic rules and regs revealed a certain embarrassing, testosterone-soaked, überpatriotic elitism that occasionally bubbled to the surface like a recurring oil spill over the next decades.

The federal government said "thanks, but no thanks" to the NRA's modest proposal but left the states free to consider—and control—the gun-toting membership who wanted to help. Three months later, when the Japanese shoved the United States off the fence and into the conflict, the NRA plunged into the fray with civilian instructors and reviews of the latest U.S. combat weapons. They even had an *American Rifleman* editor, Bill Shadel, accredited to report successes of American riflemen and review what the enemy was shooting back at us. The excellent quality of his work caught the ear of Edward R. Murrow, who recruited him for CBS Radio. He eventually worked alongside journalistic luminaries Walter Cronkite, Howard K. Smith, and Eric Sevareid in the combat theaters.

———————————————◆◆◆———————————————

Janet and I moved into the town of Arlington Heights in 1972 with our three kids and two cats to earn a few dollars and pay off the house mortgage. Twenty-four years later, we had done both and were just establishing ourselves as writers with our first hardcover book, *The American Fire Station*, when the Historical Society contacted us. Arlington Heights needed an updated history book, and the society asked us if could take on the job. We agreed to be editors and also write three of the chapters while recruiting other local writers to produce the bulk of the book. One of the chapters we chose was "Arlington Heights: The Village at War."

I was only five years old when World War II ended. Except for wondering why my parents kept two new automobile tires under their bed or why I had to either accommodate the cooking grease bucket alongside me in my stroller or carry it to the meat market every week with Mom (I did get a macaroon cookie from the butcher), home-front anxieties were a distant mystery. Looking back on those years—especially the early months—I can see that the American people were not exactly sure they were going to win. Our allies had been pounded into surrender or near starvation, and we faced enemies off both our coasts. The German blitzkrieg, the Japanese sneak attacks, and even the Italian slaughter of Ethiopians had everyone on edge. Our boys were being chased all over the Pacific and gunned down in North Africa's Kasserine Pass, and the battle for aerial superiority over Britain and the English Channel was still a near thing. What were the folks in Arlington Heights, Illinois, doing back then?

The NRA's preemptive jump at assisting civilian law, order, and safety though rifle club militias was not quite a credibility stretch when you consider the nervous, newspaper headline–fueled context. Arlington Heights is thirty-five miles northwest of Chicago, about as geographically centered in North America as you can get. And yet during the war years of 1941–1945, the village had a civil defense plan.

The police department still had a siren on its roof to alert the boys in blue to call in from the nearest phone. A number of civilian Air Raid Precaution volunteers wearing white helmets patrolled the neighborhoods to spot insufficient curtains over windows at night when the village held "blackout" tests. Airplane spotters set up stands on various roofs to scan the skies for flotillas of enemy aircraft droning above the clouds, ready to rain down steely death. At night, residents cupped their cigarettes and smoked their pipes upside down (like they had seen in British navy war movies), lest the glow be spotted by a Nazi bombardier flying at thirty thousand feet. These were real fears when every day newsreels at the movie theaters showed stacks of dead civilians after a Japanese bombing raid or streams of refugees clogging roads beneath strafing Stuka dive bombers.

Arlington Heights even had a dynamite squad. The exceptionally brave
Frank Sachs actually trained locals how to use dynamite to clear rubble from
the roads so emergency vehicles could get through to the wounded and dying
in the bombed-out buildings. Local GP Dr. Bruce Best assembled medically
adequate rescue units to apply first aid in the blast zone. Meanwhile, the Boy
Scouts and Cub Scouts practiced racing from point to point on their bicycles
carrying messages, because phone lines would be targeted by plunging
bombs. The village was a hotbed of civil defense activity.

While brochures were being passed out showing in illustrated steps how
to dispose of a phosphorous incendiary bomb that went through your
roof—using a shovel and a bucket of sand (never water)—invaders dropping
from the sky were a bigger concern. Parachutists could land in the cornfields and do all sorts of mischief if not stopped. An item in the *Cook
County Herald* newspaper mentioned resident Joseph A. Wisersky, who
hoped that "as soon as the weather permits," the Civil Defense Rifle Service
could begin blazing away at targets on a makeshift rifle range.[6] Farmers
brought out shotguns, from .410 boys' models to 8-gauge goose guns.
Winchester, Remington, Marlin, Stevens, and Model 1903 Springfield rifles
were dragged from closets. It is a tribute to the Arlington Heights Rifle
Service that not once during duty was any member inadvertently shot by a
fellow Rifle Service volunteer. Numbers of meandering livestock accidentally executed, however, were not officially recorded, but cash reimburse-
ments were distributed "unofficially."

The facts that none of the Axis powers had a long-range four-engine
bomber that could reach anywhere near Arlington Heights, Illinois, or that
they had no reason to bomb the village unless they somehow missed equally
unreachable Chicago were waved aside. People felt they should be doing
something even if it was trudging around a dark cornfield with a goose gun
on your shoulder, hoping you don't blast a foraging rooster to flinders.

Misinformation and anxiety drove a lot of home-front decisions until the
actual conditions were known—usually through trial by fire. To their credit,
the army looked at lessons learned from their past conflicts.

The new M1 Garand rifle was a clip-fed autoloader that fired eight shots
by just repeatedly pulling the trigger. This feature, in effect, increased the
average squad's firepower over the bolt-action Springfield or Enfield. Even
better for the expert rifleman, the M1 was accurate out to one thousand

yards. The U.S. Army would be the only combat force to adopt an autoloader as its basic infantry rifle. Now, how to best use it?

The tradition of America's gun culture was centered on the mythology of the flinty-eyed sharpshooter. This marksman existed in fact but never in numbers enough to act as anything but a diversion or as snipers, which was their greatest contribution. Remember, even George Washington, on seeing his "army" perform with muskets, issued the forgiving, shotgun-like buck-and-ball loads in the hope that somebody would hit something. Even in the civilian militia's greatest battle, the engagement at Cowpens in 1780, where they fought alongside the American regulars and cavalry to defeat Banastre Tarleton's punitive force, their own general appreciated their weakness. Gen. Daniel Morgan, "The Old Waggoner," only asked that his men deliver "two volleys" before they ran. They did, and the British predictably chased forward with a cheer, only to run headlong into the formed-up regulars pumping volleys of shot into their ranks and the American cavalry slashing into their flanks.[7]

Volley fire traced its origins back to the British longbow at Agincourt, where clouds of arrows climbed into the sky from archers and dropped down in a rainbow arc amid the French with devastating effect. After gunpowder was tamed, ranks of inaccurate smoothbore muskets were thrust in the general direction of the enemy and touched off. America's Civil War commanders were able to chop away at shoulder-to-shoulder bayonet charges from longer range with their rifled muzzle-loaders. Single-shot Martini-Henry rifles were employed in staggered volley fire to defeat the Zulu hordes at Rorke's Drift in South Africa. And ultimately, during World War I the British fitted their bolt-action Lee Enfield rifles with "volley fire sights" calibrated out to two thousand yards in order to lob high-angle .303 caliber rifle fire down into German trenches. The return to Agincourt was complete.

The interwar years, while darkened by the privations of the Great Depression, were banner years for civilian marksmanship training and matches at clubs and with the military. The NRA had achieved truly national status during this time as both a creator of standards for civilian shooters and a voice in political and military circles. During those days of growth, the NRA mantra declared the well-trained expert marksman to be the most potent warrior. Though they produced examples of field-hardened combat officers who supported their view, the army had the responsibility to turn out lots of trained troops from scratch. Rigorous NRA training regimens did not fit the schedule, and combat tactics had outgrown the old bolt-action era.

The battlefield tactic of fire and maneuver had changed warfare from static lines to constant fluid movement. Putting a volume of fire on the cover that protected the enemy acted as suppression, and flanking movements were attempted. For this result, the M1 rifle was the perfect infantry weapon at the time it was employed. American sniper training was virtually nonexistent in the prewar years and was only minimally instituted once the GIs came up against highly trained German snipers who were not only excellent shooters but also experts in camouflage and concealment, often showing up *behind* American lines. Even with this reality, American army sniper schooling was restricted to long-range shooting—no cover or concealment training—such as hitting a body at four hundred yards or an enemy's head at two hundred yards, which was well within the skill level of the civilian match shooter.

The NRA saw its grip on future military rifle training and influence slipping away with this minimal program needed to put boots on the ground in so many combat theaters. The proliferation of automatic weapons on the battlefield further reinforced the "firepower" concept. This was anathema to the NRA. In January 1940, a "Powder Smoke" editorial in *American Rifleman* had attempted to sway future training decisions with an agonizing analogy comparing the engine of a car with the trained shooter and rapid firing pistons paralleling spray-and-pray shooting. After hacking through the goulash of verbiage, this remained:

> We can no more hope to develop superior 'fire-power' by merely increasing the number of powder explosions a minute, than we can hope to increase the power of a streamlined motor car by merely increasing the number of gasoline explosions a minute. . . . Let no neatly turned phrases obscure the fact that fire-power and fire-superiority depend upon a rifle that is inherently accurate, handled by a man who has been thoroughly trained in the principles of accurate individual marksmanship.

Actual combat often told a different story. The American squad light machine gun was the venerable BAR. With its twenty-round box magazine, it was often unable to sustain a continuous saturation of fire required to achieve fire and maneuver tactics. After D-Day, the army doubled the number of BARs issued to squads and supplemented the Thompson submachine guns given to squad leaders with the M3 "grease gun" for close-quarters fire suppreission.[8]

The M1 carbine firing a rimless .30 caliber round developed from the .32 Winchester centerfire made for the 1905 sporting autoloader was added to the arsenal to replace the eight-shot .45 caliber Model 1911 semiautomatic pistol. The carbine pumped its bullets from a twenty- or thirty-round "banana" box magazine. In thirty-eight months, between 1942 and 1945, six million carbines of all types were built.[9] Something had to be done to counter the German MP40 submachine guns—called the Schmeisser by American troops—that gave Wehrmacht and SS attacks terrific shock power. Also, late in the war, storm troopers made use of the fully automatic Sturmgewehr 44, a remarkable weapon that set the pattern for all assault rifles that followed.

With fresh troops being churned out of the replacement training centers stateside with only weapons familiarization training, field commanders had to make do. The problem was that the NRA had a workable idea but lost ground with the military, which had a huge training quota to meet. In World War II, U.S. troops expended 25,000 small-arms rounds per enemy killed.[10] That was a philosophy of volume through technology the military would carry with them into Vietnam.

In the postwar period, combat historian Lt. Col. S. L. A. Marshall concluded, "Only about fifteen percent of American riflemen in combat had fired at the enemy." Most soldiers were more afraid to kill another human being than to be killed. Marshall further stated:

> We need to free the rifleman's mind with respect to the nature of targets. A soldier who has learned to squeeze off careful rounds at a target will take the time, in combat, to consider the humanity of the man he is about to shoot. Along with conventional marksmanship, soldiers now acquired the skill of "massing fire" against riverbanks, trees, hillcrests, and other places where enemy soldiers might lurk. The average firer will have less resistance to firing on a house or tree than upon a human being. Once the Army put this notion into practice, they bore spectacular results. By the time of the Vietnam War, according to internal Army estimates, as many as ninety percent of soldiers were shooting back.[11]

This sweeping indictment of deliberate, aimed fire from rigorously trained soldiers by a military expert published in *Infantry Journal* seemed to justify fire suppression concepts. In both Korea and World War II, soldiers did not aim so much as they sprayed as many bullets as possible where they thought the enemy could be found. Both riflemen and machine gunners covered an entire area with their fire, frequently where no enemy soldiers were visible. This study confirmed the same tactics their ancestors employed at Concord, Bunker Hill, and Yorktown. It is volley fire. Billions of bullets were sent overseas to be hosed at the enemy.

In the European theater, modern warfare utilizing artillery, tanks, and air power caused live targets to virtually disappear from the battlefields. The after-action report of the company making the deepest penetration of the Normandy beachhead on D-Day reported seeing only six enemy soldiers. Within five days of the landing, the 502nd Parachute Infantry Regiment plunged into stubborn resistance and reported seeing very few live Germans. Six enemy soldiers were bayoneted, and a few were killed with machine gun fire within forty-five feet, but when polled by army intelligence, only one man in five saw anything at the front lines resembling a live enemy target.[12]

Marshall's postwar conclusions had a profound effect on army training planners despite considerable refutation from experienced general-grade officers. The concept of putting heavy fire on an enemy rather than singling out targets would find even more credibility in Korea, where the "human wave" charges of North Korean and Chinese troops could only be halted with massive firepower.

The U.S. Marines operating in the Pacific were a different breed of cat from the much larger army forces. The Marines went to war with the Springfield Model 1903 rifle, took Guadalcanal Island away from the Japanese, and held it in the teeth of major land and sea counterattacks. In the Pacific both the army and the navy made do with hand-me-downs as President Roosevelt relented to pressure from Great Britain and decided that Germany must face defeat before Japan was dealt with, using all of America's resources. Consequently, with equipment shortages, the Marines were open to experimentation. They came to grips with the Japanese suicidal banzai charges sweeping across open ground. The five-shot bolt-action Springfield packed a punch but lacked volume of sustained fire.

Elmer Johnson designed a rifle and a light machine gun based on a recoil-operated blowback design for the .30-06 cartridge. The NRA reviewed the light machine gun and the Reising gun, an entry looking to unseat the Thompson submachine gun from its mythic position. Due to the NRA's constant courting of every gun manufacturer, the organization has rarely met a gun it did not like. This was certainly the case with the Johnson gun. The *American Rifleman* reviewer loved just about everything, from the recoil-absorbing blowback feed system to the ability to feed in single shots for accurate shooting work without having to fudge with the box magazine that fed from the left side.

The army made up its mind to stay with the plentiful BAR and were in no mood for innovation. The Marines, still burdened with the bolt-action Springfield, tried the Johnson gun. It turned out that combat conditions revealed many flaws in the basic design that did not show up on a tidy, manicured civilian target range, and the gun was dumped.[13]

The same NRA enthusiasm was applied to the Reising submachine gun, built exclusively by Harrington & Richardson, at that time a manufacturer of low-end revolvers competing with Iver Johnson for the civilian pocket pistol and plinking market. The Reising was an elegant design but had the distinction of firing from a closed bolt rather than the open bolt like most fully automatic weapons that relied on blowback from the exploding cartridge. In reality, the Reising was a very fast-shooting semiautomatic, as its mechanism performed the same complex locking and unlocking steps at every firing cycle.

Once again, when the Marines took the Reising to Guadalcanal and replaced the heavy Thompson, the heat, humidity, and grime of combat conditions outflanked the *American Rifleman*'s gushing reviews and showed the gun to be a stinker. The older Thompson, with the straight box magazine and simplified blowback action, arrived and stayed with the Marine divisions.

Not every *AR* review was rosy. One of the magazine's really blistering firearm critiques pointed out overheating, wobbly sights, jamming, poor performance at long range, a buckling barrel, and the need to add a pound of weight to overcome design deficiencies. "It is interesting to note," wrote the reviewer, "that [the rifle] does not conform to [earlier] requirements . . . published by the 1921 Ordnance Department, or the subsequent requirements released in 1929." The rifle was, of course, the M1 Garand that became a battlefield icon.[14] The same rifle was fulsomely praised by *American Rifleman* once it was officially adopted by all U.S. military services.

In all fairness, *American Rifleman* remained a spirited chronicle throughout the war despite paper shortages and the economic hardships of rationing. Supplies of gunpowder, brass, copper, and steel had reduced civilian gun and ammunition manufacture. When Britain faced Nazi invasion, the NRA urged American shooters to give up some of their guns for shipment to that beleaguered country. Great Britain had passed draconian gun possession and ownership laws that had virtually disarmed its civilians. The magazine continued to keep subscribers despite its amateurish writing, layout, and endless pages of pistol and rifle match scores, which were a blessing for local clubs that wanted to see their accomplishments in print. The NRA publishers knew their long-term readership.

To leaven pages of scores with clumps of content in the wartime issues, the *Rifleman* staff chose to run a series of fictional stories about our pioneer marksmen and their patriotic heritage. The author, Col. H. P. Sheldon, was dreadful. His stories had interesting themes about early frontier life, but he used long stretches of Dutch dialect and toothless frontier gibberish to tell large parts of his tales: "See, Henry, der flint must strike der frizzen yust so— not too soon—not too far. Too quvick der pan don'dt open—too far der sparks don'dt come. But ven it iss set yust right, der sparks go splick! Right in der pan effry time. So ve go easy mit der fixin's!"[15]

Hack your way through that cabbage for half an hour, and your brain turns into a wad of sodden pulp. Sheldon kept popping up regularly, so he must have been popular with somebody. Essentially, there were three styles running through the period of publication from the late 1930s to the late 1940s: folksy, techno-nerd how-to, and strident, finger-shaking editorials. Membership in the NRA kept growing, and subscriptions were free with the three-dollar fee. As long as membership grew, advertisers got their money's worth and continued to support the NRA and the editorial bent of the magazine.

During the war, *American Rifleman* also reviewed German and Japanese infantry weapons for their readers. The Japanese had very little to offer with their mix of antique, underpowered, but sturdy Arisaka rifles and crappy Nambu pistols, while the mechanical-minded Germans still carried their accurate Karabiner 98k bolt-action rifles and wielded the famous Mauser, Walther, and Luger pistols. The Wehrmacht automatic weapons were the most fascinating, with their cyclic rates of fire twice that of their American counterparts. Even Nazi training came in for some examination (and grudging admiration) based on prewar interviews and photographs. If anything it was more than a bit creepy reading discussions of overheating barrels, extractor designs, high rates of fire, and other shooter minutiae about the weapons that were blowing down American and Allied kids overseas. But "know your enemy" is still an important military dictum.

Ultimately, America went to war with all stops pulled out. Those who were not actually shooting at the enemy built the guns, or the platforms that carried the guns to the soldiers. Transportation carried the gun platforms and the bombs that cleared the way to the battlefields for the shooting soldiers. No battle was won until the rifle-carrying infantry stood on enemy ground. Virtually every endeavor was directed at putting bullets where they could do the most good. From 1941 to 1945, the United States was one large gun culture.

7

GATHERING THE REINS
IN A RUNAWAY WORLD

In 1945 the war ended in flaming cataclysms that engulfed two Japanese cities. Just like that, the shooting was over. Germany and much of Europe was in rubble. Japan had been devastated. China was cratered, burned, and fighting a civil war. Those countries on the periphery were politically destabilized, and most were in deep financial trouble. Countries that had backed the wrong horse were trading cigarettes for potatoes and bread. The United States was untouched except for thousands of her sons, husbands, daughters, and wives buried in remote corners of the world. Her soldiers were coming home to disrupted lives, dogged by the drone of military bureaucracy and boredom or the twitchy apprehension of "combat fatigue." For some, it was the greatest experience of their lives, and they flocked to American Legion posts and Veterans of Foreign Wars meetings to swap stories. Divisional, squadron, and fleet organizations were created to keep bonds formed in combat alive in peacetime. For others, the memories of death, fear, and killing could never be retold.

From these warriors and scarred refugees of civilization's greatest sin came our future leaders. The leadership they provided was also a mixed bag. We found ourselves facing chest-pounding super-patriots who saw America as the alpha dog in the junkyard. On the opposite side of the aisle sat those bleeding hearts who were desperate to see war ended for all time whatever the cost. In between were the majority of Americans fed up with the privations of the Great Depression, which stole their youth, to be followed by reduced lifestyle priorities. The loss of loved ones and the loss of many small freedoms such buying as many tires as you needed, getting gas to run your car, getting a seat on a train or plane, or serving meat, butter, or other rationed foods on your table, had been borne for four long years. The American people had endured degrees of want and anxiety for almost fifteen years, and they demanded a taste of the good life.

Big paychecks earned from war material production plants went away as overtime hours vanished. Though industry began retooling in 1945 for renewed civilian purchasing as unneeded military contracts were canceled, the turnaround was agonizingly slow. Women were chased off the industrial work force when men returned from overseas. During wartime production, the National War Labor Board had negotiated a labor truce between the unions and companies, extracting a no-strike pledge from the unions in return for company recognition of their "workplace scrutiny" and continued membership recruitment.

This truce guaranteed a constant flow of dues to the unions, which expanded their bureaucracy, created benefit programs, and set aside funds for political action. The "maintenance of membership" rule that kept members paying their dues excluded "free-riders" and scabs better than the violence of the 1930s. Labor leaders representing millions of voting members had war chests of millions of dollars and therefore the ears of lawmakers as well as public opinion as they pursued the prosperity promised by capitalism. This groundswell of collective power was not lost on the public sector as police, hospital workers, postal workers, firefighters, and municipal workers formed unions.[1]

The NRA was a pioneer in building its own influence base by scooping up whatever national shooting sport it could pull into its tent. For example, the National Revolver Association, founded in 1900, had trained, financed, and managed the American pistol teams through the Berlin Olympic Games of 1936. Following the war when the games started up in London in 1948, the NRA was in charge of America's international pistol, rifle, and, by 1960, shotgun competitions. To their credit, the NRA has done an excellent job of sports qualification and event management. But their tent would get even bigger.

Even as the war was winding down in 1945, the NRA was tooling up. In an *American Rifleman* editorial penned in December of that year, the association stated: "The National Rifle Association of America emerges from its third war financially sound, respected and appreciated by American officials and the American people and with a new kind of experience which will be capitalized to develop the outstanding patriotic sportsmen's organization of the world." They also determined that "we will have no dearth of shooters, but we will make no progress unless we find and develop a great corps of *competent leaders* [italics in original]."

The antigun crowd also came in for some lumps for their "subversive campaign" to register all privately owned firearms. The NRA outlined antigun advocates' goals using a Communist Party circular that urged members to "formulate plans for disarming police and loyal troops; break up groups of loyal fighting workmen; destroy, when unable to capture all tanks, cannon, machine guns, and other weapons which loyal proletariats might use." The Communists—and by association, the antigun crowd—were encouraged to join civil defense organizations as auxiliary police, and find and copy lists of registered gun owners for later confiscation sweeps.[2]

This equating the antigun crowd with the Communist Conspiracy marked an early shift in NRA influence-seeking tactics that had an all-too-familiar ring. The table-thumping would get louder as America sifted through cold and hot wars and the political and social confrontations to come.

With the postwar home front looking for high-paying salaries and the accompanying good life, politicians jockeying for the hot-button issues to ignite their ambitions, and our soldiers coming home from four years of committing or enabling regimented violence, changes were demanded. While the public sector was busy organizing, the major labor unions went into a spiraling decline, weakened by four years of "truce" with the employers; they had little leverage left as factories began retooling.

Three million workers went on strike in 1945 and five million in 1946. In 1947 the Republicans introduced the Taft-Hartley Act against "featherbedding" workers being paid for work not done. According to an increasing uproar from the public, labor had received more than its fair share. President Harry Truman needed labor support and vetoed the act. In a letter to Vice President Alben Barkley, Truman wrote that if his veto was overridden, the result would

reverse the basic direction of our national labor policy, inject the government into private economic affairs on an unprecedented scale, and conflict with important principles of our democratic society. Its provisions would cause more strikes, not fewer. It would contribute neither to industrial peace nor to economic stability and progress. . . . It contains seeds of discord which would plague this nation for years to come.[3]

Truman's veto was overridden 68–25 in the Senate. Labor was furious and flocked to Truman in the 1948 presidential election, helping "Give 'em Hell" Harry upset Republican Thomas Dewey. With the Taft-Harley Act a reality and with one of its requirements being that every union member had to take an anti-Communist oath, the great Communist witch hunt began and kicked open the door for Sen. Joseph McCarthy of Wisconsin to track down every Communist in government.

His Senate hearings began in February 1950, and he bludgeoned witnesses with wretchedly thin evidence and made being a Communist, or even befriending a suspected Communist, a virtually treasonable offense. The hearings were carried on television, in newsreels, on radio, and in all the newspapers. Americans were stunned that our former ally, the Soviet Union, could be plotting to tear down our country from within. There could be a Communist cell of agents in any block. Nobody, it seemed, was above suspicion.

My dad hated Harry Truman, and when Dewey suffered that ignominious defeat, the air went purple in our South Side Chicago apartment. My normally apolitical father was certain some "commie chump" would bomb Harry's office in the White House just to keep the country stirred up. Our neighborhood was an absolute nest of "DPs." These "Displaced Persons" had come to the United States from the rubble of Europe with their cardboard suitcases and foreign accents and "stolen" jobs away from honest Americans who had killed off all the Nazis in their terrible little countries. And now these "foreigners" were here, talking their gibberish and cooking their queer food that smelled like someone was boiling an overcoat. And we just had to take it.

Being a little kid in a one-bedroom apartment, I had to listen to all this. And most of it was baloney, as Dad conveniently overlooked the ethnicity of the owner of his favorite hardware store, whose last name was a Romanian sack full of consonants, and our Doctor Weiderborg, and my best friend, Ronny Krasnitz, and the dozen other Poles, Slavs, Italians, and Greeks we pleasantly dealt with every week. They were different because he knew them. He was pretty much like his three brothers living in Buffalo and every other blue-collar Presbyterian, Lutheran, or Methodist who believed in America for Real Americans. "Let them foreigners stew in their own juice" was the neighborhood credo.

The world turned and swirled around me in incomprehensible conversations, unreadable newspaper articles, and talk, talk, talk between old people's heads on television. I lived in a world abstracted from the plots of radio and TV programs that kept me entertained. Mostly, they were about guns and all forms of mayhem. In the late 1940s and early 1950s, radio programs still taught their moral lessons: "Crime doesn't pay." "Always tell the truth." "Be kind to those less fortunate." "Don't go into the basement of the creepy house after dark." Johnny Dollar, Little Orphan Annie, Terry and the Pirates, Tom Mix, the Green Hornet, and Sergeant Preston of the Yukon blazed away at evil every week as I sprawled in front of our console radio in the living room. The pickings were sparse on our 1949 Zenith TV. It was hardly a porthole to the world, with its four local channels, but the grainy black-and-white vista was a miracle to us.

We ate dinner off the card table in the living room on Sundays at 5 p.m. so we could watch William Boyd as Hopalong Cassidy gallop across the west on his brilliant white horse named Topper, with Gabby Hayes at his side. Hoppy's pair of nickel-plated six-guns never missed. Boyd had purchased his 1930s B Westerns and sold them to TV, making him a fortune and becoming a cultural icon to kids my age everywhere. Actually, he hated horses and kids, and never met a cocktail he didn't like, but we didn't know or care. At night, I crawled under the coffee table to watch William Gargan in *Martin Kane, Private Eye*; *Man against Crime* starring Ralph Bellamy; and *Big Town* and *Racket Squad* with the mellifluous Reed Hadley. Sky King even managed to find places to land his twin-engine airplane when his daughter, Penny, got kidnapped by spies.

When not at home bathed in gunfire, my pals and I rode our bikes to the Shore Theater on 75th Street, the Cheltenham off of 79th, or the posh Hamilton and Jeffrey over near 71st and Exchange Avenue. There, in the dark, popcorn and melting Baby Ruth bars in hand, we were wrapped in the violent worlds of *Sands of Iwo Jima*, *Battleground*, *The Desert Fox*, *O.S.S.*, *They Were Expendable*, *Operation Tokyo*, and one film I've never forgotten (nor have I ever seen it since), the World War II propaganda movie *China's Little Devils*. We watched Chinese kids our age, their parents killed in Japanese bombing raids, forced to pick up real guns to help a downed American pilot and crew escape capture. They held the fiendish Japanese soldiers off, killing what seemed to be hundreds of the enemy before all dying heroic deaths at the business end of machine guns, grenades, and bayonets.

Now, how could a kid growing up in this atmosphere not become enamored of guns, shooting, and their connection to the triumph of good over evil? I asked my dad if we had a gun in the house. Mom pitched a fit, but I was about ten years old, and Dad made the big decision. He went to the top drawer of his bureau—the one that always smelled of clean, ironed handkerchiefs and the hint of machine oil that radiated from all his casual clothes—and withdrew our house gun.

It was incredibly beautiful, made of gleaming brass with wood grips and a wood forepiece beneath what appeared to be a cylinder hung under the slim steel barrel. He opened the breech and from a green-topped tin removed a small lead pellet shaped like an hourglass. The pellet went into the barrel's chamber, the breech was closed, and he pulled the wood forepiece down and began pumping the piston that compressed air into the long brass cylinder. Five pumps seemed to be enough, and he aimed it at the bed pillows. I covered my ears. Mom started to say from the bedroom doorway, "If you put a hole in my quilt, I'll . . ."

"Snig!" The pistol fired. "Pap!" went the pillow. Dad reached into the dent in the bedclothes and came back with the pellet. With the morning *Chicago Tribune* headlines screaming about commie tanks and submachine gun–wielding North Koreans sweeping down across South Korea, the afternoon *Herald-American* showing the bloody aftermath of the latest labor riots at a Chicago steel plant, and the *Southeast Economist* editorial about gang fights erupting on the other side of 79th Street (only a half-mile away!) discussed ad nauseam at the dinner table, our home was defended with an air pistol.

The Korean War was the visible manifestation of the Communist Menace playing itself out from 1950 to 1953 with residual sputterings that hung around for decades. Already fueled at home with explosive political and social changes, the menace became real as the North Koreans—who looked to us like the Japanese we had already defeated—decided we were too weak in resolve and arms to defend their takeover of the South. They were almost right.

In 1948 the United Nations was barred by Soviet Union veto from establishing a democratic election to unite the peninsula of Korea into one nation after forty-three years of Japanese occupation. While the Soviet Union used the partition of Korea as a victorious symbol of spreading communism and poured arms and training into the northern provinces, for South Korea the United States was less sanguine. Extreme military budget cuts after the war followed America's usual pattern of downsizing its forces and its military aid to allies.

Through the Marshall Plan, named after Secretary of State George C. Marshall, the government spent $13 billion (more than $100 billion in today's dollars) on European civilian, infrastructure, and business recovery. This bolstering of economies came at the expense of maintaining the U.S. national and global defenses as the Soviet Union and China expanded their ambitions. Both North Korea and North Vietnam became recipients of Communist political and military aid.

Under severe budget cuts and General MacArthur's micromanaging, the Eighth Army garrison force in Japan was in dismal shape. Virtually all U.S. forces had been reduced, and only about 10 percent of the available soldiers were war veterans. The rest were sullen, bored recruits serving out their peacetime enlistments, out of shape, poorly trained, and counting the days until they could return to civilian life.[4] This downgrade was allowed to happen even though these troops were strategically placed to respond to any aggression in Southeast Asia.

Lt. Gen. Walton H. Walker, the new commander in Japan, was appalled at the condition of his troops and tried to appeal to General MacArthur, but the Olympian general's usual wall of sycophants barred all communication channels to anything negative.[5]

On June 25, 1950, divisions of the North Korean People's Army (NKPA) crossed the 38th parallel, the geographic line that separated the two Koreas, and steamrollered their way south. The NKPA rolled across the hapless Republic of Korea (ROK) troops who had received virtually all their arms and training from the United States. When Dean Acheson, Marshall's successor as secretary of state, telephoned President Truman about the invasion, a decision was made at once to send U.S. forces from Japan to stiffen the ROK defense until General MacArthur's Far East Command (FEC) could be brought into play. We were at war again only five years after the end of World War II. This conflict, however, was labeled a politically correct "police action."

General Walker arrived in Korea with soldiers who had been the garrison troops in Japan since the surrender. They carried small arms, bazookas, some machine guns, a modest number of cannons, and light tanks, and were led by few combat veterans. Walker took one look at the Korean situation maps and established his command at Daegu, some sixty miles northwest of Pusan with its port on the southeast corner of the peninsula. There he could receive reinforcements and supplies whenever the FEC decided to shake itself loose. Some troops went directly into the line to halt the advancing NKPA and were immediately overwhelmed and driven into retreat. They didn't have the weapons they needed, and many didn't have the savvy to use the weapons they did have.

As soon as he could, Walker improvised what he called a "mobile defense" composed of a thin screen of defenders supported by large mobile reserves that could move quickly to plug holes—the opposite of most military wisdom. Fortunately, the army and navy assumed air superiority over the NKPA Yak propeller fighters using World War II P-51 Mustangs, Vought F4U Corsairs, and new P-80 Shooting Star jets from Lockheed. On July 29 the increasingly dire situation prompted Walker to issue to division commanders what has become known as his "Stand or Die" order:

> We are fighting a battle against time. There will be no more retreating, withdrawal, or readjustment of the lines or any other term you choose. There is no line behind us to which we can retreat. There will be no Dunkirk. There will be no Bataan. A retreat to Pusan would be one of the greatest butcheries in history. We must fight until the end. . . . We will fight as a team. If some of us must die, we will die fighting together. . . . I want everybody to understand we are going to hold this line. We are going to win.

The military and political theorists decided conventional methods of training were obsolete. New weapon studies were curtailed in favor of "upgrading" World War II inventories. Secretaries of Defense James Forrestal and Louis

Johnson pushed through changes that reduced training time and produced uniformed civilians rather than professional soldiers trained in the skills of war. The ROK troops were only given "defensive" armaments, and much of them were inadequate against the NKPAV's T-34 Soviet tanks. Old 2.36-inch bazookas were issued instead of the 3.5-inch weapon that fired a larger-shaped charge. With a lot of thoughtful chin scratching, the politicians tried to fight the war using the threat of considering tactical nuclear weapons.[6]

American soldiers faced human wave charges of NKPA troops whose front ranks carried automatic weapons such as the 7.62mm Soviet PPSh-41, also known as the Burp Gun, and advanced beneath clouds of mortar rounds. Follow-up NKPA troops carried only bags of grenades and were expected to glean their guns from the heaps of their own dead in front of them.

American soldiers fired their M1 Garand rifles with eight-shot clips, often triggering their rifles as fast as possible where single aimed shots could not kill enough enemy until the hordes were plunging into U.S. forward trenches and lines. Our unprepared soldiers often threw down their guns and ran, or surrendered in embarrassing numbers. The most-heard complaint among battle weary soldiers was "The war we can't win, we can't lose, we can't quit!"[7]

Stiffened by the few combat veterans, the raw surviving American troops quickly became veterans themselves and held the lines around Pusan until support arrived and naval gunfire directed miles inland, beneath plumes of aircraft-delivered napalm, halted the NKPA.

With the reversal of the North Korean invasion, the Chinese entered the war in October 1950 to support their allies. The United States and its United Nations allies fought a three-year war that established the battle between democracy and communism as much more than a noisy social and economic debate. The new Cold War put everyone on notice that the devastation that had wracked Europe and the Far East and turned our former ally, the Soviet Union, into a pathological danger to the free world now walked down Main Street America.

The end of World War II caused stay-at-home shooters to take a deep breath and exhale. The home front had endured a constant drumbeat of the NRA and local shooting clubs to create shooters among draft-age young men who could arrive at military basic training ready to ship out loaded and locked with small-arms expertise. The home guard of civilian riflemen trained in civilian clubs sponsored by the NRA had been moderately effective. While these freshly minted shooters did not face the sobering aspect of invasion, as had the shooters turned out by the National Rifle Association of Great Britain in the war's early days, they did help focus on the need for well-trained troops. The NRA had also graduated from a haven for target-shooting hobbyists, hunters, and retired soldiers to a broad-based organization with closer ties to both the military and political upper echelons. The NRA found itself virtually in control of America's shooting culture.

With soldiers coming home looking for a job, an education, and—after a suitable bachelorhood—a house in the country with a few rugrats running around the backyard, guns were the furthest thing from most of their minds. They had lugged M1s all over Europe, the Pacific, and Korea. They wanted a new Oldsmobile, a college degree, and a Veterans Administration loan on a new home. There was also another group who had survived the war and wanted to keep the skills that they had been taught. As with their fathers, the war had been the greatest adventure of their lives, and every time they sighted down the barrel of a hunting or target rifle or even a shotgun, their hearts raced with the memories. That alignment of the front and rear sights—the "sight picture"—became an image of excitement and success, and they wanted more.

Then there were the younger kids who only knew war through movies, radio programs, newspapers, and comic books. They listened to stories told by older relatives and friends who came home from combat theaters carrying exotic souvenirs: a German bayonet, a Japanese battle flag punctured with bullet holes, a Nambu semiautomatic pistol, or a Hitler Youth dagger. The movies filled in for soldiers' memories that were too dark to relate. From the late 1940s through the 1950s, the game of choice among the kids on 78th Street was Guns.

―――――――――――――◆◆◆――――――――――――

That's all we called it. Indian attacks on stockades had been replaced with bomber crews fighting off swarms of Japanese Zeros or German Focke-Wulfs. Mom let me have a swipe with her ever-present wet dishrag when I told her the small pot-metal German airplane I traded from Ronny Adams for a handful of marbles (two shooters, a peewee, a jumbo, and three of my best clearies) was a Focke-Wulf 190. She thought I'd used the F-word.

Our city park on Chicago's South Side, around which most of us lived, was planted with thornapple trees offering low branches and wide, accommodating crotches that became machine gun positions on a B-17 or B-25 bomber. Movies like *Air Force,* showing a crew fighting its way out of Pearl Harbor after the 1941 attack, laid the groundwork for many Guns scenarios. When we were holding "Bloody Nose Ridge" in Guadalcanal against Japanese banzai charges, we played both Marines and frenzied Sons of Nippon so we could also die dramatically under a hail of imaginary machine gun bullets. From the tall grass, we called out to the defending American soldiers, remembering the Japanese had trouble pronouncing the letter *R,* "Maline—you die!" We then asked seductively, "You got cigalette, Joe?" to lure Marines from their foxholes. The movies taught us well the tricks of the wily Japanese.

Of course, our guns were cap pistols or rifles that didn't shoot anything. We had peashooters, plastic soda straws used to launch dried whole peas at a surprising velocity. One day, sandy-headed, barefoot Bernie Larsen came to our camouflaged clubhouse in the vacant lot battlefield carrying a Daisy BB gun. But it was the wrong kind, not the Red Ryder 1,000–shot, lever-action model, but the 650-shot, pump-action model that was incredibly hard to cock when it was new. While we made a fuss about it and the satisfying "snap!" it made when we finally managed to cock it and fire a copper spheroid, Bernie knew it was not the real McCoy, and he only used it to pot tin cans or annoy neighborhood cats in his backyard.

We had slingshots carved from dead branches, but their accuracy and our casual target practice caused many to be snapped in two by angry dads who had received complaints from neighbors with frightened cats, howling dogs, and reports of broken windows and scratched car fenders. With John Wayne assaulting Mount Suribachi at the Shore Theater one week and blazing away with a Tommy gun in *The Fighting Seabees* at the Jeffrey the next, we felt disadvantaged having no missiles to call our own. Dad had his air pistol in his handkerchief drawer, but touching that was a hanging offense.

But one day, the Methodist Church at 76th and South Shore Drive started up Troop 529 of the Boy Scouts.

The kids I ran with were all hooked on the promised curriculum described in the Boy Scout Handbook, and we browbeat our parents with emotional pleas and lists of things we'd learn. We'd be taught how to tie knots, cook over campfires, hew a tree with an ax, find the North Star, and imitate the call of a loon (in case a lost loon ever flew over 78th Street). For a few of us still laboring under Guns fever, a glance at the Scout merit badge list revealed a circular patch adorned with red concentric circles and the promise to "master Rifle Marksmanship." We kept knowledge of this particular badge from our parents, who were still in their "shoot your eye out" mode whenever BB guns were mentioned. We had more lethal equipment in mind.

Pat Brady's dad was an okay guy in a down-at-the-heels kind of way. He also owned an Iver Johnson .22 caliber revolver and a single-shot Stevens .22 rifle. As freshly minted Boy Scouts with Tenderfoot badges pinned to our uniform shirts, we prevailed upon Mr. Brady to teach us to shoot his rifle so we could earn that marksmanship merit badge.

This was 1952, and according to most politicians, radio commentators, and specifically the House Un-American Activities Committee (HUAC), Communists were crawling across the country like a plague of rats. Every day more American secrets turned up in Moscow cocktail parties. Back in 1947 State Department analyst George F. Kennan had written an essay, "The Sources of Soviet Conduct," that warned the world that the USSR would not rest until communism had spread like a rash throughout the Western world:

> It is clear that the United States cannot expect in the foreseeable future to enjoy political intimacy with the Soviet regime. It must continue to regard the Soviet Union as a rival, not a partner, in the political arena. It must continue to expect that Soviet policies will reflect no abstract love of peace and stability, no real faith in the possibility of a permanent happy coexistence of the Socialist and capitalist worlds, but rather a cautious, persistent pressure toward the disruption and, weakening of all rival influence and rival power.
>
> Balanced against this are the facts that Russia, as opposed to the western world in general, is still by far the weaker party, that Soviet policy is highly flexible, and that Soviet society may well contain deficiencies which will eventually weaken its own total potential. This would of itself warrant the United States entering with reasonable confidence upon a policy of firm containment, designed to confront the Russians with unalterable counterforce at every point where they show signs of encroaching upon he interests of a peaceful and stable world.[8]

President Truman bought into this "containment" concept and created the Truman Doctrine, which in 1947 promised countries the United States would aid foreign governments in "resisting armed minorities" or "outside pressure," for example, communism.

Backing up our words, the United States was deep into the Korean War against the invading Reds. Democracy was under attack by an enemy even more insidious than the Nazis or the banzai-screaming Japanese. The commies were everywhere, pretending to be patriots. Americans needed to hearken back to their Revolutionary roots and be strong once again. One way was to ensure that they retained the mythologized skills of their forbearers in marksmanship. A well-armed society of flinty-eyed minutemen who knew how to point the business end of a firearm had a leg up on any commie-facist-Nazi dictator who might come along. And they had the blessing of the Founders expressed in the Second Amendment to the Constitution, which promised that the right to keep and bear arms shall not be infringed. Or something like that.

While the postwar NRA was busy helping citizens build and operate rifle and pistol ranges across the country, it also created the NRA legislative service, which "keeps a careful eye peeled for crackpot legislation—local, state or federal—aimed at taking away that heritage."[9] By 1952 the fear of communism streaming from the Soviet Union and pouring in across our borders had grown from a steady drumbeat to a veritable tattoo.

Responding to that crisis mindset, in February 1950 Republican senator Joseph McCarthy assailed the Democratic administration with a clarion call that he had "proof" that over two hundred Communists had infiltrated the State Department. Between the developing Cold War and the need to shore up our "citizen-soldier" roots, the NRA recruiting and fund-raising campaign reverted to its wartime demands for a well-armed populace of anticommunist patriots to be on the alert for internal insurrection or attacks on our liberties and virtues. As NRA executive director C. B. Lister lectured in an *American Rifleman* editorial in March 1948, "'Crisisism' is the father—whether by accident or design—of Communism . . . and every other catch-phrase designating Dictatorship. Please, gentlemen of the law, the press, the radio and the political rostrum, may we get on with an intelligent study and quick solution of our problems and stop crying 'wolf, wolf' to the point where villagers may refuse to grab their pitchforks when they really need them?"[10]

McCarthy's allegations were a great flailing against the Democratic Truman administration, but when Republican Dwight Eisenhower became president and the Republicans swept both houses of Congress, the junior senator from Wisconsin became a political liability. The American public, seeing his blandly malevolent face on television, further dashed his dreams of power and glory.

Before he was censured and bounced from his senatorial seat to die a bitter alcoholic, "Tail Gunner Joe" McCarthy set a standard for browbeating his way into the media. His effective public raving style motivated the NRA's campaign to be vocally vigilant against those crackpots in the government who would turn against the people and take their guns. As television had destroyed McCarthy, it also showed film of the Korean War prisoner exchanges and the dismissive arrogance of the North Korean negotiators. They gave communism a modern "foreign" face and good reason to guard America's liberties.

One of McCarthy's greatest faults was his inability to distinguish between liberals, fellow travelers, and card-carrying Communists. He tarred them all with the same crimson brush. To wear any of these labels meant you did not love your country. Today the NRA makes a similar overstatement in many of its tub-thumping editorials, using "liberal" as an epithet. They step into the same swamp created by fringe pundits such as Ann Coulter, who in her 2003 book *Treason: Liberal Treachery from the Cold War to the War on Terrorism*, claims McCarthy was exonerated and was a true defender of his country's values, while liberals don't love their country.[11] NRA ideologues paint any "liberal agenda" as subversive to American values and therefore unpatriotic.

The deterioration of military marksmanship training of the American soldier troubled the NRA and World War II veterans. With the Cold War amping up, a return to the savvy combat soldier possessing all the survival and attack skills was needed. Whereas S. L. A. Marshall had been the darling of the association throughout the 1930s, his "aimless fire" concepts were alien to the NRA of the early 1950s, and *American Rifleman* editorials and articles raged against reduction of marksmanship training. Angry letters flooded into congressmen's mailbags with those editorials stapled to them. Political heat came down on the Department of the Army Infantry School, and rifle marksmanship was cranked up from forty hours to seventy-eight hours for the thirteen weeks of basic training.

Still, the NRA needed to recruit the youth of America, pry them away from those new TV sets infesting American homes, put a rifle in their hands, and teach them discipline and responsibility. And the word went out: we need a new generation of hunters and sharpshooters to keep the commies in their place.

To my folks and most Americans, the Boy Scouts were one great step to indoctrinate our youth into the legacy of American virtues. And the kids wore uniforms, too, and worked for medals and badges, tangible symbols of success. What better path was there to the corporate boardroom? To Pat Brady's blue-collar dad, teaching us kids to shoot suddenly took on an all-American theme. The Scout oath repeated at every weekly meeting with hands held in the familiar three-finger salute resonated: "On my honor, I will do my best to do my duty to God and my country and to obey the Scout law." Doing his duty to God and his country, Pat's dad decided to build us a rifle range.

While HUAC dragged suspected Communists and sweating liberals in front of its messianic committee members beneath the glare of newsreel and TV lights, the future of freedom was hard at work snaking plywood down into the crawl space beneath the Bradys' large, decaying house. The range was not a thing of beauty, and even at our pre-growth-spurt heights we couldn't avoid some stooping to avoid heads whacking joists. It was functional in a damp, earthy way. A gallery rifle range had to be fifty feet from firing line to the target to qualify as NRA "official" for scoring. An old mattress served as the firing position. The unmistakable scent of aged urine suggested why the compressed pad had been discarded. Pat's younger brother had been known as a "soaker."

The Detroit Bullet Trap was a square funnel made of sheet steel that ended in curving pipe into a removable steel cup that held the expended lead bullets. A clamp on the trap's top front edge held the "Official NRA" paper target. A General Electric floodlight bulb in a Bakelite socket fastened to an old music stand (a grim remnant of my former violin lessons) lit the black circle targets so they seemed to float in darkness. The reflected wash from that lamp and a single sixty-watt bulb hung from the trapdoor in the floor of the upstairs kitchen provided light for the shooters. A musty old sofa that smelled of mouse poop and desiccated mouse corpses entombed in its stuffing squatted behind the firing line. An orange crate-table on which lay our stack of targets and an official NRA scoring sheet affixed to a clipboard completed the furnishings.

Finally, with the Boy Scout Handbook as our scoring guide and a copy of *American Rifleman*, which showed the contortions that were the four shooting positions recognized by the Scouts and the NRA, we were ready. This was a big deal. While we were virtually oblivious to the drums and trumpets firing up the American people to defeat the Communist menace at home, we had clammy hands over the idea of actually firing a bullet.

Pat's dad may have enjoyed a beer or three, but his sober approach to our indoctrination into firearms lasted the rest of my life. He produced a bar of Fels-Naphtha soap, a brown, harsh laundry soap that was hard and—I discovered later in life dining in a sod-roofed fishing hut at the edge of Canada's Arctic Circle—smelled like seal blubber.

Solemnly, he placed the bar of soap in the bullet trap, came back, lay down on his stomach, propped himself up on his left elbow, and aimed the Stevens .22 caliber rifle. The bang made us all jump. The soap bashed into the back of the steel trap. For the first time, we smelled the sweet perfume of real smokeless gunpowder. He latched back the bolt and ejected the empty shell casing. We examined it as if the glistening brass was some sort of antique artifact found in King Tut's tomb. It was hot and blackened at the end and carried that lingering scent of action.

The bar of soap had a hole in it the size of a half dollar and was almost split in two. That soap was a lot harder than our twelve-year-old skin, so the message was clear. This was no toy. This was the real deal to be respected, and everyone became intensely aware of where that rifle muzzle was pointing at all times. The bolt that closed the breech was always open and fingers never strayed near the trigger until the "range officer" gave the command to "fire when ready." Years later, when I was teaching other youngsters to shoot at targets as an NRA instructor, I used the soap trick to achieve the same result, remembering to always sneak a hollow-point hunting cartridge into the chamber for maximum explosive effect.

In the real world, beyond that dank, smelly rifle range, the government poured millions of dollars into development of the hydrogen bomb. The NRA ramped up its political rhetoric about making sure the country had legions of shooters ready for the call to defeat communism. People were peering through parted curtains and over back fences at any possibly suspicious activity that might be some commie plot to poison the reservoir or kidnap the town council for ransom.

Me, I laid atop the nose-pinching odor of dried pee, cradled the rifle's wooden forestock across my left palm, slid a live .22 caliber Long Rifle bullet into the breech, closed the bolt, and cocked back the firing pin at the rear of the bolt. I tried to emulate the correct alignment of front and rear sights as prescribed in the Scout manual. Everything wobbled about. I held my breath, and soon my vision clouded with "spider webs" of eyestrain caused by lack of oxygen. Exhale and try again.

The trigger seemed welded in place under my finger joint. Try again. The shot startled me, and I looked up as if with my spectacle-assisted vision I could see the hole in the target. Pat Brady's dad used a pair of navy-surplus binoculars, and his delay in reporting the fall of shot caused me to fear the worst.

"It's a nine!" he shouted. "At three-o'clock! Just a cunt hair to the right of the bull's-eye!" He immediately apologized for the crude analogy, but I had missed the meaning completely. When I repeated his description of my prowess later to my mother and got walloped with the wet dishrag, I was really bewildered. I think she was angrier with me for not announcing I had signed up for the rifle marksmanship merit badge until it was a fait accompli than my innocently ignorant use of the C-word.

But I was hooked. I was at that terrible age where I had no sports skills. Mom bought my pants in the "husky" department. None of my clothes actually fit, because Mom insisted they be oversize so I "had room to grow." A few years earlier, I was the last boy in South Chicago to actually wear corduroy knickers. I ran to school, not because I loved the place, but to keep the tough kids from beating on me because I looked like a dork.

Without my glasses the world passed by in a nearsighted fog. I struggled to learn to ride my new Schwinn Liberty bike with a steel crossbar that threatened to cause my shift from alto to soprano in the music class chorus. My hockey skates gathered dust, and my right fielder's glove—I was always stuck out in lonely right field—had turned stiff from disuse. I was always the last to be chosen for teams in anything that required athletic coordination. But with a little practice, I could drill a bullet downrange into a bull's-eye hardly bigger than the diameter of the lead missile. Every kid needs a ticket, something at which he or she excels, to earn the applause of his or her parents and peers. When that empty shell casing ejected spinning into the darkness of Pat Brady's crawl space, my ticket was punched.

Totally unaware of each other, the NRA and I had stepped into new worlds at the same time.

As America lazed its way through the prosperity of the Eisenhower years, when men wore fedoras, smoked Philip Morris cigarettes, and drove Buicks with vent-a-ports in the fenders, buying a rifle or shotgun was a one-stop trip to the hardware or sporting goods store. A pistol was another matter in most urban areas. In some cases you had to prove residence and fill out a form. In other locales—except New York, where handgun sales were flat-out prohibited and only police may issue a permit because of the Sullivan Act passed in 1911—nobody cared where you lived if you had the dollars. Gun and ammunition control was a casual business for adults. For aspiring gold medal shooters, the legal tangles were a colossal annoyance.

It was easy enough to buy a gun in any of the collar counties that ringed Chicago's Cook County. But in most cases you had to be at least twenty-one years old to seal the deal. So, I went without after earning that bit of cloth merit badge for my Scout uniform sash. And then I entered high school and was startled to discover ROTC, established to funnel high school students into military careers. They had a rifle team. As mentioned before, my physical skills were wanting, and the thought of climbing the rope to the ceiling of the gym while everyone watched made me sweat at night. I forsook gym for ROTC.

That was the first of the greatest decisions I ever made as a young man. I went into uniform as an ROTC cadet private in the First Squad, Second Platoon of Company C that constituted a third of South Shore High School's battalion strength. A regular army master sergeant named Bonham was the commanding officer, and he handled the tryouts for the rifle team. Our armory was prodigious. We had two platoons' worth of M1 .30 caliber rifles, a 3.5-inch rocket launcher, four BARs, and a rack of Springfield .22 caliber target rifles dating back to the 1920s. Those Springfields used to compete against other high schools' ROTC teams.

With my Boy Scout experience behind me and having mastered the little Stevens .22, I drew my first bead on an official ROTC target with brimming confidence. The rifle was heavy (it was supposed to train shooters to move up to the old nine-pound, bolt-action 1903 .30 caliber Springfield), and the bolt had a long, slippery, self-cocking action, but its firing pin was tripped by a creepy trigger, so discharge was always a surprise. By the fifth shot, I realized I was soaked with perspiration, seeing both spider webs and sparkles of light in my oxygen-starved vision. My glasses fogged, and the iron sights wandered all over the target. I flunked the tryout. Sergeant Bonham, in his usual bored manner and Virginia drawl, yawned that I should stick to rifle drill and stay away from rifle shooting.

So much for the one sport I did well. By then I was an Explorer Scout at Troop 529, but there were no plans to start anything like a rifle club, and if I could not shoot on the ROTC range, what was left? My path to juvenile delinquency, reefer madness, and a bitter life of social rejection after a prison term for felonious mopery was wide open.

A fellow scout, Gavin Scobie, turned out to be a shooter and had his own rifle, but he ran with a bunch of guys a few blocks away from my turf. He suggested I come down to his rifle club and check it out. The second momentous decision of my early years took me by the elbow and led me to the American Legion Post 175 on 75th and Coles Avenue. I followed Scobie through a narrow, dark alley along the side of the old blackened brick building, down a flight of cement steps lit only by the glow of a forty-watt bulb wrapped in dried spider corpses, and through the door into the rest of my life.

"Chank! Chank!" The sounds of .22 caliber rifle fire reverberating off brick walls came from behind a drywall partition that spanned a low-ceiling, whitewashed basement room, its overhead laced with water pipes and an electrical conduit. At a table, a blonde girl my age loaded .22 Winchester target ammunition from its cardboard box into a square of wood drilled to accept twenty cartridges. Next to her, a club member wearing a Marine Corps fatigue hat and a padded shooting coat scored a stack of targets.

The balding, big-shouldered hulk of "Doc" Meissner, the Junior Rifle Club boss, occupied a narrow desk against the wall that divided the clubroom from the five-target rifle range. He eyed me through thick bifocal spectacles, curling cigarette smoke, and the bushy hairs of a squinting eyebrow.

Arthur Meissner, OD, was an ophthalmologist and a certified NRA instructor. His first words to me after hearing about my single Boy Scout merit badge credential and taking his peremptory visual appraisal were "Grab a rifle and we'll see if you can shoot without killing somebody."

The rifles in the nearby rack ranged from heavy-barrel Remington Model 37 Rangemasters, one immaculate Winchester Model 75 with a long 20X telescopic sight replacing the usual open iron sights, and a row of the dreaded Springfield training rifles used at the ROTC range. I selected one of the Springfields as my heart sank. One more crappy performance coming up.

This dank basement had its own unique blend of smells—mostly stale beer and rye whiskey from the American Legion saloon upstairs. Mixed with the tang of freshly burned gunpowder and Doc's ever-present cigarette, the fetid atmosphere was like a rain-washed spring morning to me as I rolled into the prone position on the shooting mat. Doc sat on a little stool next to my mat with the ammo block in his hand. As I adjusted the rifle's leather sling around my left bicep and settled the forestock onto my left palm, he said, "Try a few dry-fire shots."

Dry-fires are shots with no ammunition in the breech. You dry-fire to test the trigger pull's crispness and how much it creeps backward before tripping the firing pin, and after the "click" of the shot, you can see where your sights settle down on the distant target. The idea is to get your body and rifle naturally pointing at the target so you only have to make the fine adjustments along its length before you begin firing for real. I worked the long-throw, slippery bolt with no illusions as to the outcome. As the front sight centered in the circular peep rear sight and balanced beneath the black dot of the distant target in the six o'clock position, I squeezed the trigger. It snapped cleanly. The effort was so precise, I knew exactly where the shot would have struck the target. Somebody had worked on that rifle with a file, emery paper, and lubricant to create an action as smooth as glass.

"Take a couple more," Doc said. "Take two breaths and then let out half of the third. Get your elbow right under that stock . . . and relax."

By the time I sent the first Winchester Match Target bullet down range, I knew this was what I wanted to do, what I could do. Out of ten shots, I hit six bull's-eyes—three of them were pinwheels that hit the target dead center. Later that evening I would proudly take home the parental permission forms, and a form that would admit me into the NRA junior division.

After my brilliant performance in the prone position, Doc proceeded to show me everything I had done wrong. Precision rifle shooting follows a very strict rulebook concerning the four positions allowed on any NRA rifle range in the country. Though each position had been developed by the military, they little resembled actual shooting conditions on a battlefield. For instance, in prone, sitting, and kneeling positions, you slipped a leather loop made with your rifle sling over your bicep and snaked your hand under its tension to grasp the fore stock. That sling tension helps wedge the rifle's buttplate firmly against your shoulder. Of course, having a hoard of howling, blood-thirsty Communist soldiers chasing you through a snow-covered Korean wood doesn't allow for such civilized range practices.

Being compact at five feet five, with a big butt and short legs (all of which would change radically in three years as I shot up to five feet seven and rearranged my other dimensions during a tour in the U.S. Merchant Marine), I shot in the low sitting position with my elbows propped on crossed legs and the low kneeling position, parked with my butt on my right leg turned under me, which always fell asleep. Standing, or "offhand," was a real revelation. I learned that the best way to produce the most consistently high scores in offhand was to shoot fast once the rifle was at your shoulder. The first time your sights align on the target, shoot. At that point, you are as steady as you will ever be so, get 'er done. With target rifle triggers that have zero creep before the sear breaks, releasing the firing pin—discovering that break point—required several hundred rounds at practice.

I watched Diane Guest, that blonde girl with the soft eyes and big laugh, balance the bottom of the trigger guard and magazine floorplate of her sixteen-pound rifle on her thumb and tips of her fingers with her upper arm and elbow tucked into her right side (no slings allowed) and anchored on her thrown-out right hip. Diane was a southpaw, which made target shooting more difficult, since virtually all target rifles are built for right-handed shooters. She held the Distinguished Rifleman badge, the highest shooting award in the NRA, and shot rings around me and everyone in the club. The members loved her in a most protective, brotherly fashion. She and I are still good friends and frequent correspondents.

That range and my friends who shared my love of shooting provided me with a home away from home. No jukebox in a malt shop equaled the music of rumbling pulleys as each shooter cranked furiously to send or retrieve targets downrange that were clothespinned to target frames hung from over-head wires. Each shot echoed off the whitewashed brick and stone walls and a lead-spattered inclined steel backdrop to be muffled in the dirt floor between the cement firing surface and the targets.

On Parents and Guests Night, Doc fortified himself and the adult visitors at the upstairs bar and then led them down to our musty basement and had us send downrange wooden matches clipped to the target frames. One by one, lying on the shooting mats in front of people we cared about, we fired at the redheaded wood matches—not to shoot the small head off its stick, but to light each match with a passing bullet. It was like hitting the winning home run in the bottom of the ninth inning when that match of mine flared, along with all the others.

Master Sergeant Bonham was replaced by MSgt. Henry Harpel as ROTC commander, and after a couple of months of Friday nights at the American Legion rifle range under Doc Meissner's tutelage, I requested another try to qualify for the rifle team captained by my old friend John Stiefel. By this time the Springfield was also a familiar friend, creepy trigger and all its quirks. I made the team and rose to become cocaptain. My poor father, who had given up all hope of seeing me distinguish myself as an athlete, was bewildered when, in my senior year, he and I received an invitation to South Shore High School's 1958 lettermen's award ceremony. There, with all the baseball, basketball, football, golf, and tennis jocks, I received my sports letter that reads "Riflery" in blue stitching. That was the first time my father ever applauded me.

<hr />

Following the Korean War, the country settled into a period of relative peace during the Eisenhower years. Over this period, the NRA cemented its relationship with the Defense Department's Civilian Markmanship Program (CMP) and the Office of the Director of Civilian Markmanship (DCM). The Spanish-American War had put a point on America's badly organized rush to obtain enough trained men quickly and field an effective army. This prob lem was addressed in 1903 by the creation of the CMP. The object of this organization was to provide civilian rifle- and pistol-shooting clubs support in the form of affiliated competitions; the right to purchase surplus military-type rifles, pistols, and ammunition at discounted prices; and both awards and recognition for excellence in the shooting sports. Its concept was heartily approved by President Theodore Roosevelt.

In 1916 the National Defense Act created the DCM to oversee the CMP. This promotion of shooting embraced the NRA, and together the DCM and NRA created a virtual hierarchy of national matches where civilians and military personnel fired at targets side by side, forming a loose brotherhood under arms with the blessing and monetary support of the U.S. government.

One of the requirements for clubs to become affiliated with the DCM was to have at least ten NRA junior division members enrolled and active in the program. By 1954 the American Legion Post 175 Rifle Club built up our junior group to meet that requirement, and they purchased two M1 rifles and boxes of M2 .30-06 caliber ball ammunition. By the time I joined, the club's senior members had been shooting the M1s in DCM matches at the army's Fort Sheridan and the Great Lakes Naval Training Station. I was familiar with the M1 as a part of ROTC close-order drill, and I could field-strip one down to its basic components blindfolded, but now I had the opportunity to also shoot the rifle.

At that time, no other junior group in the Chicago area was qualified to participate in the matches. We were limited to "familiarization" shoots while we qualified for NRA-Army expert medals out at the Fox River Valley two-hundred-yard range clear across the city and deep in the northwest cornfields. Finally, Doc Meissner showed around some of the scores us "kids" were shooting, and as a test we were allowed to show up at the next military and senior club .30 caliber match and shoot the army "C" course of fire in all four shooting positions plus a nine-shot rapid fire prone. We had five shooters and two rifles.

Doc had drilled into us proper range procedure so we knew all the commands from the range officer in the tower behind the firing line. When he called out, "Ready on the right? Ready on the left? Ready on the firing line!" we were as ready as we ever would be. The targets rose from the concrete butts two hundred yards distant like a row of impregnable shields, and we commenced to fire.

Prone, sitting, kneeling, and offhand, we loaded fresh eight-round clips for each other, thumped each clip on the table top to settle the powder onto the primer, and listened to Doc as he sat behind us and watched each target through his spotting telescope. He was actually watching the heat mirage rise from the asphalt strip that ran the length of the target embankment. The wind down by the targets blew the mirage, bending it over, and that wind also blew bullets off course. Going against his coaching that required a quick shot once the sights were on target, he taught us how to work with a spotter to defeat the invisible wind at mid-range. Doc intoned a barely audible, almost mantra-like singsong: "Steady . . . steady . . . window coming up . . . window almost there . . . window!"

On "window," the reflected heat mirage was straight up as the wind dropped, and our sights swung slowly from left to right beneath the target. During "window" we could fire just as the front sight almost achieved perfect alignment. "Blam!" The M1 hammered into my shoulder, ejected the spent shell casing, and autoloaded a fresh round.

Civilian shooters from other clubs with customized rifles, retired and active sergeants with 1903 Springfields slung over their shoulders, and curious spectators drifted down to our space on the firing line beneath that hot sun and acid-blue sky to watch the kids shoot. We were models of good behavior, even though we were so damned excited we could hardly hold it back.

When the smoke cleared after the rapid-fire sequence, everyone got a kick out of our other girl shooter, Donna Brandebury, who was fourteen but looked about twelve years old. She had been battered back almost a foot and a half behind the firing line by the rifle's recoil. Our targets rose up with white hole plugs clustered within the bull and nine-ring circles. Of course, we were unofficial, having been invited as a test. But that day I shot a possible score offhand with about half the shots in the bull's-eye's center X ring thanks to Doc's "window" coaching.

There was always great camaraderie at the rifle matches, because even though team scores were posted, each shooter was alone with his or her rifle or pistol. All of us on the American Legion team competed among ourselves for NRA and DCM qualification medals and place medals at matches. We had all earned the expert classification, and I had passed the rifle instructor test. At the end of each Friday night session, we piled into Jim Preston's 1949 Oldsmobile "bubble" coupe with its 1956 V-8 engine and twin four-barrel carbs (but no floor beneath the back seat) and thundered off to the White Castle on 79th Street for a Coke and a half-dozen sliders each.

Still, there was a hole in my life. Jim owned a beautiful German Anschütz target rifle with a thumbhole in the stock and amazing sights. Gavin fired a unique BSA Martini lever-action rifle offered only by Al Freeland of Rock Island, Illinois. Everyone admired Diane Guest's Winchester Model 75. I had squat. I owned a 10X shooting coat with rubber elbow pads and a leather shoulder pad. I now cradled the club rifle on a Freeland padded shooting glove, but a new target rifle of any competitive quality cost over $150. Those were big-time bucks on the South Side in 1956.

One day, out of the blue, my dad asked me to ride with him down to the hardware store to help him carry something home. We didn't go to the local store, but one further south. He had recently bought an Iron Fireman window air conditioner there—the first one in our building. While he wandered off toward the tool aisle, I spotted a rack of rifles behind a counter where pistols and revolvers glistened under glass. The elderly Polish owner came over and gestured toward the rifles.

"See anything you like?" he asked in his heavy accent.

"Let's see that one," said Dad from behind me, pointing at the end of the rack.

The old man lifted with some effort a heavy-barreled Winchester 52C, called the King of the Target Rifles, mounting Redfield iron sights and a fold-down Schuetzen buttplate that hooked under the shooter's armpit to help leverage the fifteen-pound package. He handed it to me, and I have it to this day—with a 10-34X telescopic sight because my eyes are no longer as good as they were when I was sixteen. I was so intensely happy I could not speak the whole way home.

In two years, I was off to college at the School of the Art Institute of Chicago and the University of Chicago night school for my academics. I was no longer a chubby kid but had leaned out some and began trying to find my patch of sanity in an increasingly chaotic world. As the 1960s approached, life began to round off my edges, but shooting and firearms in some form would always return, as do the memories of those first small victories.

———————————◆◆◆———————————

After a rush of sales orders during the Korean War, handgun manufacturers faced a skidding market. Colt hunted around for a buyer to take over their company once the bloom was off the venerable .45 caliber Model 1911 semiautomatic pistol that had been a cash cow. The army was looking to replace the big-bore pistol with the more shooter-friendly 9mm round, which also permitted greater magazine capacity in the grip. Colt's line of revolvers was old and gasping on tradition, with only one star attraction, the Colt Python .357 Magnum. This horse of a gun was offered in 1955 with a tight lock, laser-bore sighting, and under-barrel weight with a ventilated rib-sighting ramp on top. The revolver was gorgeous in nickel or blue but a handful even in its 2.5-inch barrel version. An eight-inch-barrel "hunting" model, offered with a Leupold telescopic sight, was the first such handgun sporting package offered by a major gun manufacturer.

Smith & Wesson became the largest manufacturer of pistols and revolvers in the United States and, in the early 1950s, had a pistol in the hunt for the new army contracts. The Model 39 chambered the 9mm Parabellum in an eight-round-single, stack magazine. Essentially, it was a knockoff of the World War II Walther pistols, but its double-action safety (trigger pull cocks the hammer) saved time over the need to either work the Model 1911A1 Colt slide to chamber a shot or carry the pistol at full cock with the safety catch engaged (scary but popular with some law enforcement agencies). The pistol was rejected by the army and offered to the public in 1955. The Model 39 turned out to have manufacturing quality issues, and after the Illinois State Police tried the gun and dumped it, other police agencies backed away from automatics in favor of revolvers for the next decade. The S&W reputation for semiautomatic pistols was rescued in the 1970s by following the Browning Hi-Power lead with a fifteen-round magazine for the 9mm and copying the European Glock polymer frame design (and getting sued by Glock for copying the design a little too closely) in downsized double-action pistols for concealed carry.[12]

While Colt was playing musical chairs with a number of buyers to save its brand name, and S&W engineers were searching for the magic formula by reverse-engineering Europe's latest high-capacity lightweights and trying to make revolvers seem "innovative," along came Bill Ruger. After striking out with a postwar machine gun design, he turned his use of low-cost stampings into a very good-looking .22 semiautomatic pistol. Enlisting the investment and enthusiasm of wealthy art student and gun fancier Alexander Sturm, he formed Sturm, Ruger. Their first product was the Ruger Standard pistol, which resembled the German Luger in balance and natural pointing that was an extension of the hand. Using low-cost manufacturing processes, the Standard challenged the High Standard and Colt Woodsman pistols, which were the only two comparable match-grade semiautomatic designs.

An *American Rifleman* review lauded the pistol's reliability, ease of pointing, inherent accuracy, and low price: $37.50 compared to Colt's $50. The gun took off as an entry-level match target pistol and was soon followed by the Mark I version with a heavy barrel, which took away the entry-level stigma. With only six employees and $50,000 in seed money, Ruger had gone all in and opened up the handgun market, inspiring future manufacturers such as Taurus and Kimber to spur competition. Ruger's introduction in 1960 of their Colt Peacemaker knockoff Single-Six following Colt's discontinuation of the model helped ignite a raft of cowboy revolver makers in the United States and overseas as a flood of Western television shows sent millions of buyers back to their gun shops. Eventually, all the handgun markets would flourish even more in the twenty-first century.

As I tackled my studies and before I discovered the world of photojournalism, my shooting needs changed. Graduations had split up the American Legion post gang, and I realized how important the friendship was to the shooting experience. Also, I was a bit burned out and carrying a heavy scholastic load as well as my art studies. I still lived at home, still slept on a day couch in the dining room, and still needed to flee the house at regular intervals.

I discovered that the 53rd Street YMCA had a pistol range on its top floor. The Y was only a short electric train ride and a two-block walk away, so I visited. "Blam!" "Pow!" "Bang!" The noise of exploding cartridges sending hot muzzle blasts into the dark range was excruciating to my unprotected ears. Though each shooting position had partitions on either side of where the shooter stood, the blasting cacophony during a rapid fire sequence with five shooters hammering away at their targets sixty feet away thoroughly intimidated—and excited—me.

Competitive pistol shooting is essentially a three-gun affair. There is a definite distinction between Olympic-style target shooting and combat or "practical" competitions. At the time I learned this sport back in the late 1950s and early 1960s, civilian and military/police shooting was done with one hand.

The gun was held extended from the shoulder as the shooter stood at a right angle to the target. Your free hand usually ended up in your pants pocket.

The three guns were a .22LR (usually an S&W K-22 Masterpiece or a Colt Woodsman semiautomatic), a Colt or S&W centerfire (in either a .38 Special or .32 caliber) revolver loaded with sharp-edged wadcutter bullets, which punched a perfectly round hole in the paper target, and a semiautomatic, clip-fed pistol firing .45 caliber ACP, .38 Super, or .380 caliber. Slow-fire and rapid-fire strings were aimed at a standard bull's-eye target at twenty yards and scored. It was all very fussy and treated the short-barrel handguns pretty much like the rifle competitions except you stood closer and had only one position to learn: standing upright, pistol extended like a duelist at dawn.

I found it very hard to learn. The slightest deviation from a perfect hold or sight picture threw the bullet strike out of the black bull. If you held too long with your arm outstretched, the sights took on a life of their own and wobbled all over the place. Of course, once again, I had to use borrowed guns sighted in for their owner, which I told myself made all the difference. Thus began my campaign at home to obtain my own target pistol. Determined, I sought out the last resort of a college student. I looked for work.

Job number one was as an usher at the State-Lake Theater in downtown Chicago. I wore a maroon suit with black stripes on the legs, a double-breasted jacket with huge shoulder pads, a white cardboard dickey with a wing collar, a black bow tie, and white gloves. I saw *The Vikings* with Kirk Douglas thirty-four times, *Man of the West* starring Gary Cooper more than fifty times, and *Separate Tables* with David Niven and Burt Lancaster about twenty-five times before going quite mad after a particularly nasty clean-up job at midnight in the women's toilet.

My second job had me sailing with the merchant marine as an ordinary deckhand across the Great Lakes hauling shiploads of really expensive dirt (iron ore) to make steel. Its result, besides extending my vocabulary into a realm that earned me another swat from my mother with her handy wet dishrag (did she carry that thing in a holster?), was enough money to afford a Ruger Standard .22 pistol. I also bought a pair of unformed walnut grip blanks to carve and sand so they fit my hand.

Dad got into the spirit of my handgun shooting and made some micrometer measurements of the muzzle and produced a mechanical drawing, which he sent to a metal worker he knew at the Sperry Gyroscope plant in Cleveland.

In two weeks a heavy brass tube about four inches long arrived that slid over the muzzle and front sight of my pistol and locked there with an Allen wrench. Three 1/8-inch cuts had been made in the top surface of the tube extending down to half its diameter. The end of the tube was filled with an aluminum baffle drilled with a hole just barely larger than a .22 caliber bullet and sweated into place. The weight of the brass tube slowed the too-slender barrel wobble, while the cuts acted to vent the gun powder gas upward away from the tube plug counteracting the muzzle's rise at each shot.

My scores climbed, particularly in rapid fire. I began lifting a weight to strengthen my right bicep and forearm. I won some NRA qualification medals and some competition brass. Everyone in the range was friendly, and it was like the American Legion post experience all over again.

And then, one evening during a match, I was shooting slow-fire when a hand thumped my shoulder. I jumped. It was a damned rude interruption in the middle of a string being fired for score. The thumper was the range officer for the opposing team. He pointed with his finger. My hip was touching the edge of the shelf in front of me. I quickly stepped back, but he solemnly shook his head. In a few moments, my target for that string was disqualified. I was called for cheating. My scores for the following rapid-fire were included in the team total, but the way the other shooters watched me, looking for any repeat infraction, made me sick to my stomach.

To this day, decades later, I remember the incident vividly. Did I cheat intentionally? Did I just fail to notice my hip against that shelf? How badly did I want to do well? I came back to the range a couple of times after that, but while some members 'fessed up their own stories of rules lapses with chuckling wave-offs to take away the sting, I left the team and used my pistol for squirrel hunting. I've used the Ruger at other indoor and outdoor ranges over the years, but never in competition. I shoot only against myself now.

--- ◆ ◆ ◆ ---

In 1956 pistol and rifle target shooting in the United States was a popular, although niche, sport due to the absence of spectator appeal. However, the Olympics held in Melbourne, Australia, that year confirmed that the American team was considered by the international shooting fraternity to be the Olympic doormat; our team managed only one third-place medal. There was actually no American Olympic shooting team. Every four years, independent shooters gathered from their various leagues to try out and then were packed off to the Olympic venue. Nominally, the NRA was in charge of rifle target-shooting while the United States Revolver Association (USRA) selected the pistol shooters (from its membership).

It is no reflection upon the skills of the individual American shooters who were selected that they were trounced at every Olympics. It is just that the NRA and the USRA looked upon international shooting rules with an upturned nose and jingoistic disdain. American ranges were measured in yards while the "foreigners" used meters. The bull's-eye target was official NRA size, while the folks across the pond used a smaller bull with less space between the concentric rings. The Olympics featured strange matches using a free pistol with impossibly long sight platforms, wrap-around wood grips, and single-shot breeches that harkened back to the old Remington Rolling Blocks of the 1880s. The free rifles were equally strange, especially for the "running deer" matches where the target zipped across an open space while the shooter got off rapid shots. They didn't use proper Winchester, Remington, or Springfield rifles but employed expensive Hammerli, Anschütz, and Walther target specials. When American shooters arrived, they carried borrowed guns and had only a short time to get used to the smaller targets. Worst of all, for the 1960 Games the Soviet Union racked up seven medals to the U.S. effort that netted one gold and one silver.

This pitiable showing reached back to the revival of the Olympics in 1896. According to shooting historian and writer, Col. Charles Askins:

> Yet no one should have been surprised that we lost the [Melbourne] Olympic shooting; we have been losing Olympic shooting matches in large numbers and with great consistency throughout the 60 years since the modem revival of the ancient games. In all those 60 years we have won the Olympic shooting championship only twice, the last time in 1924. We have won exactly one golden first in Olympic pistol competition in the past 32 years. Our rifle record is not much better, with a total of six firsts since 1920. The best we have been able to tally in the past three decades in the overall Olympic shooting aggregate was second in 1948. We placed fourth in 1952—two places below the Soviets, who had not entered Olympic competition since 1908.[13]

Matchlock musketeer. *Library of Congress*

A Civil War Union sniper, one of Hiram Berdan's sharpshooters. *Library of Congress*

Native Americans with white officials at a fort's trading post in the late nineteenth century.
Library of Congress

The firing line at Creedmoor Rifle Range circa 1880. *Library of Congress*

A line of pre–World War II U.S. Navy recruits take aim with Colt Model 1911 semiautomatic pistols. *Library of Congress*

Practicing with my Smith & Wesson Chiefs Special Airweight revolver.

Standing at the far left with my South Shore ROTC rifle team.

The NRA junior rifle team at the American Legion Post 175 rifle range.

Standing on the firing line of the Fox Valley two-hundred-yard rifle range in 1957.

Dressed in my uniform for the Arizona State Guard and Detective Agency.

Youngsters with a BB gun in a yard.
Library of Congress

Fanning my Colt near Big Timber,
Montana, in 1969.

Awaiting my call on a
Western film set.

The 1980 Lake Placid Olympics.

Smith & Wesson Military & Police .38 Special.

My old 1955 Winchester 52C rifle.

Busting clays.

If the three gold firsts won by the Soviet Union had been awarded to the American team, the United States would have won the 1956 Melbourne Olympics. As it was, the Russians walked away with bragging rights. The Communist press lost no time playing up their athletic superiority, achieving a propaganda prize of world-shaping proportions.

This attitude was nothing new. As far back as 1900, Americans lost to the French, who beat them 8–1 at international shooting. The Games held at St. Louis in 1904, on their home turf with only seven nations competing (the World's Fair was running in St. Louis at the same time), the Americans did not even schedule shooting matches. When they returned to Greece for the next outing, they got hammered again. And so it went until 1920 when, inexplicably, they cleaned up thirteen events at the Antwerp games and came back in 1924 with a string of five firsts out of twelve events. Of note, our best shooters on these two teams were all military personnel, so the marksmanship training for World War I service proved its value in the long run.

And then, in 1928, the system manned by the NRA and USRA caught up with their own good fortune and, through inaction and a shrug, allowed the International Olympic Committee (smarting from the American victories) to cut shooting events from the Amsterdam Games. From that time forward, Americans stunk out the house.

Management of Olympic shooting in the United States stumbled along until after the war when the NRA assumed full control except for shotgun venues, but we continued to lurch along until 1978 when the U.S. Olympic Committee designated the NRA as the sole national governing body for Olympic-style shooting. This official sanction and implied mandate spurred the association to create its International Shooting Sports division with its headquarters office at Colorado Springs. The following year, after passage of the Amateur Sports Act, the NRA International Competitions Committee produced a forty-page report mandating the establishment of national teams and development teams in each Olympic shooting discipline, a national coaching staff, year-round training programs, and a headquarters and training site for Olympic shooting sports. Organizations such as the Amateur Trapshooting Association (ATA), the Pacific International Trapshooting Association (PITA), and the National Skeet Shooting Association (NSSA) actively govern and develop American-style trap and skeet shooting in this country.

In 1992 the NRA ceased to be the national governing body for Olympic shooting, and in April 1995 USA Shooting was formed and became the full-time national governing body for international shooting sports in the United States. The NRA is now one of many sponsors of this far-reaching organization. In 2000 the NRA chose not to be a member of the National Three-Position Air Rifle Council. The NRA is not directly involved in the practical pistol competitions conducted by the International Practical Shooting Confederation and International Defensive Pistol Association, or in cowboy action shooting. These types of events have grown dramatically in recent years.

Pistol competitons and innovations were way below the radar of U.S. manufacturers after World War II. Souvenirs from Europe had given American shooters a taste of design style and durability, especially in regard to semiautomatic pistols. Firepower coupled with hitting power was the name of the game as shown by combat in the Korean War. The Colt .45 ACP Model 1911A1 was an antique used only by hard boiled fictional cops like Mickey Spillane's Mike Hammer. Law enforcement—the primary handgun market—was looking around for new solutions and better training. Robert Dyment, in his 1957 article in *Guns Magazine*, cited two instances of disappointing police performance at that time:

A few years ago, a lieutenant on a big city police force appeared at a gun repair shop with his service pistol wrapped carefully in a hotel dinner napkin. Trouble? The gun was cocked. The officer had cocked it in anticipation of trouble which had not developed and he did not know how to uncock it without pulling the trigger.

Then there is the one about the officers who were called to dispose of a large dog that had bitten several children in a school yard. The policemen approached within a few yards and commenced firing. They ran out of ammunition. The dog, no longer amused, went home. The police followed, and the scene was repeated. Nobody knows (or will tell) how many shots were fired, but all agree that the dog was not hit. The dog catcher was called, finally. He caught the dog.[14]

Dyment goes on:

The great city of Chicago, with well over 10,000 men in its police and detective forces, allots just $23,000 for firearms training out of an annual budget of nearly $55,500,000—less than one-half of one-tenth of one per cent! Lieutenant Bernard M. Dier, Rangemaster for the Chicago Police Department, says that the budgeted allotment for firearms training has not increased in recent years, is not sufficient for adequate training because of increased man-power and increased costs of ammunition. Lieutenant Dier's report concerning the failure to increase firearms training allotments to meet increases in police personnel and increases of as much as 100 percent in equipment costs is echoed throughout the nation. Only 14 percent of the enforcement agencies contacted by our survey report any increases at all, over the past few years, in firearms training funds.[15]

Besides its hunting programs and new magazine, the NRA considered the police problem a worthy avenue of training, and police departments added their grateful support to the association. A special police school had been reinstated at Camp Perry in 1956. The NRA became the only national trainer of law enforcement officers with the introduction of its NRA Police Firearms Instructor certification program in 1960. Today there are thousands of NRA-certified police and security firearms instructors. Additionally, top law enforcement shooters compete each year in eight different pistol and shotgun matches at the National Police Shooting Championships held in Jackson, Mississippi.

Revolvers, still the primary sidearm of police officers as they began lifting their skill levels in the 1950s and 1960s were expensive to build due to hand-work and tight tolerances to achieve cylinder lock and prevent gas escape. There was also the maximum cylinder capacity of six shots of even medium caliber. Like the military, the nation's police forces were tradition-bound, and domestic handgun production was bogged down in wheel-gun sales.

But if new guns were lacking in innovation and volume of production in the postwar period as mentioned earlier, imported handguns and military weapons found a growing market. The story of the postwar gun boom really began immediately after V-E Day. At that time, American weapons could be purchased in Europe for bargain-basement prices. For example, genuine Colt 1911 .45 caliber automatics sold as new for only $16. Smith & Wesson revolvers went on the block for $8.40. Colt Lightning .38s, like new, needed only $4.20. Winchester lever-action rifles, old models in fine working order, went for $1.50, and Remington cap-and-ball .44s with perfect bores were flogged for only $6.[16] These were the actual prices paid for these American firearms in the postwar years in Europe. And on the flip side of this European fire sale, America faced a gun shortage. After four years of all-out production of military guns, there was little left for the hunting and sport shooting population. Manufacturers suffered from reconversion—dusting off prewar tools and dies to restart production of civilian guns—steel controls, and other material shortages.

When the Germans failed to invade England and were finally rolled up by the Allies in 1945, the British were dollar-poor but had one major export they could send to America: the firearms they had scoured from the United States before the war. But the British, hoping for a future increase in value, were not anxious to immediately send their warehouses full of guns back where they came from, or so they insisted in 1947. The sudden flow of cheap guns back to the United States was due to the machinations of a Mr. Bland.

This gentleman—whose first name no one in the United States seemed to know—bought up the warehouses of used, captured, and surplus guns from the Port Authority as an investment, cagily guessing their potential value. The cash-strapped Brits needed pound sterling on the barrelhead and went along with the deal Then, Bland died. His estate's executors decided to sell off the whole pile in small lots and dumped the accretion of antiques, war booty, and American collectibles on the U.S. shore. Most were sold as is, and bulk crates were dropped on the dock at prices per ton. The sudden flood of weapons set off a buying spree in the States and sowed the seeds for the postwar gun hobby boom.[17]

When Colt stopped building its Single Action Army "cowboy gun" in 1947, they allowed all claims for that design to lapse. This monumentally bad idea opened the door to gunmakers in the 1950s and 1960s as the quick-draw phenomenon swept out from Hollywood into tie-down holsters across the country.

For the latter half the 1950s, Colt operated as a wholly owned subsidiary of Penn-Texas. In 1959 Penn-Texas changed its name to Fairbanks Whitney, following its acquisitions of two larger companies, Pratt & Whitney, a Connecticut manufacturer, and Fairbanks Morse & Company, a diesel engine firm based in Chicago. Colt was a minority player in the conglomerate's business but had the highest-profile name recognition. In 2002 the company became Colt's Manufacturing Company, which produces firearms for the civilian market, and Colt Defense, which deals with the military, law enforcement, and private security contracts.

The Vietnam War escalated in the 1960s and brought a new rush of business for the Firearms Division of Colt Industries. The M16 rifle was delivered to Colt in 1959 by designer Eugene Stoner for export, until it was discovered that many of the countries that loved the rifle could not order it because it was not being used by the U.S. military. After intense Colt lobbying that included an informal test shoot by air force general Curtis LeMay on some watermelons, the first big government order for M16s came in 1963 when the air force agreed to purchase twenty-five thousand to replace its M1 and M2 carbines. By 1966 the division had sixteen hundred employees, nearly half of them engaged in putting together M16s.

Eugene Stoner, who transferred to Colt Industries, had created the new M16 rifle design around a smaller-caliber, high-velocity cartridge that produced lower recoil than the .30-06 bullet dating from the 1903 Springfield rifle of World War I. Battlefield statistics from World War II determined that most combat targets appeared well within three hundred yards, and it was important to enable soldiers to put enough bullets downrange to suppress enemy fire.

The army had embraced the concept that aimed shots gave the average soldier too much time to think about his target, resulting in the low numbers of soldiers who actually shot at the enemy. The primary infantry rifle of the late 1950s and early 1960s was the M14. This was, essentially, a full-automatic version of the M1 Garand with some wood removed to keep the weight down and still accommodate a twenty-round box magazine loaded with 7.62 NATO (.30 caliber) rounds. Unfortunately, at full automatic the M14 was virtually uncontrollable, as the big NATO cartridges hammered through the breech. The rifle was developed as the T44 during a period when NATO was trying to create a unified weapon that could counter the legendary Kalashnikov AK-47. After much bickering over the British EM-2 firing the .280 cartridge and the Belgian FN FAL (which chambered the 7.62 NATO), the U.S. military cobbled together the compromise M14 using much of the tooling that had built the M1.

The small-caliber cartridge that Eugene Stoner adopted for his new rifle was the .223 Winchester, a .30 caliber case necked down to a .22 caliber bullet and loaded with "stick" gunpowder that produced high power and clean burning. The M16 rifle was made of metal stampings and forgings turned on oil-splashed routers, grinders, and augers into finished assemblies. It offered the soldier single shot and full automatic at a high rate of fire—the original model AR-10 design emptied its twenty-shot magazine in two seconds, or six hundred rounds a minute. With the M16 weighing only six pounds as compared to nine pounds for the M14, the soldier carried more ammo in bandoliers of twenty-round plastic box magazines. The first shipments of the rifles for actual combat were sent to Vietnam in the mid-1960s for the South Vietnamese troops and their American advisers. Everyone who tested the rifle loved it.

The final hurdle was the new small bullet. The .223 Winchester, from which the 5.56mm round developed, was a "varmint" cartridge, and dropping down from the long-standing .30 caliber round was anathema to the U.S. military, using the same logic as they had with the British .280 in the NATO trials. Firing into blocks of ballistic gel eased their worries. Shooting the 5.56 into the gelatinous slabs that imitated the resistance of human flesh revealed the killing power of the M16. The bullet entered the gel with a small entry wound, but as it met resistance, the slug began to break up and keyhole, tumbling sideways and achieving heavy tissue damage. The smaller slug was a real man-stopper.

Then word came in from the jungle battlefields. The M16 had a major jamming problem, and soldiers were dying with inoperable weapons in their hands. Stoner had specified the high-energy stick gunpowder for the .223 round, now dubbed the 5.6mm by the army. To save money and use up surplus supplies, the army ammo sent overseas was loaded with slow-burning, high-carbon "ball" powder granules. These caused a buildup of corrosion in the rifle's breech, especially in full-automatic fire, which was employed most of the time. Empty shells stuck in the breech and had to be pried out, or loaded cartridges failed to seat in the breech so the bolt could fully close.

The problem was solved by heavily chroming the breech to minimize the carbon buildup. An external hand-operated "forward assist" button jutting out from the receiver was installed that allowed the soldier to physically seat a single round in the hot breech with a punch from the heel of his hand and eliminate the jamming by making sure the extractor clamped on the shell rim. Finally, full-automatic fire was reduced to a "three-tap"—a three-shot burst with each trigger pull to reduce ammo use. Cleaning kits and comic book instruction manuals on lubricating and cleaning the redesignated M16A2 were included with every weapon.

The Vietnam War produced two icons immediately recognized today: the Huey (Bell UH-1 Iroquois) helicopter and the M16A2 rifle, which has gone on to be the longest-serving infantry rifle in U.S. Army history. Today the M16A2 serves our troops overseas compressed down to its M4 configuration with a collapsible stock and shortened barrel, topped with a variety of light-gathering optical sights.

Surprisingly, though the M14 had the shortest tenure of any official U.S. Army rifle, the weapon coexisted with the new rifle as a squad sniper weapon with a telescopic sight. As a semiautomatic, it is prized at the Camp Perry annual civilian rifle matches for its accuracy and reliability.

The irony of the long-serving M16 is that while Americans are proud of their troops who are on duty in Iraq and Afghanistan, those same rifles were in the hands of the fathers of this generation of warfighters. In the 1960s and 1970s, some of those fathers came home to be cursed and called "baby killers" by a rabidly antiwar minority of the American public. A shift was occurring across the country at the extreme ends of patriotism and antiwar sentiment.

This shift was also fueled by the assassinations of John F. Kennedy, Robert Kennedy, and Martin Luther King Jr., plus the widening civil rights movement and its confrontations between whites and blacks. People were nervous because the OPEC gasoline embargo of the 1970s forced Americans to ration gas, and foreigners now dictated how much U.S. citizens could travel in their own country.

In Vietnam, the January 1968 Tet Offensive saw isolated bands of insurgent Vietcong suddenly launch planned, full-scale attacks on U.S. bases, major South Vietnamese cities, and remote firebases. Only after heavy casualties and furious counterattacks were the Vietcong almost wiped out as an effective force below the 17th parallel. But on TV and in the newspapers, this bloody battle demonstrated that the United States was up against a formidable enemy and faced a long slog.

Added to that heavy combat were the 1968 Democratic Convention in Chicago, a deep recession, the revelations of the Watergate scandal, President Richard Nixon's resignation in 1974, and the inflammatory rhetoric of the

Black Panthers. There was an undercurrent of insecurity in neighborhoods across the country fueled by a constant media drumbeat. The average American was catching it from all sides.

During my time with the American Legion Post 175 junior rifle team, I became interested in teaching others the fundamentals of precision marksmanship. I watched Doc Meissner and the senior club members teach rifle handling basics and then went on to earn my own rifle instructor qualification from the NRA. I would continue to follow that path, earning a bachelor of art education degree and graduate honors in photography from the School of the Art Institute of Chicago and the University of Chicago and teaching everything from art and photography to writing and video production.

While studying to be an artist, one year when I could not sail as a deckhand in the merchant marine, I took a job with a boy's boarding school that had an enrollment of disturbed and "problem" teenagers. My first professional teaching job was showing juvenile delinquents, children of divorce, and accused felons awaiting trial how to shoot.

Each summer the boarding school staff took all the boys to a summer camp in Wisconsin for two months of fun in the woods. Besides swimming, canoeing, hiking, arts and crafts, field sports, and woodcraft, the sport of target shooting had been added. I was responsible for keeping track of the rifles, .22 rimfire ammunition, and targets; range maintenance; scoring shooting awards; and adding the gift of rifle marksmanship to the skill sets of these at-risk kids.

I had learned that teaching is not hard if the kids want to learn. All these kids wanted to do was get their hands on loaded guns. There was a lot of chatter as I led my first class through the woods and tall grass to the makeshift rifle range set against a high dirt berm about a half mile from camp. I had given each one a rifle or ammo carton to carry. The bolt-action rifles were a motley collection, having been donated or bought cheap from sporting goods stores. They held them as though they were made of golden crystal, caressing the steel and wood with their fingertips. When we reached the range with its six firing points and paper targets pinned to wooden frames fifty feet distant, they all seemed disappointed when I showed them the diminutive .22 cartridge.

"What can you kill with that?" asked one tall, skinny kid.

"Anyone here," I answered. "Let's try something." From my shoulder bag I removed my trusty bar of hard, yellow Fels-Naptha soap and passed it around. "Squeeze it. Try to break it," I said. When they handed it back, I had one kid take it down to the targets and set it on top of a frame. When he got back, I picked up one of the crappiest rifles, opened the bolt, and loaded a hollow-point .22 I had kept hidden in my hand for the demonstration. "Let's see if I can kill that soap," I said. "You should," muttered one of the kids sniffing his hands. "It stinks."

I raised the rifle, aimed, and fired, and the bar spun off the frame. "Go get it," I told the kid who had carried it down to the frame. He ran down, rummaged in the grass between the frames and the dirt backstop and then called out, "Holy shit!"

He brought back the mangled bar of soap, blown open where the forty-grain, copper-plated, hollow-point bullet had mushroomed on impact at a muzzle velocity of 1,255 feet per second.

"That little bullet does the same thing when it hits your skin," I said. "Now we'll learn how to safely shoot these weapons so nobody gets killed or has an arm or leg blown off." As they passed the bar around, the only sound was the birds in the trees.

The next month, just as routine had settled in at the camp and the kids' target scores were getting better, a gray school bus arrived that had cyclone fencing fastened across the windows. In Chicago the juvenile offender jail was full, and a busload of accused felons awaiting trial filed out. These were really tough kids, African American kids from the inner city where reaching teenage years was an accomplishment. They looked at the mostly white camp kids like wolves regard chickens. I had to teach these guys how to shoot, too.

The new guys were quiet, off balance away from their city turf and out in the woods. But anything was better than the concrete confines of juvie. First, out came the old reliable soap demonstration for the new arrivals, which quashed the "Shit, that ain't no real piece" and "I could catch that little pecker with my bare hand" comments. They became thoughtful as they passed around the blasted soap bar.

Making it up as I went along, I had a group of my better shots show the newcomers what we did on the range. Each of six camp kids fired five shots on a target. Fortunately, their nerves held under the glowering scrutiny of their audience, and their groups of shots were all in the targets' black circles. With fresh targets pinned in place, I asked the audience if they wanted to try their hand. Trying not to exhibit great enthusiasm, the tough guys grabbed the rifles and flopped down on the shooting mats. Each got five bullets, and I gave the command to fire when they were ready.

These kids scared me. I grew up where the tough kids were white Catholics—Poles, Irish, and Hispanic in the blocks nearer the steel mills. The black neighborhoods were strictly off limits. My parents and all my relatives in Buffalo were casual racists, as were the blue-collar parents of my neighborhood pals. Rainbow Beach, where I swam all summer, was, despite its name, a "white beach," and nobody thought anything about it. I went to white schools, and there were only two African American students in my class at the art institute, an interior designer who was so gay he almost burst into flames and an older man married to a white woman. Both were professional, well spoken, and worked harder than most of my other student friends. They were just artists like me trying to figure things out. These guys whom I was arming in a Wisconsin woods were the "off-limits" guys who were not welcome in my old neighborhood unless they were delivering groceries or mending the potholes.

Only one of the six shooters managed to hit the black circle, and he hit it three times. The rest were fuming. I knew exactly how they felt, remembering my tryout for the ROTC rifle team.

"If you want to learn how to hit that target every time, I'll show you, but you've got to work at it."

As they left the rifles on the shooting mats and returned to their group behind the firing line, it dawned on me that they were scared, too: defensive and scared, hassled and scared, out of their turf and scared. I looked at the kid who had hit the target. He was ebony and slender and stood up straight as he regarded me with alert brown eyes.

"Good shooting," I said.

"My brother taught me," he replied. "Ain' no thang."

A heavyset guy a little older than the rest pulled a toothpick from his mouth. "Shut up, fool," he grinned. "The man wants t' make you a house nigger. Say 'thank you, Massa.'"

I piped up. "You know there's a cash prize at the end of the month for the best scores? These other kids have a month's head start. Want a piece of it?"

"What kind of score we talkin' about?" asked the bad mouth around his toothpick.

A trickle of sweat rolled down my back. Cicadas had joined the birds in the background chaos beneath the warm summer sun. "Fifty bucks," I said. "Twenty bucks for second best and ten for third."

If the shifting eyes could have made a sound like shaking dice, the birds and bugs would have been drowned out. I had everybody's attention.

"We just gotta beat them?" asked my top shot of the new arrivals as he looked across at the cluster of white boys. The white boy who had fired the best score earlier was no patsy. He folded his arms and mimicked, "Ain' no thang."

I was trying to tear down a fence here. The black kids had lost face big time, and I thought I knew exactly how they felt. But I didn't, not really. My failure to make the team in high school was only a failure of marksmanship. These teenagers thought they were the alpha dogs in this pack—and here was whitey on top again. It wasn't until I assigned a white kid to each of the black shooters on the firing line to get them talking to each other that the freeze began to thaw. They all had more in common than was apparent. Each kid had received a raw deal in life and was working his way through it. They still talked trash at each other, but the barbs were blunted and spiked with dry humor. Results downrange started to add up. If there was an outsider, it was me. I had more to learn than they did. First, I had to persuade the camp officials to pony up eighty dollars in prize money now that I had shot my mouth off. I thought they would see the value. They agreed the money was well spent, or at least their half of it. The other forty dollars came from my pay. At the end of camp, I went home knowing at least no one got shot. And when the gray school buses with the barred windows pulled out heading back to juvie, I waved good-bye, and a few of the kids inside waved back.

The post–Vietnam War semiautomatic "assault rifle" challenged America's state and federal gun laws. These civilian clones of combat weapons became the poster children for both pro–gun rights and antigun factions, which now faced off to recruit the most supporters among the population and the legislators. It took some time, but the M16 became a cash cow for the firearms industry. Gun manufacturers from Smith & Wesson to Bushmaster cranked out civilian AR-15–type rifles as "tactical" weapons marketed to *Soldier of Fortune* wannabes and a segment of shooters who loved anything military. There was also a growing group of ordinary shooters and hunters who wanted something nasty looking for what they termed "home defense." The gun magazines supported the manufacturers' marketing with reviews of the type quoted by the Violence Policy Center (VPC), a national tax-exempt 501(c)(3), nonprofit antigun organization based in Washington, D.C.:

> The gun industry itself deliberately used the military character of semi-automatic "assault weapons" and the lethality-enhancing utility of their distinctive characteristics as selling points. The German company Heckler & Koch, for example, published ads calling their civilian guns "assault rifles" and stressing their military lineage. "The HK 91 Semi-Automatic Assault Rifle from Heckler & Koch . . . was derived directly from the G3," a German army weapon, said one full page ad (below). Another described the HK 94 Carbine as "a direct offspring of HK's renowned family of MP5 submachine guns." An Intratec ad said the company's TEC-9 "clearly stands out among high capacity assault-type pistols." Magnum Research advertised that the Galil rifle system to which it had import rights "outperformed every other assault rifle."[18]

There is no doubt that the gun manufacturers could not support the sale of M16 and other AR-15–type weapons by selling only to law enforcement agencies. Military contracts to various governments make up another sales segment. The testosterone-sodden advertising that features camouflaged warriors rising dripping from soaked rice paddies into the moonlit night with big, black, glistening weapons gripped in grimy hands are aimed straight at the wallet of the clerk in accounting, the mechanic at the garage, and the retired actuary who reads Clive Cussler novels. This is the American way—sell the sizzle, not the steak.

The NRA and the firearms manufacturers formed a comfortable synergy. The years following the Korean and Vietnam wars—though they flew in the face of the NRA mantra of "one shot, one kill" on the battlefield—were also kind to the NRA-military relationship. The AR-15–type rifle, with its hint of illegality and later the attempted assassination of President Ronald Reagan (which gave birth to the Brady Handgun Violence Protection Act), set up the pins in other alleys for the NRA to roll against, wrapped in the American flag and with the full weight of the Second Amendment.

———————————————◆◆◆———————————————

By the start of the volatile 1960s, I had graduated college. After living at home in that South Side apartment for twenty years, I packed my gear and headed west. A school chum, Paul Clinkunbroomer, had started an advertising agency in Phoenix, and I would become designated photographer. The agency was circling the drain when I arrived and resulted in my job as an officer with the Arizona State Guard and Detective Agency, discussed earlier. When I landed a day job teaching art in the P. T. Coe Elementary School, I went back to Chicago; married my college sweetheart, Janet; and returned to Phoenix.

Even with our three salaries, we were barely making a go of it when I read a wanted ad for a photographer-writer needed in Yuma. The salary was low, but so was Yuma's cost of living in 1963. We moved into former Marine Corps off-base housing and shopped for groceries at a nearby railroad salvage store. One time we bought a slightly scorched case of canned goods for $2.00 and ended up with twenty-four cans of garbanzo beans.

My new employer was the *Yuma News Enterprise* weekly newspaper published by the *Yuma Daily Star* as a tax dodge and once-a-week sponge for really local news. It was also a printing shop and a throwback to the old days of cast-lead type set in metal chases that were trundled around the print floor on wheeled "turtles." The *Star*'s photographers were older guys with 4x5-inch Speed Graphic cameras with the flashgun virtually welded to the camera and loaded with Sylvania Press #6 flashbulbs. I had a 2-1/4-inch Minolta Autocord twin-lens reflex, a 35mm Miranda single-lens reflex, and a Mercury Univex half-frame camera that gave seventy-two shots on one roll of film, plus had a built-in motor drive. The employees at the *Star* looked at me as if I had just crawled out of a flying saucer.

I was happy beyond measure, shooting, writing, and laying out double-truck (two pages wide) center spreads of my photos and words, shooting days, nights, weekends—whenever there was work to be done. Yuma's heat was crushing. The pressroom combined its simmering lead cookers with the hot, churning presses that filled the air with a mist of machine oil. My closet of a photo lab reeked of high-energy developer, acetic acid, hypo, and me after a two-day shoot in the cantaloupe fields.

In the evening as the desert cooled, Janet and I packed some iced tea, sandwiches, and crunchies and drove out into the scrub and dunes in our little Renault. We also packed our pistols and a few boxes of .22 bullets. I had traded in my S&W Chiefs Airweight cop gun for a High Standard nine-shot revolver for her. I carried my Great Western .22 Colt single action replica and a cardboard box full of empty bleach bottles and milk cartons. We had created our own private pistol range a couple of miles from town in a dry wash among the dunes. Bullets were cheaper than movie tickets or dinner in a restaurant.

Even after Janet gave birth to our charming daughter, Damienne, and while I drove back and forth to press conferences with Republican presidential candidate Barry Goldwater, we kept our evening shooting dates. Damienne sat in her little canvas seat on the hood of the car as we put holes in plastic and cardboard while the sun set on the vast emptiness and silence. Our Yuma interlude turned out to be just that. For six months our life was a whirlwind surrounding these oases of calm, punctuated by the bark of our revolvers, as I thought only about making a bleach bottle jump into the air and not about story deadlines or learning how to read type set upside down and backward in the chases.

Shooting pictures or shooting bleach bottles, I practiced the same skills over and over again—and in Yuma with about the same effect on the world events in 1963. I was luckier than most backwater photojournalists, because my beat covered the Army's Yuma Proving Grounds, where they pushed tanks out of airplanes to see if they would bounce, and the Marine Corps Air Station, where the Blue Angels flight demonstration team came to practice on their way to San Diego, California. I flew with the Blue Angels in an F9 Cougar, hammering across the desert, arcing up into the deep purple, and was weightless as we reached the apogee of the climb and nosed over in a parabola before diving flat out for the earth. From watching my camera float up toward the cockpit canopy to the crushing pull of six Gs as the pilot hauled back at the bottom of that dive and invisible fingers clamped my arms to the seat and clawed down the skin on my face—the wonder of it. I flew up in a GI parachute and came down with the army's Golden Knights parachute team. Covering my agriculture beat had some thrills too. For want of a place to sit, I stood on the lower wing of a Stearman biplane crop duster, squinting through goggles and feeling the prop wash tug and ripple my jacket and jeans as I fired frame after frame of the pilot and his insecticide trail above the lettuce fields at seventy miles per hour.

I assembled a collection of those center-spread photo stories and shipped them to United Press International, the Associated Press, and the *Chicago Tribune*. While Jan was back in Chicago visiting relatives with our daughter, the *Tribune* sent me a letter. I called her and told her to stay in Chicago.

After transporting all our goods back to the big city, I became a news photographer for the *Chicago Tribune* in 1964. We moved into the mecca of hippies, flower people, writers, artists, and tourists called Old Town, just off North Avenue and Wells Street. We relished our good fortune. Now we were in the action and ready to rock and roll. Part of that "action" came from our neighbors on Sedgwick Street. We lived only a short block away from the high-rise housing project known infamously in bloody headlines as Cabrini-Green.

This collection of multistory buildings rose like a forest of festering pillars from the formerly affluent neighborhood that bordered Old Town, where the old money that lived in the Gold Coast and Lincoln Park met Michigan Avenue, all forming the "Magnificent Mile." The apartment building where we lived was originally called the Marshall Field Apartments, built by its namesake who owned the big department store downtown. Its new name was the Old Town Garden Apartments. What had been a successful experiment in upper-middle-class housing had become a border bastion of young families, singles in the creative arts, Muslim families, Hispanic families, and educated African Americans with good jobs on their way up.

The apartments were a fortress where you exited through the imagined portcullis onto Sedgwick Street, always turning left toward North Avenue and the civilized joys of gentrification. One never turned right toward the projects, except when I had to dash across the street to the parking garage where I stowed my black Peugeot sedan. Usually, I was carrying a shoulder bag filled with cameras and lenses; I was a junkie's wet dream. My combined value on the hoof was worth a day's score of smack, a large bag of weed, or enough blow to while away the afternoon in transcendental bliss. That's why I ran.

Even the police refused to go into Cabrini-Green. The Gangster Disciples ruled, and watchers manned every street corner around the complex perimeter. Dope dealers clustered in groups, like prides of lions along the edge of a wildebeest herd. We had parties with our neighbors, joined the Old Town Gardens Community Theater, smoked our first joints, and put on old clothes to wander in a high buzz on Wells Street so the tourists from Iowa could take our pictures ("Look, Catherine! I think that's a hippie.").

At work, it was a different world. Being the new kid, I worked the 1 p.m. to 10 p.m. shift. Newspaper photography, as practiced by the *Tribune* at that time, was incredibly boring, punctuated by moments of giddy chaos orchestrated by a collection of old timers—seniority got you promoted, rather than the quality of your work—whose knowledge of photography and its capabilities ended somewhere before the Korean War. You walked into the editorial room, and the smell of tobacco smoke mixed with flowery aftershave that masked the sweat-damp clothes was overpowering. In the photographers' lounge, the olfactory mix of acidic photo chemicals crashed against mounds of damp, dead cigar roaches heaped in big, turkey platter–sized ashtrays resting on yellowing pages of newsprint. Old 4x5- and 5x7-inch press cameras peered out from yellowed glass-front cabinets like forgotten criminals and gut-sprung leather couches lined the walls. An editor would stick his head in the door, squint through the ever-present fog of tobacco smoke, point his finger at the next shooter up to bat for an assignment, and shout, "Grab yer box!"

Also, being the new kid meant I was the lucky one who got to accompany the long marching lines of African American civil rights demonstrators on their well-publicized wanders through the Near South Side neighborhoods, ending up in front of Mayor Richard J. Daley's house in Bridgeport—or as close as they were allowed by a phalanx of beefy policemen. President Lyndon Johnson had signed the Civil Rights Act in 1964, and a wave of attention-getting marches swept across the country. On this pilgrimage, my job was to watch the rooftops for snipers and side alleys for ready-to-rumble oxymoronic Nazi patriots, and stay near enough to the head of the march to get off a shot just after the first bullet hit Southern Christian Leadership Conference leader Ralph Abernathy. According to *Tribune* policy, I wore—or carried—my white hard hat with a clear plastic gas shield that lifted up when not needed. Nobody shot at Abernathy. I wore out shoes.

When the marches became routine and no one had been killed or maimed, I was sent over to watch the goings-on at the Auditorium Theatre, where Elijah Muhammad was addressing the Nation of Islam. To make sure no one interrupted his talk, the room was ringed with huge guys in tailored suits known to law enforcement organizations everywhere as the Fruit of Islam, a semiparamilitary group of really touchy bodyguards.

Standing outside under the sidewalk canopy—the media was forbidden to enter—I was helping a young Canadian journalist find his way around a Chicago guidebook. The doors of the Auditorium suddenly burst open, and the Fruit of Islam pushed out a blood-spewing, tromped-upon black gentleman wearing what remained of his ripped suit and marched back in and slammed the door. I had gotten off one shot. The Canadian guy began to babble into his tape recorder's microphone. The victim made off in a crablike scramble, probably with a rearranged rib cage and spinal column, and disappeared into a waiting car's rear seat.

I extracted my roll of film, waved over a taxicab as I scribbled a quick caption, and handed the roll of 120 film to the cabby wrapped in a $5 bill. He saw the *Tribune* name on the caption card, touched his cap brim, and gunned away from the curb.

The Canadian watched and asked, "Is that how you do it in Chicago, eh?"

I answered, "The cabby will get another fiver from the *Trib* elevator man in the lobby who'll send the film up to the inside guys to be souped for the evening edition."

He chuckled. "I have to be off. Going to New Jersey for the Democratic Convention. Here's my card. Thanks for the help. I'll try that restaurant." And then he was in a cab and gone. His card said he belonged to CTV National News and his name was Peter Jennings. I figured I'd keep an eye out for his work on television—if he got lucky.

The photograph of the beating victim won me an award from the Chicago, Press Photographers Association and a $5 bonus from the *Trib*. Not too long after that, I was sent into the neighborhoods ruled by the Blackstone Rangers, Latin Kings, Vice Lords, and, in Uptown, the Thorndale Jagoffs. The paper wanted me to photograph and interview Republicans, because it was hunting for Goldwater support in Chicago. Looking for a Republican in these wards where all the good jobs came from Democratic political patronage was a real long shot. Ending up in my underwear, head-down in a dumpster in some rat-infested alley was about a 50-50 bet.

Curiously, I did not get savagely beaten or worked over with a blowtorch and an electric drill. After two weeks on the mean streets, the *Trib* sent me up to the northwest suburbs to seek out Democratic voters. In all the collar counties, I think I found about six. Life didn't stay dull for long.

Bullets whined off brickwork, and concrete chunks caromed off police cruisers on my next hazard-pay outing as the Latin Kings went on a hot summer rampage and riots boiled down neighborhood streets. Overweight cops, puffed out even more in riot vests, dashed from doorway to doorway as the snipers potshot away from rooftops and rock throwers darted out from between parked cars. As bullets sent up puffs of cement dust off the sidewalks, I wondered, as I accompanied some cops in doorway dashes, if any of those young shooters had learned their trade at my summer camp rifle range. I snapped a couple of photos of rock throwers I knew the paper would never use, because the cops cowering behind squad cars and holding garbage can lids over their heads while skinny teenagers lobbed rocks was bad press for the city. Not a whole lot of selfless heroism was on view as I ducked behind a sheriff's cruiser already dented from thrown missiles. A couple of bricks bounced off the roof's flashing light deck as I dropped down out of sight.

I was not alone. Curled up on his knees against the driver-side door, a man in a dust-soiled Burberry raincoat and fedora held his collar closed over a suit and tie against the swirling brick dust and the rolling black stink of a car fire down the street that blazed where no firefighters would go. He turned his face and looked at me mournfully though thick glasses.

"Hello, Sheriff Ogilvy," I said, trying to smile.

His eyes scanned down to the camera wedged into the crook of my arm with its tiny illuminated "power-on" LED blinking beneath the strobe lens.

"Son," he asked, "I would appreciate it if you did not use that camera right now."

The idea of sending in a shot of Richard B. Ogilvy, sheriff of Cook County, crouching behind an embattled police cruiser in the middle of a riot was already half-framed on my ground glass as I looked down. A half-inch to the left . . . Then I remembered. He was a Republican. That shot too would never see the light of day, and my career with the newspaper would condemn me to the near West Side where blacks, Hispanics, and shot-and-a-beer drunks battled to stay off the bottom rung of the social ladder. Combining self-interest with a smack of pity, I reached up into my jacket pocket, brought out the camera's twin lens cover, and slipped it in place.

"Too much dust," I said.

"Thank you," he said.

I lasted on the *Chicago Tribune* until December 19, 1965, when they finally canned me for being "too creative," sneaking 35mm cameras into my workbag and threatening the 1954 status quo. The Luddite chief photographer said that "them 'minicams' got no place in newspaper journalism." Sheriff Richard Buell Ogilvy was elected governor of Illinois in 1969 and served one term.

Starting with the Marines landing boatloads of troops on the beach on March 8, 1965, near Da Nang, South Vietnam, unrest continued building as the war escalated. Their job was to defend an American air base from guerrilla attacks. A crowd of news media greeted their landing with lights, cameras, and microphones, sending antiwar protesters, whose publicity attempts had been gaining steam, into positive overdrive. On May 5, megaphone-shouting activists at the University of California, Berkeley, marched on the Berkeley draft board, and forty of them gathered to burn a draft card, which every male American over eighteen years of age was legally ordered to carry at all times. The Selective Service System, with offices throughout the country, had control over who went to war and who stayed home after receiving deferments. In late July, conscription quotas were raised from 17,000 per month to 35,000, a law was passed making it a felony to burn a draft card.

The war controversy, compounded by the growing civil rights demonstrations after Malcolm X was gunned down on February 21, 1965, and the assassination of Martin Luther King Jr. on April 4, 1968, became a full-fledged race, class, and education collision at the 1968 Democratic Convention in Chicago. Busloads of zealous black and white college students—many facing the draft—rumbled into the city and set up tents in Lincoln Park. Hippies, druggies, and activists, who always knew where the cameras were, flooded into public spaces with their North Vietnamese flags, and megaphones, and burning effigies of Uncle Sam and Lyndon Johnson. They screamed, "The whole world is watching!"

And it was. Captured by the media frenzy to record every instance of violations of free speech and assembly, incitement to riot, and indecent exposure, middle-class America was fascinated and appalled. Demonstrations hooted and marched up and down neighborhoods where people worked for a living, raised families, and were often first- and second-generation Americans. Television sets blazed with the outrage and carnage. Gradually, from out of the side streets and the alleys that bordered the marches and American Legion halls, came the mobs of "patriots" wearing construction hard hats and thrusting American flags in front of them like spears. Sawed-off broom handles, short lengths of rebar, and baseball bats brought bored cops to attention. Police watch commanders on the scene, conspicuous in their white shirts and polished brass, called headquarters for instructions. Then the neo-Nazis showed up just to crack heads and recruit the disenfranchised from both sides.

Homes on streets across America found that much of the unrest had come rampaging to their doorstep, both on television and churning past their front porch. Polls conducted in 1968 discovered 81 percent of Americans were certain law and order was breaking down. Gun manufacturer David Ecker, president of Charter Firearms, said in a 1981 interview while looking back on the riot-torn 1960s, "You had a terrific civil rights problem, with riots all across the country. There was a terrific boom in firearms sales. So any firearm that was being manufactured or imported was being sold."

With the addition of foreign imports, the number of handguns that poured into the American civilian market during the 1960s was almost three times that of the preceding decade.[19]

After I left the *Chicago Tribune*, I joined the Chicago Park District as a public relations photographer. Each park has a multipurpose community fieldhouse, and mostly I documented the Fieldhouse Frolics, a sarcastic term used by the staff to describe fashion shows, senior citizen reunions, model sailboat races on the Jackson Park lagoon, beauty pageants, and handshakes at shovel-turning ceremonies. I wielded a 4x5 press camera and was thrown back into the 1930s–1950s era. The only thing missing was a "press" tag stuck in the hatband of my fedora. But it was a job. Only President Johnson's New Frontier saved me.

While stirring a hot-tub-size water basin filled with two-dozen prints from the same negative to be given away as VIP gifts, I overheard a conversation just outside the print darkroom. The Chicago Committee on Urban Opportunity (CCUO) had lost its photographer. Johnson had inherited John

F. Kennedy's poverty program and continued it, lumped in with his "Great Society" civil rights initiatives. The City of Chicago had created the CCUO as a federally funded neighborhood outreach program. I hung my rubber apron on a nail, left the photo prints to soak, quietly walked out to "have some lunch," vaulted down the stairs to my car, and drove like an insane person to our apartment to snatch up my portfolio. I returned to the CCUO's Loop offices and skidded to a halt, trying to look professional. My enthusiasm, brilliant work samples, and the fact that I knew the boss who had been a *Daily News* reporter carried the day.

To celebrate my good fortune, Janet and I decided to see a movie, *Don't Look Back*, about folk singer Bob Dylan. We had moved out of Old Town and into a small North Side apartment on Sawyer Avenue. The movie was playing in Piper's Alley on Wells Street near North Avenue. We saw the mobs of hippies and demonstrators about three blocks east in Lincoln Park on the lakefront. It was a colorful assembly, and the megaphones could just barely be heard. A group of overweight Shriners with "Kansas" stitched on their red fezzes had gathered on the corner to listen with cupped ears and frowning faces. After a late dinner in the Old Town Ale House, Janet and I saw the movie as dusk was settling into a warm summer night.

At the film's conclusion, we drove our car from a lot east on North Avenue, and we could see lights and red flares and hear noise from the gathered demonstrators through the Peugeot's open sky roof. We had to reach Lake Shore Drive, which was east of the park, past the mob's improvised tent ground. Police cruisers formed a bumper-to-bumper barrier along the circling curbs. Cops with flashlights examined us as we picked our way slowly over the debris.

"Pop!" "Pop!" "Pop!" "Pam!" "Poom!" We were suddenly ignored by the cops who began moving toward the trees and baseball field. "Pop!" "Pop!" "Pop!" Bright halogen lights switched on, and a huge fog was illuminated rising from the park. Screams rose above the shouting. I saw a cop duck past us, pulling on a gas mask and clutching a shoulder-fired grenade launcher.

"Tear gas!" I shouted at Janet. We frantically cranked up the side windows, crunching along over broken glass, cardboard cups, and burger boxes. More screams, more shouts. I could see the haloed orange lights along Lake Shore Drive, and then the fog swept over us. I had forgotten the car's sky roof.

I slammed the roof panel shut so hard its handle cracked off in my hand, slashing the soft skin between my thumb and forefinger. Blood drooled down my forearm. The gas had flooded in, and were tearing up and coughing. There was no way to get it out as long as the choking mist surrounded us. Through the tears, I managed to turn up the ramp to the drive, and the breeze off the lake pushed the fog toward the west. We cranked open the windows and rolled about a block down the wide parkway before we pulled over and put two wheels up on the right curb.

Other cars had pulled over. Ahead, a big Cadillac crouched at an angle off the pavement with its doors flung open while its driver, an elderly man, threw up his expensive dinner as his frightened wife watched. Eventually, when we could see and breathe again, we drove off and went home, our good clothes and car seats stinking of tear gas. Our city was bleeding, and the whole world was watching.

If the 1960s held a jarring note for the signature publication of the NRA, the association's magazine achieved national publicity in 1963. Lee Harvey Oswald killed President John F. Kennedy with three long-range shots from an Italian 6.5 mm Carcano carbine purchased via a Klein's Sporting Goods advertisement in the February 1963 issue of *American Rifleman*. He paid $19.95 plus postage.

American Rifleman's editorial and pictorial display policies changed considerably beginning in 1966 with a new editor, Ashley Halsey Jr., an experienced magazine writer for the *Saturday Evening Post*. Almost at once, his penchant for investigative editorials touching politics and their effect on national gun laws locked horns with powerful antigun legislators and lobbyists. Senator Thomas Dodd (D-CT) felt the wrath of the NRA when he proposed restricting firearm sales across state lines. Besides this strident new voice, the *American Rifleman's* pages displayed color photographs for the first time in 1971. This new slick publication then needed more room for its editorial overburden, and in 1973 the backlog of hunting articles were spun off into a new magazine, *American Hunter*, that showed a profit after only two years.

8

THE ME GENERATION
UNDER FIRE

After a few years of world travel and adventures with my cameras—in "The White Man's Grave" along the coast of West Africa; the cracked and wasted desert of Tunisia; Madrid, where my Spanish took on a lisp; Copenhagen, where I shot stories of expatriate Americans—I won my dream job: telling the story of an entire country. The Society for Visual Education, a division of the Singer Corporation, wanted a series of filmstrips shot in the British Isles. After Janet and I treated the girls to a vacation in the Hawaiian Islands, in May 1974 I packed my cameras, a British-to-American dictionary, a new pair of sneakers, and the shooting outline of a dozen stories, and departed. My contact in London was the Central Office of Information on Lambeth Road, a short walk from my hotel at Elephant and Castle. They made the assignment a success, passing me from England to Scotland to Wales with helping hands and infinite patience.

I burned through a hundred rolls of 35mm film and wore out my new sneakers in the first month. London, Bath, Edinburgh, and then off to the Orkney Islands for hours in the North Atlantic with the fishing fleet. The quirky English weather held, and frame by frame each story was told. Melancholy Wales, with its village names that sounded like someone having a coughing fit, offered up starkly beautiful images. After documenting the queen's birthday and crawling into excavated Viking burial mounds, I returned to London. On August 8, 1974, I stayed up late in my Basingstoke hotel room to listen to Richard Nixon resign the presidency. That event marked my final two stories: the north and south of Ireland.

The ferry from Great Britain bumped along the quay of the terminal in downtown Belfast. My assistant at this time was a young lady from Edinburgh who had offered her estate van (small station wagon) as transport, and it was loaded full of our gear as soon the boat's ramp lowered to the dock. That was the last easy time we had after arriving on the Emerald Isle. This was during "The Troubles." At once, the British soldiers who met each ferry gave our car a going-over while other soldiers waited with their FN rifles unslung. My papers from the COI bought us some directions to our hotel and an introduction to the army public relations officer in the morning. It was suggested we not leave the hotel for sightseeing that evening, the city being still "a bit unsettled." The Catholic Irish Republican Army (IRA), fighting for the reunification of largely Protestant Northern Ireland, ruled by the British, and the independent Republic of Ireland, was in bitter conflict with UK security forces and loyalist paramilitaries.

After an uneasy night listening to some distant tat-tat-tats and muffled booms somewhere out in the dark, we trimmed our equipment to a portable minimum and set out for downtown Belfast as a squadron of gray clouds swept in from the sea. We drove past the pillared façade of the Irish Parliament closed down by the British government, to the fenced, barbed-wired, and patrolled enclosure that surrounded the British Army headquarters.

The army, we were told in the PR officer's spartan quarters, had been deployed under Operation Banner to support the Royal Ulster Constabulary, the civilian police combatting the Belfast brigade of the Provisional IRA and its various factions. Army casualties just two years previous had been 172 killed. Sniping, bombing, and ambushes were the "Provos'" primary tactics. Sometimes bystanders got caught between the "Taigs" (Catholics) and the "Prods" (Protestants) in confrontations or assassination attempts. He looked at my long 50-300mm zoom lens fastened to one of my Nikons.

"That's a big lens. You plan to use it in town center?"

When I nodded, he added, "It could be mistaken for a rifle, or a grenade launcher. That'll catch our lads' attention. And the only thing the Provos hate more than an aimed rifle is a pointed camera. Two British scribblers—one with a camera—were jumped near the Falls Road. Beat half t' death they were. No Provo wants his photo taken."

I gather he thought we looked a bit stricken. He reached for his phone. "I'll send a sergeant along with you. That'll tip our lads at least." He pushed some papers at us. "If you'd just fill out these forms. In case we have t' take you out in a rubber bag, no one can say you weren't warned." He grinned a crocodile smile.

No automobile traffic was allowed in downtown Belfast. Our keeper, a short, dark young man built like a beer keg and obviously committed to a long, long life and many grandchildren, drove us near to the main street in a scout car, stopping finally at an army checkpoint in a narrow, blockaded avenue. We all disembarked, and he had a word with the corporal on duty. From there on, we were on our own, with our keeper staying at least ten paces to our rear, armed to the teeth with a radio.

The smell of an urban combat area is always the same: brick dust, burned window frames, wet concrete, and if the combat was recent and bit hard, the coppery smell of blood and gunpowder. Rain had fallen the day before, but instead of freshening the air, the puddles held the taint of diesel and petrol from the army lorries that passed on the road, with troops sitting on the tailgates covering us with their rifles as they passed. The first thing to find out was who is where. Instead of Chicago cops, I had soldiers in full battle harness and green camouflage kit, useless in the grays, blues, and muted colors of the overcast day reflecting cement hues off stone facades and potholed pavement.

The lack of automobile or truck traffic gave the downtown main street an eerie postapocalyptic feel, but that did not discourage the shoppers who were out and about, carrying their own shopping bags. There were only a handful emerging onto the main thoroughfare from unblockaded streets, further up Falls and Crumlin Roads. Most people walked in the deserted streets clear of storefronts that might suddenly vomit their guts in a cough of flame and debris. Downtown Belfast was a dirty gray mall with broken glass crunching under foot and bordered by swept-up piles of scorched wood and busted bricks.

Every time I raised my big-lens camera to shoot a passing troop lorry or pedestrians trudging near a sandbagged pillbox manned by two or three soldiers, our keeper turned into a storefront entry to admire a fine selection of childrens' toys or a well-presented display of bedpans and wheelchairs, a move that also took him out of the line of fire from many high rooftops with their beetling cornices. I shot, my assistant watched the street and roofs, and our keeper ducked in and out of doorways. So we proceeded until I sensed a movement across the street to our right.

We were passing the army HQ, which was secured in a comandeered building block flanked by blockaded streets. This gray eminence was ringed with razor-wire concertinas, and its entrance lurked beneath a tarpaulin awning overlaid with barbed wire strung taut to defeat tossed grenades. At each corner, a cinderblock bunker reinforced with sandbags housed an automatic weapon. As we walked, two machine guns tracked us, their two muzzles vectoring us into their field of fire. I wanted to shoot the building, but there is always some clown who doesn't get the word. We walked on.

"Jaysus," my assistant whispered in her soft Edinburgh burr.

We came to a checkpoint before a major intersection. These points had full-height turnstyles and were manned by a squad of Scottish soldiers with their FN rifles slung. My shoulder bag was thoroughly searched, and a corporal asked to look through my long lens. I latched it loose, and he verified it was just a lens and not a cleverly concealed rocket launcher. As were gathered our minutely examined belongings and walked away, my assistant looked over her shoulder and sniffed derisively, "Glaaascow!" with a hard nasal "a."

We headed toward the city hall, passing a bomb-gutted department store. A loud "clankity-bang boom!" to our left made us jump. Hunkered between two buildings in a narrow alley crouched a Saracen armored car. Its diesel engine had just turned over as we passed, and the two faces framed in its slitted windows were unreadable behind reflecting goggles. It squatted there, a malevolent thing on six wheels, all angled steel plates and comb-toothed radiator beneath a top-hat turret sporting a gun barrel and a rack of gas canisters. The engine idled with its deep-throated "brum, brum, brum, brum," amplified by the pressing masonary walls as its turret slowly rotated in our direction and stopped. Our keeper was still chatting with the guards at the checkpoint.

I said aloud, "Fuck this" and walked to the middle of the street, turned, raised my camera, framed the shot, and photographed the armored car in its lair. "Clackita-clackity-clack!"—a three-shot burst. As I returned to my assistant, who had scooted a couple doors down the block, I mumbled over my shoulder, "Bang, you're dead."

While we passed through the final checkpoint before I could get a clear shot of the hulking pile of Victorian masonry that was the Belfast City Hall, a scene assembled itself to my right. A father and his son—the resemblance was unmistakeable—stood on the sidewalk in front of a dark doorway. The boy was about six years old and held a small, tin toy locomotive that had seen much play. He looked up at his father, who had his hands raised as a soldier patted down his jacket. Another soldier held his FN rifle on the man until the search was finished. They went through the cloth shopping bag at his feet, dumping the contents out on the sidewalk. When they were done, they walked away, and he was left to pick up his few groceries.

I had it all on film and felt embarrassed for them. My son at home was going on two years old. My girls were nine and ten. What if they had to watch that public frisk, watch their father searched at gunpoint, helpless. Just another "Taig"? Who was the victim? Was it the soldiers who had their humanity burned out of them by ambushes and assassinations against their ranks? Was it the Provisional IRA with their bloody insurgency, where scouring the street with an automatic weapon was better than throwing darts at the pub and collecting the dole? Was it the Protestants, with their self-righteous, entitled march to the beat of the Orangeman's drum? Or was it just the father and his son, enduring what had to be endured to carry on?

Later, when photographing the Harland and Wolff shipbuilding works, I shot a photo of the dark-lit dressing hall where the crews changed in and out of work overalls. A row of pegs ran down one wall. I chose to photograph the flat cloth caps on the pegs, all the same pattern, the caps of Catholics and Protestants mixed together. After a couple of hours, when I'd made my way to the top of one of the huge cranes above one of the world's largest dry docks, where the *Titanic* had been built, I watched the shift end. The tiny workmen streamed from the crew room dressed for home, and the press of men split into two quick-stepping columns, the Catholics carrying their lunch pails down toward the row houses crammed into the Ardoyne district, while the Protestants strolled up the street toward Woodvale and other like-thinking enclaves. The flat cloth caps still looked alike.

The me generation of the 1970s launched the dot-com revolution of the 1980s but first had to endure the OPEC gasoline embargo that nearly drained America's fuel reserves and sent the automobile industry into a tailspin. Besides pushing drivers into small, cheap cars in 1973, a deep recession ganged up on the country and lasted sixteen months. On top of the recession came inflation caused by the United States going off the gold standard and printing more money: too many dollars chased too few goods. Prices were inflated by President Nixon's introduction of wage-price controls. High costs reduced demand. Wage controls caused companies to lay off workers and freeze wages. The result of these combined problems—over which the average American had no control—was three negative quarters of gross domestic product growth in 1974 and 1975.

While the me generation sputtered along, deep into an LSD trip and wearing questionable fashion statements beneath way too much hair, the media sunk its teeth into a series of chilling events. On 1970 the anti–Vietnam War group the Weather Underground engaged in a series of attacks against government sites in Chicago, New York, and San Francisco. Presidential candidate George Wallace was shot while campaigning in Laurel, Maryland, and ended up paralyzed for life. Lynette "Squeaky" Fromme was captured with a loaded pistol waiting for President Gerald Ford in 1975. Two weeks later, Sara Jane Moore actually got off a couple of shots in his general direction. President Carter spent one term living down both his brother's Billy Beer promotion and a failed rescue of American hostages in Iran—a brilliant and compassionate man wasted in public office.

The 1980s started with President Ronald Reagan stopping bullets from mentally unstable John Hinckley Jr. on March 30, 1981, at the side entrance of the Washington Hilton Hotel. For more than a decade, these stress tests for the American public elbowed each other aside to create fresh headlines or a sound bite for the nightly TV news.

We had leeched out the last of our troops from Vietnam in 1973, leaving behind images in 1975 of fleeing civilians crowding Saigon airports. North Vietnamese trampled under the brave but corruptly led South Vietnamese army to roll onto the Saigon palace lawn in Soviet T-54 tanks. American soldiers discarded their uniforms at airports rather than be connected with a war that was not theirs to fight but once committed were commanded by Washington politicians, not by soldiers in the field.

If the American populace felt the need to hunker down and fort up against all these slings and arrows of outrageous fortune, getting a gun to poke out between the sandbags was becoming a tougher proposition. While gun control laws had always been in effect, they existed in varying degrees, depending on geography and the social inclinations of the different states. The northeastern states throughout the 1970s and 1980s saw 25 percent of gun ownership in the home, while the east southcentral states claimed that 60 percent of homeowners owned guns. Across the board, 45 to 50 percent of Americans kept guns in their homes.[1] And yet no statistics have been found to equate simple firearm ownership with gun violence.[2]

During those chaotic years, the huge number of guns legally available to American citizens did not escape the notice of lawmakers. They also saw the gun manufacturers shifting back from wartime contracts once again to the civilian market looking for sales opportunities. Disgruntled returning Vietnam vets, spillover of druggies from the late 1960s, civil rights activists forcing face-offs to keep awareness alive, Hispanics and African Americans dueling to stay off the bottom rung of the economic ladder in cities, civilian militias gearing up in the West and South, and labor having faceoffs with scabs at shut-down industrial plants all contributed to combative confrontations with possible deadly outcomes. These confrontations inspired the courts to act on any solution that might take guns away from troublemakers.

Unfortunately, as with many knee-jerk reactions, the courts in California set an example with far too wide a net. They based their particular solution on a previous decision passed in the 1970s concerning alcohol-related accidents and deaths. If a driver left a bar drunk and got involved in an accident because of DUI, the bar was held equally guilty and liable because they sold the drinks that resulted in the driver's intoxication. Taking this same "dramshop law" concept, California governor Gray Davis signed AB 496, which accused gun manufacturers of "negligent marketing" of guns. If a robber used a gun to shoot people while committing the crime, under AB 496 the gun manufacturer would be held liable. Product liability lawsuits could put gunmakers out of business by draining their financial resources through constantly defending themselves in court every time someone stuck up a bodega.

The original dramshop law involving saloons, drunk driving, and liability was struck down by Civil Code §1714. The California legislature said, in effect, "The furnishing of alcoholic beverages is not the proximate cause of injuries resulting from intoxication, but rather the consumption of alcoholic beverages is the proximate cause of injuries inflicted upon another by an intoxicated person." In other words, the drunk ran you over, not the saloon or the host of the party. Sue the drunk driver.[3]

Regardless, a wave of product liability lawsuits flooded the courts, aimed directly at the gun manufacturers. The true goofiness of the logic employed in some of these convoluted fishing expeditions can be demonstrated by an example from Clayton Cramer, a progun drumbeater. Despite his bugle-blowing style, the naked facts of the incident he cites are enough to chill anyone with an ounce of common sense.

On Christmas Eve in Riverside, California, four police officers responded to a 911 call claiming that a woman was asleep in a car in a closed gas station. Her friends had called the cops, fearing she might be in trouble. The black nineteen-year-old sat in the driver's seat, sleeping off a large quantity of celebratory gin. A pistol lay in her lap. The cops knocked on the closed window. No response. The car engine was running, so the police might have become concerned about possible carbon monoxide poisoning. The situation spiraled downhill rapidly as soon as the cops smashed her side window. Roused from a boozy snooze, the young lady naturally snatched at the pistol she had placed in her lap. One of the cops probably shouted "Gun!" The officers poured a fusillade of gunfire into the vehicle, shooting many holes into the startled young woman.

This monumental lapse in judgment caused the four officers to be fired. The police chief resigned, civil rights leaders flocked to Riverside to rant and stomp about this racist slaughter, and lawyers tripped over each other diving for their business cards. Drawn into this shabby whirlpool was the manufacturer of the young lady's pistol. The City of Riverside sued Lorcin Engineering for "negligently marketing and distributing the .38-caliber gun (the victim) had. . . . "[4] At no time had the victim's gun been fired, but the Riverside lawyers claimed that Lorcin's advertising and marketing of that pistol was responsible for her death from twelve bullet wounds delivered by the guns of the four cops. These third-party firearm lawsuits were eventually forbidden by the Protection of Lawful Commerce in Arms Act, which was enacted in 2005.

The dissatisfaction, recession, and denial of idealism of the 1970s overflowed into the 1980s. This edgy disappointment caused two tragic statistics. A spike was noted in the number of adolescent suicides as well as a rising trend in suicides among adults aged seventy-five and older. The primary cause of 50 percent of these deaths was firearms, mostly handguns. During this decade, dominated by the dot-com bubble inflating within the computer industry, handgun sales took a dive because of market saturation. Manufacturers yet again began seeking out new revenue generators. With middle-aged males packing heat, logic dictated the distaff side for exploration. The 1980s became the decade for peddling handguns, long guns, shotguns, and anything that would go "bang!" to women. Collaborating with the NRA, gun manufacturers' designers, advertising agencies, and media shills set out that women must be armed.

The high-ticket selling point on the prefrontal lobe of the male-dominated firearms market was rape. All women feared rape. Fear of "radicals" and "troublemakers" had fueled gun sales in the South during the height of civil rights confrontations. Fear of having the Second Amendment carjacked by skulking liberal socialists fired up millions of people who had a gun moldering away in a dresser drawer, nightstand, or basement closet. Sportsmen, target punchers, and militia members fired up their typewriters with letters to legislators and op-ed columns in the media. Fear of that loss blazed from the pages of *American Rifleman*'s editorial pages. Now the Big Gun turret swung in the direction of women as they were targeted by the testosterone-bubbling gun world.

To allay any concerns that male NRA members would soon be attending Tupperware parties or carrying man purses, NRA Personal Protection Program director Tracey Martin said in 1988, "Millions of intelligent, self-reliant women have chosen to defend themselves." And if the female members of the NRA were looked upon as beer-swilling, tattooed, ballbusting rednecks in biker drag, that was also a misconception. In articles and advertising, women were portrayed as competent, pleasant, no-nonsense folks who, besides being businesswomen, high-powered shooting champions, or former Dallas Cowboys cheerleaders, could also defend themselves. That was the key comment from all the quoted female shooters: "I can defend myself." Believe that, because in an NRA sales instruction pamphlet titled "A Question of Self-Defense," the NRA text against a blood-spattered background warns, "You're a woman. Someone's going to rape you. You'd better buy a handgun. People buy handguns out of fear, and rape is perceived as what women fear most."

"Tell them what rape is," the pamphlet shrieks. "Be graphic. Be disgusting. Be obscene. Make them sick. If they throw up, then they have the tiniest idea of what rape is!"

Another NRA pamphlet, titled "It Can Happen to You," shows the picture of an elderly woman, and the text oozes: "In nature, the predator preys on the weak, the sick, the aged. It stalks. It waits patiently for the precise moment when the victim appears defenseless. Then, it strikes. . . . There is no way of telling a criminal predator by the way he looks. He might be a potential suitor."

A 1987 self-defense advertisement shows a man in a stocking mask beneath the headline "Should You Shoot a Rapist Before He Cuts Your Throat?"

And a further warning and admonition sums up the potential dangers: "The days when you thought you'd never be the victim of a rape—that it 'can't happen to me'—are over. We all know of friends or family who have been raped, beaten, robbed or burglarized by thugs who don't think twice about hurting someone. You might be the next victim."[5]

The answer for the modern 1980s woman was a snub-nosed .38 Special. Through the 1980s, the revolvers were still the most popular self-defense firearms, while the semiautomatic pistols (easier to conceal) were just trickling in from overseas. But by the end of the decade, the manufacturers had the technology and new packaging mostly to rein in this new female segment. Smith & Wesson came up with the Ladysmith, a diminutive series of four .38 caliber revolvers targeting women.

For women purchasers desiring a bit more punch on the receiving end, Detonics offered .45 caliber weapons in their Ladies' Escort line. The Royal Escort came in purple with a gold-plated trigger, while its twin sisters Midnight Escort and Jade Escort shimmered in deep black and emerald green, respectively.[6] The Lady Lorcin from Lorcin Engineering begged, "Ladies, don't become a target" and offered them a gun "with you in mind" in pearl pink and chrome finish. There was the Titan Tigress, a gold-plated .25 caliber semiautomatic pistol with gold lamé carrying purse, its faux ivory handle inscribed with a red rose.

Even though the trend did not end in the 1980s and 1990s—in 2010 Charter Arms offered snub-nosed .38 Special revolvers in pink (Pink Lady), lavender (Lavender Lady), and gold (Goldfinger)—the striving to create a "pretty" gun for "fashion-conscious" females tapered off. Treating women's tastes in firearm décor as though they were inmates in a redlight district whorehouse was counterproductive. Real, dirty black and blue guns were sold along with actual training on how to use them. In the beginning, the NRA wanted to build its membership base, and the gunmakers wanted to move iron off the dealers' shelves. The women—those with any sense of dignity—did not buy into the manipulation and fearmongering.

However, as usual, the NRA had an excellent sense of its audience and knew how to play the power of paranoia. In 1988, according to a Gallup poll, gun ownership among women had jumped to twelve million, or 53 percent. Those women just thinking about buying a gun expanded to nearly two million.[7] When the 1980s began, American women owned roughly 10.5 percent of the guns in the United States. As of 2008 that percentage remained the same.

Criminologists Frank Zimring and Gordon Hawkins wrote in their 1987 book *A Citizen's Guide to Gun Control*: "The American woman of the late 1980s and 1990s [is the] leading indicator of the social status of self-defense handguns in the more distant future. If female ownership of self-defense handguns increases dramatically, the climate of opinion for drastic restriction of handguns will not come about."[8]

After Barack Obama was elected president, the number of guns in the United States climbed to more than two hundred million.[9] Many feared he would pursue harsh gun-control measures, which has not come to pass. However, the radicalization of America's political scene by the Tea Party movement, the collapse of the housing economy, and the continued high joblessness rate produce that uneasiness, which has motivated Americans to defend what they perceive as the only fragments of personal dignity remaining in their control. The entire pitch based on actual self-defense incidents, even in a less secure society, has proved to be a paper tiger. According to most statistics, more people are struck by lightning each year than use handguns to kill or wound in self-defense.[10]

Historically, despite the ramped-up sales effort, the gun industry had a poor decade during the 1980s, which threatened to overflow into the 1990s. In 1992 the federal Bureau of Alcohol, Tobacco, Firearms and Explosives (ATF) estimated that 74 percent of America's 250,000 retail gun dealers did not operate storefront businesses such as gun stores or sporting goods outlets. Most gun dealers operated out of their homes—often in violation of state and local laws. Some of these "kitchen-table" dealers were involved in high-volume criminal gun trafficking. At gun shows covert independent dealers did not have to require Brady Act background checks of gun buyers while federally licensed gun dealers had to comply. Some show sponsors adopted a "nudge nudge, wink wink" attitude concerning under-the-table sales not unlike during Prohibition in the 1920s when restaurants and nightclubs served booze in coffee cups. The ATF figured this was another conduit of illegal guns to the streets for criminal use.

What confuses most average shooters and opponents to gun ownership is the use of statistics to "prove" a point. Any college masters degree candidate can tell us that the manipulation of statistics is an art as much as a science and can be used to "prove" black is actually white (which is true). As Oscar Wilde noted, "He uses statistics as a drunken man uses lamp-posts—for support rather than illumination." This statistical sword cuts in both directions as gun opponents and gun advocates lunge at each other. A recent example in the self-defense debate fueled much interest in turning around the gun industry's sagging fortunes in the 1980s.

Professor Gary Kleck of Florida State University and his colleague, Mark Gertz, offered up a statistic resulting from a survey that people defend themselves with guns 2.5 million times a year. Cheers and hoopla from the NRA and the gun industry greeted this scientific finding that "proved" there was great value in packing heat. However, Professor David Hemenway at Harvard's School of Public Health closely examined the work of Kleck and Gertz and stated in *The Journal of Criminal Law and Criminology* that their survey contained "a huge overestimation bias" and that their estimate is "highly exaggerated."

To further illustrate his point, Hemenway cited an ABC News/*Washington Post* survey that asked people if they had ever seen an alien spacecraft or come into direct contact with a space alien. He then applied Kleck and Gertz's methodology to the survey's results and "proved" that almost twenty million Americans believe they have seen an alien spacecraft and more than a million have met the rascals face to face.[11]

If you live out Roswell, New Mexico, way, you might ask, "What's your point?" And that would be exactly the point. If statistics can appear to flood the country with vacationing space aliens and their zippy transportation, number manipulation can add or diminish instances of gunning down miscreants, or being gunned down by miscreants, depending on who is punching the calculator keys or programming the software. So we rushed through the 1980s and 1990s with the extreme ends of the pro–gun rights and anti–gun rights scholastic defenders bopping each other with Nerf bats that were supposed to represent the truth. Flying flags that cried out "*Veritas!*" both sides rushed toward the twenty-first century.

While the scholars began their joust, the anti–gun control quest was further pursued by the high-media-profile murder of John Lennon and the attempted assassination of President Reagan. Cities and states began cranking out every kind of "get the guns off the streets" legislation they could dream up or statistically justify. The feds also began pushing for more widespread regulations. In 1985 the Law Enforcement Officers Protection Act made it illegal to manufacture or import armor-piercing Teflon-coated "cop-killer" bullets capable of penetrating "bulletproof" clothing of that period. Penalties were also made harsher for previously convicted felons involved in gun crimes. The Brady Act required a (not unreasonable) five-day background check waiting period for handgun purchases from a licensed dealer. Soon, computer electronics allowed these background checks to be accomplished the same day on the phone using a law enforcement database.

With state and federal regulations heating up, both the gun manufacturers and the NRA needed something to get people excited about owning guns and belonging to a like-minded club. They needed to win a good war. In 1990 it was offered up on a plate when Iraq, led by Saddam Hussein, occupied the Middle East oil kingdom of Kuwait and stood with the largest army in that region to wait for the U.S. reply. The response—in cooperation with the Saudi Arabian government and other allies—came in the form of a coalition called Desert Shield during the troop buildup and then progressed to Desert Storm.

With overwhelming superiority in technology, organization, planning, and execution, the coalition led by the U.S. armed forces steamrollered the Iraqi forces. They were pounded from the sky, hammered by tanks, and assaulted by troops and artillery; the war was a walkover. The United States lost 148 killed and 487 wounded. Iraq lost about 100,000 killed and 300,000 wounded. The shooting war had lasted from January 17, 1991, to February 28, 1991, when Kuwait was liberated and the Iraqi Army had nothing left with which to fight. The Gulf conflict had been the perfect war. America had won, and that was all that counted. The returning American soldier and all his battle-winning gear came back to a firearms industry waiting with open arms.

Also waiting on the dock for this new image of an American war hero was the NRA. Americans had been fighting for freedom, and one of the critical freedoms that needed defending was the Second Amendment to the Constitution guaranteeing the right to keep and bear arms. The American military had been a threadbare symbol of freedom fighters since they were evacuated from Vietnam in 1973. These new kids in their chocolate-chip camo and carrying guns built to shoot buckets of bullets, not to look pretty, were the new role models—and they were winners.

For me, the 1980s and 1990s put behind the scramble for survival as a freelance photojournalist. Travel assignments had sent me all over the world, from the bleak oil fields of Puerto Ordaz in Venezuela to picking flies out of my calabash of creamy white palm wine before washing down the crunchy flame-puffed pupae of the Goliath beetle in the forest villages of Liberia. Back in the States, after I covered the 1975 Indianapolis 500 and the 1976 Montreal Olympics for Motorola, they offered me a full-time job in their marketing services department. Just as I became used to a normal life, waking up each morning without wondering what country I was in, they pulled me away to begin another round of world travel.

With two very bright daughters harboring college ambitions and Janet becoming a sculptor, scorching up the basement with her propane torch while she worked as a full-time advertising artist and mother to our new son, Collin, my guns were once more mothballed for the duration. But at the same time, I picked up a cinema camera and became a documentary shooter who later began videotaping, writing, directing, and eventually producing industrial, commercial, and television programming. I dusted off my pen and ink from my Art Institute school days and began drawing editorial cartoons for newspapers and illustrating children's books. It was anything-to-earn-a-few-bucks time, and blasting clays or punching holes in paper targets didn't figure into our days at all.

One of my Motorola assignments took me back to the British Isles, out to a factory near Bath to document the company's innovative use of two-way communications to regulate a series of pumping stations. Normally, returning to Britain after spending four months there in 1974 would have fostered a sense of homecoming. I loved the Isles, from Land's End to John O'Groats and beyond to the Orkney Islands. But my departure from the mother country had been more like flight to avoid prosecution than departing with a wave and a tear in the eye. Back then I could not wait until my Boeing jet took off from Heathrow Airport with my cameras, exposed and undeveloped film, and two weeks of toxic laundry. My last stop had been in Ireland, and I might have been just a step ahead of an arrest warrant. My return to Great Britain stirred a few chilling memories of shouted orders, interrogations, and staring down the muzzles of submachine guns.

Crossing the border into the Republic of Ireland from Northern Ireland in 1974 put behind us the feeling of eyes on our backs. We had driven through one scarred town after another, but the bullet pockmarks in walls, the charred automobiles dragged into side alleys, and the quick step of watchful shoppers along the narrow streets thinned as we left the outskirts of Belfast, Londonderry, and the other battlegrounds. Following our Ordnance Survey map, we passed into the Republic on a road where there was no checkpoint. We were just there, and as the trees and cottages whipped past, we rolled down the windows and took deep free breaths.

Dublin was congested but dotted with elegant architecture. The moment we turned onto O'Connell Street, textbook photographs came alive. The General Post Office, an encrusted Victorian pile, sat on its block in the swirl of foot and auto traffic that flowed down the street, past the monument to Daniel O'Connell, the nineteenth-century Irish patriot; toward the O'Connell Bridge, wider than it is long; across the River Liffey; and past the jarring, modern Guinness Storehouse, where that black beer rises to a caramel foam.

It was a bustling city beneath bright blue skies and divided by a pea-green river that belched up gaseous black bubbles. It was a city of boisterous pubs and bloody fistfights between opposing football team fans swathed in their colored scarves. It was a city where beautiful girls became second-class citizens in the eyes of the government once they were married. It was a watchful city until the first round for the house was bought at the bar during the pub lockdown at midday called "Pope's Hour."

Kilmainham Gaol was a shrine to the deaths and imprisonments of Irish patriots who stood shoulder to shoulder, aiming German-provided guns at British soldiers during the April 1916 Easter Rising. Fighting for Irish independence was better than submitting to conscription into the British Army for shipment to French trenches and dying under the Union Jack. Irish militias sprouted like mushrooms on a log. The Irish Citizen Army, a 250–man, well-armed and -trained collection, defended workers and strikers from the frequent brutality of the Dublin Metropolitan Police. There was the Irish Republican Brotherhood, the National Volunteers, the Hibernian Rifles, Fianna Éireann, Cumann na mBan, and the National Foresters. After the formation of a Provisional Irish government, they joined together as Óglaigh na Éireann—the Irish Republican Army.

The Easter Rising was called the "Poet's Rebellion" for the seven men wearing makeshift uniforms who marched down O'Connell Street that April 24 morning to the General Post Office with old rifles on their shoulders, took over the building with hundreds of their followers, and read out the proclamation that drew other Irish patriots to their side. James Connolly, who led the small band, was a poet and socialist who headed the Dublin Brigade of the Irish Citizen Army. He and the men at his side were poets and writers whose works had helped fire the desire for Irish independence from Great Britain. In 1903 Connolly wrote this verse from "A Rebel Song":

> Come workers sing a rebel song,
> A song of love and hate,
> Of love unto the lowly
> And of hatred to the great.
> The great who trod our fathers down,
> Who steal our children's bread,
> Whose hands of greed are stretched to rob
> The living and the dead.[12]

I stood in the courtyard at Kilmainham where James Connolly was brought on May 12, 1916, tied to a stretcher with only a few days to live because of his bullet wounds. He was roped onto a chair in front of a gray stone wall and shot as prescribed in his hasty sentence for treason. A cross marks the spot, as does another cross at the far end of the courtyard where his fellow poet-militiamen were lined up and dropped with a volley.

It seemed that wherever we went in Ireland, death, destruction, oppression, and revolution followed—usually accompanied by a song or a verse. Kilmainham Gaol is a museum today, but the scuff of boots on its iron staircases leading to the name plaque cells where the martyrs served their brief sentences reminds the visitor not to look too deep beneath the Hibernian charm.

Departing for the countryside demanded another deep breath of fresh air. We skimmed along the country roads past some of the most beautiful views in the Western world. We passed from the grit and bustle of Dublin to plunging cliffs and thatched crofts spotted at the boundaries of rolling fields behind low "drystane" walls. All was charm, tradition, and good humor from village to village until the first submachine gun poked into our car window.

Timing is everything. We had come to a stop at a temporary lift barrier flanked by two sandbag bunkers, each manned by two Irish Army soldiers pointing FN FAL–type assault rifles at us. The exact type of rifle was not noted because I had a hard time looking past the black muzzle aimed at my eye. Slowly, I removed one hand from the steering wheel to roll down the hand-cranked window. The submachine gun two inches from my cheek was a Carl Gustav 9mm with a thirty-six-round magazine clamped in place—a bit of a relic but effective. It was supported by a canvas sling around the soldier's neck. The collapsible wire stock was folded shut. He peered first at me and then at my assistant, who tried to smile confidently, but her eyes were also fixed on the steady muzzle of the Gustav. A police officer in a black Garda uniform jacket and cap knocked on her window, and she almost soiled the car seat when she jumped. I jumped. The soldier, who could have turned us both into garbage, jumped, and the Garda officer stepped back. She cranked vigorously, and the window slid down.

In a soft Irish accent, the Garda officer—a slender, close-shaved, middle-aged man who looked like he should be delivering the mail—asked us for our papers. We had transferred our critical papers from the Central Office of Information and our passports to a single envelope for convenience. He thumbed through them, comparing the passport photos. He seemed disappointed.

"But where are your Irish government permissions and documents?" he asked.

"We're not visiting any Irish government offices or locations," I answered, "We're just tourists trying to tell the story of Ireland to schoolchildren in the United States."

"How do you do that not bein' Irish?" he asked more as an actual question than a rebuke, handing back our envelope. The soldier, meanwhile, surveyed our messy back seat: open crisps packets, a fragrant bag of half-eaten Chinese takeaway, and layers of maps and guidebooks. He held out his hand for the car keys to look into the boot (trunk), and I quickly surrendered them.

I considered my interrogator's question. "The same way I did in Wales, Scotland, the Orkneys, Britain . . . and now I am here." My assistant shot up her eyebrows. "We are here," I added.

All this time, as though they were part of a waxworks display, the armed soldiers behind sandbags and beneath helmets kept us covered. The soldier at my window handed me back my keys and nodded at the Garda officer.

"Be alert," the officer said as he stepped back. "Some IRA boys blew their way out of a nearby prison compound with plastic explosive and are on the loose. Don't pick up no hitchers."

And so we proceeded from village to village to town and to checkpoints between counties, handing our papers in their eventually dog-eared envelope to nervous men with automatic weapons and no sense of humor whatsoever. It was late in the day as we arrived at the remains of an ancient Roman fort on my shooting list. We had stopped at a few looming castles and rock piles listed as "castles," but this was the oldest ruin of them all and would be the last of our Irish shoot.

The walls of the ancient fort were only a foot high in places and formed a large ring around internal partitions that were overgrown with grass. Only the ruin's geometric pattern betrayed its presence. We parked in a lay-by next to the road and unpacked the tripod as the sun was setting behind us, catching the edge of the wall and hitting the top quarter of a rising ridge about a quarter mile away. I got the wide-angle shots quickly because I would lose that edge-lighting sun on the low wall first. Then my assistant called out, "Gerry!" and pointed at the distant ridge.

Four trotting shire horses climbed the ridge. Each stood almost seven feet at the shoulder and clopped on giant hooves with feathered, untrimmed hair floating behind each stride like dark gonfalons. Perched on the bare back of each horse was an Irish youngster, eight to ten years old, farmers' kids in Wellington boots and flat caps, two boys and two girls. They clung to fistfuls of thick mane and straddled the broad, jouncing backs as if they had grown there as part of the horses' anatomy. While I watched, the line of farmyard cavalry broke into a galumphing canter, and each small rider leaned forward above their mounts' necks to allow for the rising ridgeline. I shook myself out of my trance and dove for the car boot to fetch my 50-300 zoom lens while my assistant, reading my mind, unlatched the wideangle camera from the tripod's head.

Brought forward in the telephoto lens to an upward sweeping diagonal, each horse and rider edge-lit in setting sun against a sky of deep blue-gray, the silent scene caught in my throat as I pressed the shutter button on the motor drive, adjusting the shutter speed in increments to bracket the exposure. In a few short seconds, they were gone to the far side of the hill. We both stood for a moment, and then I checked my film supply. One shot was left on the roll. I had fired off just eight frames. In those days before digital photography, that meant at least a week would pass before I could see what I had captured. The odds were eight to one in my favor.

I unlatched the big lens and camera from the tripod, and it was then we saw the three military scout cars top the ridge in line astern and plunge down the grass and bracken slope toward us, fanning out to three abreast as they drew nearer. Each car held three soldiers in camo green. Brass caught the setting sun on one of the passengers in the center car. They braked to the left, right, and directly in front of our small estate van in need of a good wash. Dismounting, each man leveled his FN rifle at us while the officer shifted his Gustav 9mm submachine gun to grip it under his arm. I began to strongly dislike that particular gun. Everyone's finger was on the trigger.

The officer asked something in Irish Gaelic. I answered him in American English. I went through my patter about the Central Office of Information in London, the educational film strip we were shooting, our stopping to photograph the ruins of the Roman fort—which they had almost flattened, I almost added—and how we were heading to our bed-and-breakfast in the next town.

"Then why were you photographing our watchtower?" the officer demanded.

"What watchtower?" I demanded.

He pointed toward the ridge. "There! That's restricted!"

I raised my camera and saw one of the riflemen tense, shifting his rifle's buttplate from his hip to his shoulder. My mouth was like cotton as I refocused on the ridgeline. Behind the ridge, against the blue-gray sky, was a darker gray silhouette of the top part of a timbered structure that was barely discernable when I lowered my telephoto lens. I had been so intent on the horses and riders, I had panned right past the vague outline.

"What is it?" I asked lowering my camera very slowly.

"You don't know that's military ammunition stores over there?" the officer snapped.

"The first time I knew there was military around here was when you came over the hill. We came to shoot that Roman fort. When the kids showed up on their horses, it was a bonus—a beautiful scenic shot . . . and very Irish."

The officer gave me a raised eyebrow and spoke into his two-way radio in Gaelic. I slung my camera over my shoulder, listening to the conversation, though I didn't understand a word. And then, out of the blue and for what reason, I had no idea, the voice at the other end said in clear English, "Whatever happens, get his film."

The officer turned to us. "Pack your gear and come with us. Follow me in your car." He turned away and motioned for a private to stay with us as I packed the boot. Walking to our estate van, I whispered to my assistant,

"Chat up the soldier. Keep his attention."

She blinked, nodded, and turned toward the approaching soldier, who was all kitted up in ammo pouches, combat harness, and sheathed bayonet and glowering at her from under his beret. The muzzle of the big FN automatic rifle pointed at the ground. As she began talking in his direction in her Edinburgh lilt, I furiously rewound my roll back into its cartridge. As he answered, I slapped down the legs of the tripod, making an exaggerated meal of the project and undid my camera's back. I bent into the trunk to shift a couple of bags. With a flip, I tossed the roll into the canvas bag filled with our day's exposed film rolls and plucked a fresh roll from my pocket. My assistant was in full cry like a magpie on speed while I poked, prodded, and sorted gear and wound forward the blank roll with the motor drive. The officer crunched up.

"Come on! We've not got all day!" He gave the boot a cursory once-over, and I slammed it shut. My assistant skipped over to the passenger door, smiled back at the grinning soldier, and waved. "Tah!" she chirped and slipped into the car.

Our little parade ended a few miles along the road at a whitewashed Garda building bustling with black-clad police uniforms and sour looks in our direction. The prison breakout had the countryside in a panic, and our timing could not have been worse. It was Sunday, and the American Foreign Affairs Office in Dublin was closed, as was the COI in London. My blizzard of paperwork was as good as toilet tissue. They put us in separate rooms with a couple of constables who reminded me that Americans were responsible for money and arms going to the IRA. My assistant's Scottish roots did her no good, as it was in the North that most of the troops on garrison duty were from Scottish regiments, not here. An hour of interrogation ensued.

Eventually, we were hustled before the desk of the duty officer. He handed me back our papers and—thank heavens—our passports. Our stories would be checked tomorrow, and they knew where to find us if the need arose. Oh, and by the way, "Please give me your film."

I put up a stiff argument for the film that had other photos on it that would have to be retaken, photos of castles and scenic views and Irish farmers at work and driving cows. All my windy protests were to no good purpose. I was escorted out to the car, removed my camera, marched back in, and made a great show of rewinding the film and dropping the cartridge from the camera onto his desk. He scooped it into his desk drawer and pointed at the door.

"Good day t' you, sir," he said with a bureaucrat's winning grace.

We shuffled out the door with me in a foul mood. "You drive," I barked and slammed into the passenger seat. The army was still parked out front, and as we drove past their scout cars, her private soldier waved, and she waved back, and I stared straight ahead in a peevish funk. When the Garda village had disappeared from the rearview mirror, we shook our heads and had a good laugh but never mentioned the switched roll of film. The Irish are a crafty people, and who knew what kind of radio transmitting bug may have been planted to catch them up an American gun smuggler and his Scottish tart sidekick.

In Dublin a note from my employer in Chicago was waiting for me at the hotel. They wanted me to stay in Ireland to embed in a unit of the Irish Army and go into the field to do a story on a young soldier who was taking part in NATO combat exercises. If there was a last place on earth I wanted to be, it was with the Irish Army. As it was, I kept waiting for the boot against the door and a room full of angry troopers demanding to know why I had slipped them a roll of blank film.

Thus, my assistant drove back to Scotland, and I trudged off to test fate one last time surrounded by every firing and stabbing implement known to modern warfare. When I wasn't absorbed with pumping rolls of film through my Nikons and Leicas, in my fevered brain the morbid, dank cells of

Kilmainham Gaol creaked open and beckoned with their mossy walls and the stench of despair. I just wanted the hell out of there.

The kick on the door never came, and instead of processing my film in London as had become my habit, I bolted for Heathrow and finally drew a deep breath as the wheels of my jetliner lifted off. I'd had enough automatic weapons shoved in my face by sweating young men to last a lifetime. I wanted to go home and stay for a while, to enjoy the company of my lovely and talented wife, my bright and busy kids, and our usual herd of cats who provided comic relief. As for Ireland dropping away below, there were oases of friendly charm and breathtaking beauty. For the rest, as my Scottish grandfather used to say, "Plow it under and plant corn."

The parting shot to my British Isles adventure came at Chicago's O'Hare International Terminal customs inspection, where I had hand-carried my film off the plane and waited while my equipment bags were compared to my boarding list of four months ago to make sure I had not sold anything while overseas. The customs officer moved to my personal foldover bag and requested that I open my bulging laundry sack stowed inside.

"You do not want to open that," I said.

Sensing she had a live one, she seized the opaque plastic bag. "What's in here?" she demanded.

"Laundry," I said without elaboration.

Casting the cruel eye of suspicion, she wrenched down the zipper.

There are times in life when memory is indelibly stamped: your girlfriend's first kiss as your wife, your daughter's first words, the first time a huge marlin hits your hook, and the sad, career-shortening expression on the shrunken face of a customs inspector who has wrenched open your two-week old laundry bag.

Toward the end of the 1980s, as American society was hard-charging into the computer age and the sign-carrying hippies and viral antiwar vegetarians of the 1970s were putting on respectable suits as part of the dot-com explosion, "More is better and less is better still" became a mantra. While the dot-coms trimmed, Wall Street piled on as mergers, acquisitions, and takeovers altered the economic landscape. Corporate America and the dot-coms fueled each other's rise, as more data could be crammed into less space, and decisions that once required hours were launched in split seconds. Computers were just beginning to find table space in American homes and start-up businesses, balancing finances and accumulating new research to test social and hardware limitations. Kilobytes grew into megabytes of memory. The capacity for more horsepower was designed into smaller cars, which used less fuel. More bullets were being loaded into smaller pistols, and bigger bullets were being slid into the cylinders of smaller revolvers. This computer-driven, Wall Street–implemented, uploaded, downsized mindset bolted into the 1990s and got a bump from the Gulf War.

In 1987 pistols caught up to and passed revolvers in popularity for two good reasons. Pistol manufacturers discovered that double-stack clips allow more cartridges to be carried in a semiautomatic pistol's grip magazine. Pistols could be made lighter, flatter, and shorter while still pumping out man-stopper bullets. Revolver makers, meanwhile, found hardened steel cylinders could support hefty cartridge loadings in the Magnum range, while using reinforced aluminum and stainless-steel frames kept the weight down, and ergonomic grips helped control recoil.

If there is a signature gun that set the bar for the 1980s–1990s rush to revolutionize pistol manufacture, it was built by a maker of curtain rods. Besides the rods, crates of shovels, utility knives, kitchen storage boxes, and machine gun ammo belts rolled from the small plastic plant in Austria owned by Gaston Glock. One day in 1980, he overheard two army colonels bemoaning the fact that gun manufacturers had not been able to meet their needs for a new military pistol. Though curtain rods paid the bills, guns had the ring of high-profile profits. He asked if he could submit a design. The colonels said yes, but hurry—the request for proposal was due to expire. He and his people turned to what they knew best and came up with the first "plastic pistol," the Glock 17.

The slide, grips, and other nonstressed parts are made of carbon fiber wrapped around a steel barrel and the steel-moving elements of the mechanism. All the black semiautomatic Glocks look alike, with changes in caliber from the original 9mm to .40 S&W and .45 ACP. They are designed to be held in two hands with a squared-off trigger guard face but sit in the hand with a natural pointing angle of 21.5 degrees. The Austrian government ordered twenty-five thousand Glocks to replace the antique Walther P38 that was its current duty pistol.

Loading ten rounds, the Glock made headlines around the world as security agencies went pale at the idea of a plastic pistol that would defeat all their steel-based gun-detection screening devices. Its arrival sparked interest for other manufacturers to investigate new materials that could withstand heavy-caliber cartridges in lighter platforms, and the race was on.

This pursuit of new opportunities also arrived with the conclusion of the Gulf War. Once the military had decided that the NRA target-range concept of warfare training was not compatible with actual battlefield conditions, the M16 rifle was adopted to meet the needs of the modern infantry soldier. Based on the AR-15 developed by Eugene Stoner, the original Sturmgewehr 44 rifle cobbled together by the Germans late in World War II, and the ubiquitous Soviet AK-47 assault rifle, the American M16 went to war in Vietnam. It stumbled over some army-mandated money-saver blunders and recovered, and the M16A2 became the longest-serving infantry rifle and an icon of the Vietnam War and the Gulf conflict.

The M16A2 had been built by Colt for the military, and their civilian versions used the "AR" designation for "Armalite" instead of the common nomenclature: "Assault Rifle." This product was a cash cow for Colt, as its revolver business was flat. It was also the AR civilian version that caused a political stink, as ordinary folk began buying the semiautomatic version of the designed-for-combat weapons. But to step back a bit, the conflict in the Gulf showed another flaw that had not been a problem in Vietnam. The M16A2 was a full-sized rifle with a twenty-inch barrel and a fixed, plastic shoulder stock. While it was easier to control the 5.56 round in either the full automatic of the original M16 or the three-shot burst of the later version, the M16A2 proved to be clunky to carry, especially in the confines of a Humvee, Bradley Fighting Vehicle, or other armored vehicle in urban warfare situations. Enter the M4 carbine.

Also built by Colt Defense, the M4 has a 14.5-inch barrel, collapsible tubular plastic stock, and numerous surfaces of Picatinny rails on which to mount a vast number of accessories. The M4 has sacrificed about one hundred yards of effective range with the shorter barrel, but modern battlefield combats are mostly close-range encounters well within its accuracy range. The M4 in full-automatic, burst, or even semiautomatic fire capability modes allows average troops to put down consistent suppressive fire while designated snipers seek single critical targets and other weapons, such as squad automatic weapons (SAW) and M30 grenade launchers, maneuver for position. The M4 has proved to be a highly flexible and effective combat rifle.[13]

Meanwhile, back in the American gun culture, the M4 success kicked open the door to a thundering herd of testosterone-dripping copycats as gunmakers sought to dip their bread into the battle-proven gravy. One of the best features of these civilian "black rifles" is they could be cranked out, just like Eli Whitney showed us how to do back in 1801, by clanking, stamping and drilling machines with very little human intervention once the computer button was pressed. Essentially, the rifle is three tubes: the plastic stock, receiver group, and barrel. To date, more than eight million rifles copied from the original M16 have been shipped, and there is no end in sight. The next generation being tested by the Army in a $10 million development program includes the Heckler & Koch HK416, an all-weather, piston-operated version with the familiar M16 layout, but with a higher rate of fire, no overheating, and more compact dimensions.

With the M16 breaking the mold of what is considered a classic rifle, combat weapon designers have gone far afield with Frankenguns that are polycarbonate plumber's nightmares. One example of this rogues' gallery is the XM25 Counter Defilade Target Engagement System. Not to be seen on a hunting trail near you, this semiautomatic rifle pumps out a 25mm slug that contains a chip tied to the rifle's radio signal emitted from its laser-targeted gunsight. Enemy hiding behind a wall? The 25mm smartslug zips over the wall, and one meter past the protecting masonry, it detonates, killing everything behind the wall. Each shot costs about $15, but is cheaper than ordering up an F-16 Fighting Falcon jet aircraft to drop a 500-pound bomb on a 180-pound bad guy.

Extrapolating this technology, do we see a 12-gauge smartslug shotgun with electronics bolted on to drop a deer or a felon with a minimum fuss or a minimum of training for the laser-sighted, radio signal–guided marksman? Never say never.

With the ability to march boxcar loads of semiautomatic-only M4 clones off the shipping dock under the euphemisms of "AR15-type rifles," "modern sporting rifles," or "modular rifles," the only need was for a market. What antler-flaunting deer could stand up against a thirty-round magazine full of tumbling 5.56 rounds while framed in a starlight night-vision telescopic sight with built-in auto rangefinder? The target downrange became an idea, not a critter or some inanimate target. As the NRA put it, "Nothing insures [*sic*] domestic tranquility like an armed citizenry." *American Rifleman* became the tract of a political action committee with some added gun articles. Local state rifle associations followed the NRA through its hard-right turn in its newsletters and hustled down to statehouse front steps for progun rallies.

Between the plastic pistols, heavy-caliber revolvers, and the AR15-type rifles, the riot shotguns and retro black-powder rifles, the laser sights and the concealed-carry weapons, the gun culture reinvented itself into the twenty-first century. The sport also found itself pushing a big political rock uphill.

9

PUT THE GLOVES ON THE BOSSES AND LET 'EM DUKE IT OUT

When I discovered I could make a decent buck pushing words against each other on a variety of subjects for a variety of publishers, I began to ratchet back. After I spent eleven years writing, directing, and producing video and programming for corporations, organizations, and commercials, the media company I had worked for said good-bye to me on the same day my resignation landed on my computer hard drive. I was pooped. The business was strangling on bad judgment calls, trying to save a bloated dinosaur in a new land of fleet-footed boutiques. Janet and I started our own media company, and my former employer dissolved in two years. As I said before, timing is everything.

"Ratcheting back" as a writer is an oxymoron. Since 1997 we've had forty-eight books published by mainstream publishers while traveling around the world and across the United States on research and pleasure trips. I was still shooting photography to illustrate our books and Janet's magazine articles, but I needed something to wash work out of my brain from time to time. I discovered fishing, to which I am hopelessly addicted—from marlin and bluefin tuna off Mexican beaches to Coho salmon and bass in and around Chicago. I considered following my daughter back into horses but got night sweats over that idea. Besides, the thought of hauling my antique hulk up onto that patch of hunter seat leather drains all my initiative. Finally, between bouts of polishing a chair in front of my computer, I returned to my love of firearms.

If you have read this far, you will know my life has been inextricably woven into the American gun culture. It was my salvation as a boy, sustained me as a young man, put money in my pocket as an adult, and ended up pointed at me as a photojournalist. Now, it slides neatly into place as a hobby and a diversion that still gives me great satisfaction. Sadly, the infrastructure of that uniquely American culture of which I consider myself a part now suffers from the ravages of our times and the use of fear that overshadows its future.

Looking at handguns as a bellwether for the shift in gun ownership priorities, the large jump in handgun sales occurred in the mid-1960s just as the civil rights marches began to amp up and anti–Vietnam War protests began spreading. In 1945 only 24 percent of handgun sales comprised the U.S. market. The rest were exported. A year later, 11 percent of firearms manufactured were handguns, and of that number, only 8 percent were on American dealers' shelves. In that time, though, there were financial difficulties in the postwar period, and race riots and labor strikes were contained and localized. As violence against the war and civil rights clashes spread and gasoline rationing and recession added to daily uncertainties, handgun sales continued to rise.

When the World Trade Center and Pentagon were attacked on September 11, 2001, and President George W. Bush declared war on terrorism, handgun purchases were further accelerated. And finally, the ultimate fear was exploited: the election of Barack Obama as president of the United States. What could be worse than a black liberal Democrat who already has attracted a babbling herd of mouth breathers claiming he's not a citizen, that he's a Muslim (like that's a nasty thing), and, most grievous of all, that he's out to snatch away our guns and our American constitutional freedoms and join us with socialist Europe?

But back to the handguns. The NRA, in its feverish need to find new ways to acquire members, jumped on the concealed-carry bandwagon that allows ordinary folk to pack heat on their belts, around their ankles, in hidden jacket pockets, in shoulder holsters, and in Mom's purse. Legislators suddenly found themselves besieged by gaggles of aroused citizens demanding they be allowed to "defend themselves" with the use of a concealed, or at least an "open-carry," handgun.

As the NRA and state gun-advocate associations and clubs pounded their chests and their drums in the various statehouses, the gunmakers put their engineers and designers under the lash to come up with carry-able and con-ceal-able guns to fill the holsters of Americans who were in desperate need of defense. Considering their desk-pounding belligerence, it is not difficult to understand why. And if antigun think tanks and lawmakers ever needed ammunition for their claims that handguns are only good for killing people, so the fewer on the street the better, just pick up a copy of *American Rifleman*.

A prime example of the killer handgun is the Taurus Judge snub-nosed revolver, which fires .410 shotgun shells or .45 Long Colt cartridges in any combination. The beauty of this gun is that with one loading of its five cham-bers, it can punch out a solid man-stopper bullet, a fist full of birdshot, a string of double-ought buckshot, or a special load belching twelve pellets of BB shot, plus three wad-like "defensive disks," as fast as you can pull the trig-ger, and blow that carjacker into a rubber bag. Best of all, by putting out that hail of missiles, only minimal training is needed. Anyone can take their Judge out of the box and, without even going to the range, know for certain that someone or something in front of that muzzle is going to stop a missile.

The Judge migrated into various versions, including a long-barreled model, a plastic polycarbonate frame version being super light and just barely con-trollable, and a carbine version revisiting the old Colt revolving rifle that cooked the wrists of its nineteenth-century owners. The Judge engineered out that prob-lem with its forearm stock design, leaving you with a spiffy-looking hybrid. To soften the "death and destruction" image of this blunderbuss that draws grins wherever it shows up, Taurus is attempting to lure owners out to the skeet or trap range, using the .410 shotgun ammo to blast flying clay targets. Buffalo Bill used .45 Colt shot shells to pop tossed glass balls at a range of twenty to thirty feet in his Wild West Show, which proves anything is possible.

The VPC antigun think-tank scenario opens the door on Granny Good - cookies down the street with the Magnum hawgleg that can crack an engine block and who has decided that the barking dog next door has interrupted her afternoon TV stories for the last time. Consider sweaty-palmed Pops McGregor at the corner Stop N' Shop who produces a nineteen-round Glock and turns a loud, nasty-looking, complaining customer into a mess all over the Pepsi machine?

Destruction and mayhem are only funny in Tom and Jerry cartoons. In reality they are brutal and can destroy lives at both ends of the gun. The handgun, for all its cold efficiency and specialization, is marketed to people with the least firearms training. For the training-challenged—whose large numbers are not unexpected, considering the limited number of pistol ranges in most communities—there are visual aids such as the laser gunsight pointing device that can be retrofitted to just about any handgun. It projects a red dot on the target indicating the weapon's point of aim. A big advantage of this device is its psychological effect on the intended target when that dot appears on the still-breathing anatomy, knowing that death is only a four-pound trigger pull away.

For a little more bulk—mostly suited for a house gun than concealed-carry use—there is the high-intensity, narrow-beam flashlight attached to the barrel. A mini–Picatinny rail system allows this mounting on handguns in the same fashion as the assault rifle applications. With the red dot or the high beam of the flashlight riveting the miscreant in place, the next concern is the intestinal fortitude to drop the bugger in his or her tracks. Once initiated, this can be effected in two ways: a hail of lead or one high-velocity hammer blow that ends that activity then and there and sets in motion a whole new chain of events, often including lifelong sorrow and regret.

The Taurus Judge revolver has already demonstrated the "hail of lead" principle that owes its concept to our Revolutionary War buck-and-ball cartridge, which gave our untrained musket-wielding militiamen an edge over the British regulars. The high-capacity, semiautomatic pistol also offers the firepower solution. Gangbangers and adrenaline-charged police use this fire-hose method of target suppression through sheer volume of metal. The unfortunate side effect of "spray and pray" is collateral damage within a mile of the discharged rounds.

Of course, no hard-charging handgun toter is truly satisfied with a small-caliber, short-barreled, light-frame noisemaker. While 9mm and .38 Special cartridges were once the standby rounds of centerfire handguns, law enforcement agencies found, beginning in the 1930s, that they needed a more potent handgun to put down amped-up druggies, stop motor vehicles, and shoot through things to get at bad guys. The .357 Magnum of 1935 filled that bill, and heavy-frame Smith & Wesson and Colt revolvers were built, harkening back to the old 1846 Walker Colts so big they fit into saddle holsters for the Texas Rangers.

The big-bore war moved on to the Smith & Wesson Model 29 .44 Magnum revolver, the "Dirty Harry" gun used by Clint Eastwood in the movie of that name. Even locked into a heavy frame with stout grips, it is a punishing round to shoot. These revolvers were all heavy and chunky, but as new hardened steels, carbon fibers, and tighter tolerances became available, they shrunk. Finally, the old and much-maligned .32 caliber slug was dusted off, and the .327 Magnum made its appearance, allowing up to eight shots in a cylinder.

The bore war can never end, but it has achieved the largest production revolver made today. The Smith & Wesson Model 500 is a .50 caliber weapon topping the other bruisers: the .454 Casull Magnum, .475 Linebaugh Magnum, .480 Ruger Magnum, .44 Desert Eagle Magnum, and .50 Auto Express. The Model 500 is so large in its hunter version that it needs a leather shoulder sling, but it also comes in a four-inch barrel model that has a built-in muzzle blast vent, suppressing enough recoil to actually allow attempting a second shot. Usually just seeing one of these stainless steel cannons hoisted into shooting position is enough to make most miscreants surrender.

To cool the fevered brows of the overheated antigun wonks, the gunmakers call these great big sidearms "trail guns." The drama here is that the hunter in the field has something useful to reach for when he's caught on the latrine by a giant maddened grizzly bear or charging Cape buffalo rather than an inquisitive chipmunk.

Glock, Beretta, Sig Sauer, Smith & Wesson, and other pistol makers raised their calibers to the .40 S&W, .41, and .45 ACP in the small semiautomatic handguns. When combined with lightweight carbon-fiber materials, small grips, and short barrels that produce a huge muzzle flash, these miniature heavy hitters are a handful to shoot. Curiously, of all the latest advances in firearms technology, the most popular pistol design is still based on John Browning's Colt Model 1911 from World War I and II. The original flat slab has been forged in stainless steel, trimmed, accurized, skeletonized, barrelshortened, and extended. It's also had new sights added, had parts removed, had other parts engraved, been fitted with lasers and flashlights, morphed into .22, .380, 9mm, .38 Super, and the ubiquitous .45 ACP, been stamped with a variety of makers' marks, and often caked with egregious layers of gaudy "commemorative" engraving and inlays.

Handguns have forced the American gun culture into a retro mode for which the ownership of a handgun has become a symbol of fear. People without handguns fear those who want to carry them concealed or in the open. People without handguns fear those guns in the hands of criminals, the mentally deranged, and trigger-happy radicals. To many of the people who own the more than two hundred million guns in the United States, that gun represents fear of the loss of the individual constitutional right to keep a gun. It represents fear of a government strategy to strip away all guns from the American people.

The belt-holstered gun represents the final bulwark against an imagined political tyranny that one day will come boiling down our streets. That gun represents fear of superheated minorities who will stop at nothing short of savage rampage to grab a bigger piece of the action. If this sounds harsh, it also burns way down beneath the patriotic platitudes of the gun ownership superadvocates.

Carrying a handgun as a daily accessory represents a failure of American society. For the statistics buff, the VPC claims that between May 2007 and early 2011, persons licensed to carry handguns have killed 286 private citizens and cut down 11 officers of the law. Closer inspection reveals that over this same period, there have been 60,000 homicides in the United States. Using these numbers, gun permit owners were responsible for one killing in every 200 murders. For every permit holder who shot someone, 20,000 did not shoot anybody. And with their usual sweaty-palmed statistical overkill, the VPC included nonfirearms deaths. In Florida one handgun permit holder strangled his victim. In most states where horror, rampage, and Armageddon were promised by the VPC and other antigun groups if handgun permits were issued willy-nilly, murder and crime rates plummeted.[1]

For anyone who has strapped on a loaded gun and walked out into the day-to-day routine of living, that extra bit of weight represents the fear of using it, of having to make a judgment call accelerated by adrenaline, those two extra cups of coffee, the argument at the breakfast table that morning, or a dozen other life distractions all arriving at a halted moment of time when a "self-defense" decision must be made. It is not a movie scene played by actors. It is not a freeze-frame mouse click in a video game. It is not a few sentences in a book or a moment under the lights on the legitimate stage. And it is not at a target range with a patient instructor at your side.

At both ends of the gun ownership issue, fear is the chosen tool to advance their agendas. And both ends of the argument flaunt this tool with cynical outcomes in mind. The gun superadvocates shout and stomp and rend their garments to wrap themselves in the American flag in defense of our liberties while making money and building political influence filling the holsters of the fearful people with the gunmakers' products. The antigun crowd is drowning in the loopy logic that somehow those two hundred million guns will go away, that a billion-dollar industry is going to start engraving serial numbers on every bullet, and that Americans will simply surrender to a chronically understaffed and underfunded police force that cannot enforce the gun laws that exist today. In between these warring camps are the men and women and young people who enjoy the many facets of the shooting sport, the law enforcement agencies that need training, and the kids whose only families are the gangs, who are dependent on the drug lords who buy their loyalty with the illusion of respect. Tub thumping, torch carrying, and megaphone blasting are poor substitutes for education and programs that can make a difference, because these programs are the right thing to do. History has shown that while the American people are not big on turning the other cheek, they are quick studies when turned loose on attainable goals.

Self-defense and personal liberties have a long tradition in our history. Searching the pages of America's formation back to the Revolutionary period, as our gun and antigun advocates are wont to do, reveals that while our freshly minted government struggled to govern, the people in their sovereign states were busy sorting out the extent of their new "liberties." This process required more than three hundred years of political, martial, religious, and social mayhem, compromise, and confrontation to arrive at today's polarized agony over the right to handgun self-defense.

Historically, one of these issues involved the rights of a gentleman, as understood in the new post-Revolution society. Wartime entrepreneurs and bankrupts, plus the hoard of loyalists fleeing to England and Canada, shuffled about some of the continental wealth. One of the "rights" that was new to those who had recently gained gentleman status through the acquisition of abandoned, foreclosed, or stolen property was the tradition of dueling to settle disputes of honor.

While the Quakers and Yankees of the Northeast frowned upon the practice, the Scots-Irish who flooded through the South were a bit more sanguine. Honor, courage, and reputation were treasured and defensible with dirk, bowie knife, sword, and pistol. The original planters who manipulated southern society from their statehouses and the balconies of their plantations found former farmers and tenants of the lower class now wearing brocaded silk and taking up space at what had been exclusive clubs. These interlopers also had argumentative attitudes and opportunistic friends who got them elected to state office. Throughout the South intolerable situations erupted, resulting in shots fired in the dewy dawn and "grass for breakfast." Duels became so common that newspapers stopped printing stories about who dropped whom at how many paces.

In Kentucky lawmakers grew tired of seeing old chums punctured and passed an antidueling law in 1812 making both parties punishable. However, a humbug arose with this solution. When a red-faced shouting match developed, instead of retreating to the *code duello* rules, the wronged parties took satisfaction on the spot. If both parties were openly armed, self-defense became a solid plea in court. If, on the other hand, neither party appeared to be armed, but one of them snaked out a pocket pistol and put a ball in his opponent's boiler room, the survivor could tell the judge he acted fearing his late opponent might be about to draw a lethal weapon.[2]

The dueling code was replaced by street assassinations, which forced Kentucky to pass the first concealed weapon law in 1813 (only to be repealed a short time later for infringing on a citizen's Second Amendment rights). Author Clayton Cramer has assembled a considerable body of research of early America's passage and removal of both concealed and open-carry laws in his book *Concealed Weapon Laws of the Early Republic*. While Cramer is a gun ownership–rights advocate, his body of scholarship turns a neutral and useful light on this early nineteenth-century period. We are still living with the consequences of that post-Revolution and pre–Civil War era when our population was transporting its predilections, moral judgments, attitudes, and Manifest Destiny into an untamed and unspoiled land in the West.[3]

One of the telling aspects of the early legislation was the most feared weapon of the time. Throughout the southern states, which had the most widespread reputation for violence, the bowie knife was the prime target of lawmakers. This tells us a lot about this early culture where a misused word, social slight, public insult, or property dispute often resulted in both parties resorting to brutal violence.

The bowie knife, as popularized by Jim Bowie, who cashed in his chips at the Alamo in the Texas War of Independence, had a foot-long blade roughly three inches wide with a broad hilt and a grooved handle for a good grip. One blade edge was fully sharpened along its length, while the other edge was sharpened for about three inches of its sloping tip and for the remainder of the blade topped with a soft brass strip to catch and parry any other knife's stroke.

It was a fighting knife, most often carried in a scabbard hung down the owner's back, where it could be drawn over the shoulder, or at the hip beneath a long coat. Its closest relative was the Arkansas toothpick, a long, double-edged knife built for stabbing or cutting. The dirk was a slim-bladed fighting knife designed not to spoil the line of an elegant coat. The French-imported *Châtellerault* had an S-shaped cross guard and a stylish pearl-and-ivory trim, very chic in New Orleans and often designed to latch into action from a spring in its handle.[4]

Wielding a long-bladed knife says something about a person who prefers that weapon to the pistol. There is an intimacy to being close enough to your opponent to drive a three-inch wide blade into the human body; smell the exhalation of breath; and feel the suction as the blade withdraws, scraping against bone; and see the splash of hot arterial blood spurting on your hands. It is a visceral act that makes the pistol ball seem surgical beyond arm's reach.

In 1837 a documented event occurred near Natchez, Mississippi, on the steamboat *Galenian*. The captain demanded an unruly passenger leave his ship and brandished a knife to make his point. The passenger turned to depart, but the captain hurried to his cabin and returned with a pistol. During his admonitions to the exiting passenger, the gun accidentally discharged, slightly wounding the passenger with its single ball. In a rage the passenger turned, grabbed the captain by the throat, drove him onto the ground, produced a dirk, and proceeded to carve up the flailing victim, repeatedly driving the blade home to its hilt. The passenger was acquitted of murder, since the captain had shot him as he was obediently leaving the boat.[5]

This event also demonstrates the unreliability of the pistol in the early nineteenth century. Lugging about flintlock pistols was extremely clumsy due to the complexity of their mechanism, and dealing with loose priming powder was challenging.

The percussion cap simplified the process and reduced the size of sidearms. Still, cap nipples became clogged with pocket lint, and snuff and tobacco bits blocked the primer's flash path to the barrel's powder charge. Hammers lowered on caps to keep them in place could ignite the charge if dropped on a hard surface. Also, the pistoleer had only one shot in an adrenaline-pumping situation, two if he carried a brace of pistols, as was the custom.

On January 30, 1835, President Andrew Jackson attended a funeral in the Capitol for Congressman Warren R. Davis of South Carolina. As he passed the casket, a demented former housepainter, Richard Lawrence, who believed himself to be a descendant of the British royal family, stepped up, drew a pistol, and fired at point-blank range. The percussion cap ignited, but the ball failed to discharge. Jackson, a duelist by nature and reputation, was not packing that day, but he stepped forward with his cane. The would-be assassin drew a second pistol, and its percussion cap ignited. That pistol also failed to fire its ball. Jackson proceeded to beat on Lewis with his hickory cane until officers bundled the bleeding lunatic away to spend the rest of his life in a government-run asylum. The odds against both pistols misfiring were about 125,000 to 1.[6]

If Lawrence had waited one more year for his attempted murder, Samuel Colt's Paterson revolver—the first truly practical revolving cylinder handgun—would have offered three more .36 caliber shots. While some historians couple this improved technology of Colt's growing line of reliable handguns with the increase in condemning concealed weapons in the early republic, there were alternatives predating that invention to counter that consideration. The pepperbox was a popular, close-quarters, multishot handgun. A number of barrels, from as few as four to as many as the designer's imagination could devise, rotated about an axis. Each had its own percussion-cap nipple, and a single hammer fired the shot as the loaded barrel rotated into place.

A later Allen & Thurber double-action pepperbox, where the trigger both rotated the barrels and tripped the hammer, unleashed a smoky barrage of lead in the general direction of the soon-to-be perforated target. However, sympathetic detonation was the bugaboo of the pepperbox design, where one trigger squeeze caused all the barrels to ignite. Adding to the collateral damage in the immediate vicinity of the intended victim, digital truncation and rearrangement was also a possibility for the shooter.

Of course there had to be a design where such multiple mayhem was desired. That would be the duckfoot pistol, which provided gents of low self-esteem and shaky hands a means of clearing a room with a single squeeze of the trigger. One percussion cap touched off an array of loaded barrels splayed in an arc from its center point, looking like a duck's foot. Originally a naval weapon used to flatten a mutiny with a minimum of fuss, it could also clear a poker table of sore losers. Personal portability was its biggest hang-up—it was like concealing a ping-pong paddle. The twister was the mini version of the multi-barrel guns. Two barrels rotated beneath a single hammer. If the percussion cap didn't fall off its nipple while bouncing around upside down in a vest pocket, the shooter had a second shot.

It is apparent that advancing technology had less to do with the adding and repealing of handgun open-carry or concealed-carry laws in the volatile southern states than the desire to control the level of that violence. In Georgia foreign travelers noted that dueling was an everyday event to settle grievances, but "outright crimes such as robbery or murder for financial gain were at a minimum" because the "common practice of most men going about fully armed was, the travelers felt, undoubtedly a strong deterrent to those who might have been criminally inclined."[7]

From the Louisiana docks that thrust into the Mississippi River came a vast detritus that encrusted flatboats from the north and west. These were the Kaintucks, riverboat men bringing goods and backwoods manners from Kentucky to the melting-pot port of New Orleans. Louisiana courts passed concealed- and open-carry laws not to curtail the actions of the multiethnic, multiracial, class-mixed local civic stew but to help control the flood of murderous river trash. This was an early manifestation of the cowboys arriving with their herds in western prairie railroad terminals looking to hoorah the towns. Untroubled by any previous experience with law and order in the backwoods wilderness, the flatboat men sought their pleasures with a lusty and often brutal enthusiasm.

The southern states were a hotbed of touchy people. And remember, the laws passed by the various antebellum legislatures were generally against concealed weapons. Some states tried to pass laws where concealed weapons were illegal if the owner had "aggressive intentions." Let the lawyers sort that one out. The populace could roam the countryside and most city streets fairly bristling with arms. Why was that? In the northern and northeastern states, some communities even disarmed their police officers because the display of guns made people uneasy. The best theories today have all pointed at the South's one unique commodity: slaves.

Generally speaking, when the Scots-Irish arrived in the colonies, they already had Britain's bootmark on their backsides and were looking for a fresh start. They found all the top jobs taken in the North by the Yankees and the Quakers and in the South by the cavaliers (the gentleman class running the large plantations). But the country was big, and opportunities were many as long as no one messed with your stuff. Very little prosperity was needed for a bottom-feeding southerner to buy at least a couple of slaves and jump up a notch in class.

Those who could not make that leap worked for the owners as slave over-seers or bumped shoulders with the free blacks, Creoles, quadroons, and back-country sharecroppers for that ever-present bottom rung of the social ladder. Many headed into the Appalachian wilderness and inbred there for two hundred years, scratching a living out of the stony mountains and Virginia ridges. Because justice was slow and often corrupt in the "good old boy" southern courts, it was easier to grab an ear, gouge an eye, or filet your neighbor over the price of bottomland if you already had some human property who could work the ground.

Always, throughout the South, slave owners looked over their collective shoulder to keep aware of any disturbance in the status quo that might lead to a slave revolt. Slaves were not allowed near any kind of firearm. Fear of whipping, hanging, being chained by collar, or sent down the river to New Orleans to be sold into a short, brutal life on sugar plantations kept most slaves in line. Those who managed to escape but were recaptured endured having ears cut off, branding, or having their Achilles tendon severed. But the fear of a revolt, of black African demons rising up to slaughter their masters and defile southern womanhood—that deep-down terror motivated packing deadly weapons, even to church.

It can't be easy growing up with this sense of entitled obedience from another human of a powerless class. This implied racial superiority converted any refusal to obey a southern white's demands or disagreement with their opinions into a personal insult requiring punishment. That attitude produced an intractable and coarse individual. As with all countries that held social, intellectual, and physical dominion over a huge underclass, the United States grappled at both ends of those searing words that defined the people who stood on her soil: "All men are created equal."

The southern economy depended on slaves to harvest cotton and tobacco, the backbones of the agricultural society. Slave buyers went to regular sales as though buying a sack of potatoes or a barrel of sorghum molasses. Light-skinned "negroes" went to the plantation houses as servants, and "darkies" went into the fields. Families were split up according to their market value. In today's money, men went for $1,000, women brought $800, and children went on the block for $500. Women were fattened up like prize hogs before a sale to give the look of good breeders. Children and men were checked for whip scars on their backs and chests to weed out troublemakers.[8]

The northern states were not innocent bystanders. The belt-driven power loom turned raw cotton into thread, and fortunes were made off the sale of both woven cloth and ready-to-wear clothes. Whole families and towns worked in the mills, with little girls preferred in the bobbin racks because of their small, agile hands. The power loom with its hole-punched cards dictating which thread colors went where to produce patterned cloth by saying either "yes" or "no" created the binary system that translated to open or closed switches when electricity arrived. This in turn laid the groundwork for today's computers. None of this could have become the catalyst for the Industrial Revolution without the cheap cotton harvested and ginned by southern slaves.[9]

An upwelling of abolitionist sentiment flooded through the North, stoked by books such as Harriet Beecher Stowe's *Uncle Tom's Cabin*, published in 1852. John Brown's raid on the arsenal at Harpers Ferry, Virginia, on October 16, 1859, was supposed to rally slaves to his abolitionist cause. The army of former slaves would empty the arsenal of its thousands of rifles and pistols and begin an open rebellion. Not only did the slaves not rise to Brown's cause, but Virginia citizens began firing on him and his raiders where they holed up in the fire engine house. Finally, Col. Robert E. Lee's U.S. Marines arrived, stormed the besieged gunmen, and killed or captured the lot. Brown was expeditiously tried and hanged, becoming a martyr to the abolitionist cause and celebrated in song and legend.

The result of the Civil War was a humiliating slap in the face to southern manhood and the women who had to bear up under that disgrace. Heading west was one way to leave behind the reminders of defeat and reestablish their independence and self-respect. Except that the White Knights of the Ku Klux Klan remained behind to keep fear alive among the former slaves who were either rudderless in the South or traveling north and west to start new lives. The war started more than it finished. It started a long, long road for African American self-determination that continues in the presidency of the

United States. It accelerated the industrial revolution that turned out plows, typewriters, and steel girders, as well as rifles, pistols, cannons, and ironclad ships. It made everyone aware that it is possible to lose a way of life through rebellion. It showed that Americans were capable of fighting to the death supporting the most horrific and demeaning causes.

The Civil War demonstrated how thousands of deaths can be caused by "patriotic" words and how fear can flow from intractable principles. The residue of that distant conflict put a twist in the American character that shows up today in the idea that carrying a handgun out the door each morning is as common as pocketing your house key. The right to own a firearm should not be in dispute, but the need to carry it openly in public only flaunts our weaknesses and failures.

Before we leave this subject, let us make one more observation. The Scots-Irish were not totally to blame for this gun culture mess we are in today. Yes, they arrived with a chip on their shoulder, but remember, just about everyone except the trading company owners who came to these shores strictly for profit were either transported here against their will as indentured servants or slaves, or they had run away from some intolerable situation. The Irish fled the potato famine, the Germans starvation and military conscription, the Scandinavians crop failures, the Quakers and Jews religious persecution, and the British an overcrowded, closed-class society.[10] As for the Pilgrims, Oscar Wilde suggested there should be two Thanksgiving holidays: "one in America to celebrate their arrival and one in England to celebrate the fact that they left." We all share a piece of the blame.

At stake is the idea of carrying a handgun when you leave the house in order to feel safe. The idea has become more important than the actuality of the experience. Finish putting breakfast dishes in the washer, set out fresh water and kibble for the cats, gather up cell phone, car keys, house key, quarters for the parking meter, credit card, wallet, BlackBerry, iPod, gun, spare ammo clip, aspirin, and you're all set to go. Then there's your work gun, your evening-wear gun, and the gun you take to the beach in the summer. There's the water-proof gun for outdoor and water sports. And you need a house gun—maybe one for upstairs and one for downstairs, both with laser sights. The car gun should be accessible while driving—you know those road-rage assholes.

Like golf clubs, there are different calibers for different situations, unless you settle on one of the small Magnums like the .327 or the old-fashioned

9mm. Gunmakers wake up soaked with orgasmic night sweats over dreams of this brave new world.

Ever really look in the garage at all the stuff gathering spider nests? Nerf balls, tennis rackets, lawn darts, snorkeling masks, cross-country skis with no boots, the CB radio, two old desktop computers, and the ColecoVision game set, complete with cartridges? How long before the gun cases end up in the hall closet next to the income tax records for 2003–2007 and Dad's collection of hats he never wears anymore?

While the antigunners and progunners trundle up their paper artillery and their respective acolytes gather together, yelling into their megaphones and stirring their mud pots, somehow the shooting culture continues to offer sport and challenge. Everything the gunmakers build is not a tool of Satan. Some of the latest products of the gunmakers' art take us back to our roots, when the shooter had to bring more to the party than high technology.

The sporting gun we use today that is closest to our eighteenth-century roots is the smoothbore shotgun. Not the eighteen-inch-barrel, six-shot, pistol-gripped riot gun loaded with double-ought buckshot and hiding behind camouflage paint, but the real shotgun that begins, like all good long guns, with a fine piece of wood. A smooth, light-triggered, quick-shouldering autoloader with an old-timey feeling is a joy to shoot when it fits like you were born with it in place.

A shooter does not have to look into a spotting scope to see where his lead went with a shotgun. A clay target explodes in a puff of dust, or a pheasant drops into the field, and the dinner bell rings. A couple of hours busting clay targets builds character, and it's also a decent spectator sport when the doubles and triples start flying.

The gunmakers have gone even further retro to build even stronger interest in our shooting roots. The single-shot black-powder rifle is with us again and gaining in popularity. Hunters are once again placing all their bets on making the one-shot kill after a close-range stalk. The new muzzle-loader rifle, shooting over open sights, offers the modern features of high-technology materials and ballistic efficiency that would make an eighteenth-century long rifle woodsman weep. These new guns are hybrids, a modern interpretation of two or three different eras spanning two hundred years.

While a few reproductions of antique long rifles are available—and some in kit form—most of the new breed combine the look of a rolling block cartridge breechloader with the percussion-cap muzzle-loader, stocked with camouflage-pattern plastic complete with thumbhole cut-out grip. Some offer a bolt-action receiver, while a few come complete with battery-operated electric ignition for the muzzle-loaded charge. It is a joy to peer into the ears of the designers and watch the gears turn, mesh, bind, strip out teeth, and grind on, trying to determine what to keep and what to dispose of from the sport's elegant forbearers.

On the gun rack, you can always spot the muzzle-loader by the ramrod slung in ferrules beneath the barrel. All the various actions are nothing more than clever takes on the Remington rolling block, Sharps under-lever, Martini-Henry drop block, or Ross and Mauser bolt-action, breech-access systems. All these systems are for cartridge rifles, but they give the shooter something to do when it comes time to press the #209 modern percussion cap onto its breech plug nipple. Their only redeeming quality is that they offer a degree of safety. Should a cap rupture into shards of flying copper, the breech actions hold the cap in place, and they allow for a flat receiver top where the shooter can mount a micrometer, light-gathering, or telescopic sight. The sights normally provided are light-gathering, chemical, optically enhanced, open sights that allow the sight picture to be seen clearly in very low light.

The other major upgrade for muzzle-loader riflemen improves on the original lead ball and speeds up the loading process. Needless to say, once a muzzle-loader discharges its black-powder plume of smoke and loud bang, the chance for a swift follow-up shot are nil. By the time the former location of the missed critter can be glimpsed through the pall, the venison steaks and hat rack are halfway to the next county and just beginning to really accelerate. Muzzle-loaders are not about quick second shots. That is one reason they are popular with the real hunters who don't go into the field looking like a SWAT team member laden with a loaded combat harness who plants an ample backside in a chair halfway up a tree and keeps an eye on the motion-detector screen while playing with an antler clacker until some horny deer wanders into range, sniffing in lusty doe hormones sprayed in the trees.

The sabot has replaced the lead ball projectile. Shaped like a Minié ball, the pointed-nose sabot is encased in its own "patch" made of plastic that seals the slug into the bore, keeping all the exploding powder gas behind it. The slug, once just plain old lead that could be melted and cast in the field by a ham-handed backwoodsman with broken fingernails, is now coated with platinum or copper in place of icky bear grease. The slugs are designed with boat-tail shapes for a higher ballistic coefficient, hollow-pointed for expansion to the size of a dessert plate on impact, or fitted with a polymer tip for high velocity, high impact, high penetration, and high price.

Where once the deer slayer was strung with powder horns that later became cartridge boxes and stayed that way from flintlock through percussion eras, the modern muzzle-loader has been pelletized. Lugging about a sack or horns filled with touchy black gunpowder has been sanitized into .50 caliber pellets that can be rammed down the barrel until they achieve the 150 grains usually recommended for the shot. The sabot then slides down on top of the stack. No more black teeth from ripping the head off a paper cartridge. See-through plastic speed reloaders allow the sabot-pellet-powder package to be set atop the muzzle and rammed home.

The propellant charge has changed since its eighteenth-century standardization of 75 percent potassium nitrate, 15 percent softwood charcoal, and 10 percent sulfur, all measured, mixed, and poured down the barrel. While the muzzle-loading hunter can carry powder measures for exact charges in the field, pellets allow more precise loads for consistent results. Today there are new "smokeless" nitrocellulose-based black-powder brands on the market used in guns specifically built for their higher pressures. There are also "sulfurless" powders such as Pyrodex that use dicyanamide, which requires the user to "avoid heat or flame" and "when heated to decomposition emits highly toxic fumes of cyanide." But so do cigarettes, so choose your demon. Flatter trajectory and a cleaner barrel have their price.[11]

Besides gunning down woodland critters for the dining table or to eliminate depredations, the sport of target shooting with muzzle-loaders, which began in the 1930s, has grown considerably. In the 1970s most American manufacturing was in decline due to no investment in new plants, foreign competition, entrenched labor unions, and a general lack of innovation. Toward the end of the decade, the product liability legal smoke screen was dogging firearms makers and building a very negative public image.

At the same time, people were fascinated by the hippie commune way of life, as publications such as the *Whole Earth Catalog* ran articles and advertisements about back-to-basics living, wood stoves, churning butter, and creating large gardens. Among the basics was hunting with the old muzzle-loading, single-shot rifles. At a time when firepower was the firearms makers' mantra, collectors were buying up old Pennsylvania rifles and shooting them.

Entrepreneurs began looking for ways to turn the artisan skills of the old village gunmaker into an industry (translation: significant money), and the muzzle-loader sport was reborn.[12]

The Muzzle Loaders Associations International Committee (MLAIC) was created in 1970 and fired off its first world championship in 1971. That same year, the *Last Whole Earth Catalog* offered a "Golden Age Mountainmen" flintlock rifle kit for $104.50 plus $5.00 postage. Fully assembled, the same rifle cost retro worshippers $295.00 plus $3.00 shipping. To give you an idea of the catalog's style, one of the authors of a 1971 article on the gun advertisement page suggested the following:

> Join the NRA. The NRA establishment freaks want to repeal all gun laws. They're all perverts, but join them. It's a good cause. What the world needs now is a better anarchy.
>
> Peace
> Crazy Bill
> Allston, Massachewsit [*sic*]

From that marvelously hazy, drug-drenched time of school bus communes, bare feet, and shaggy beards, old-timey survival has matured into a sport that has grown. Today many states have muzzle-loader rifle hunting seasons each year, which compete with shotgun-slug hunting for popularity. Even the great muzzle-loading, long-range rifle matches from the Creedmoor days when the Irish teams invaded our shores have been resuscitated.

If there is another .50 caliber long gun that can compete with the muzzle-loader for the hearts and minds of American shooters and also make antigun activists grind their teeth, it is the high-velocity, long-range sniper rifle. Snuggling down behind a Barrett M107 semiautomatic, its bolt-action cousin the Model 416, a McMillan Tac-308, or even the AW Super Magnum—a Swedish bullpup design pushing out the .338 Lapua cartridge—gives the shooter the feeling that enough gun is available for any contingency. All these collections of engineering overkill require are wheels to trundle them from one well-situated location to another. They are a lie-down-behind kind of gun with surprisingly light recoil and with a harder slap at the other end, even if the target is a mile away.

These big-bore rifles owe their existence to the World War I tank killers sent into the field with Russian and British soldiers. They entered service early in the war after seeing some success against thinly armored cars. The British Boys antitank rifle is a good example. This bolt-action brute carried its 7.92 rounds in a detachable box magazine and was effective on 15mm of armor at four hundred yards or 30mm at one hundred. The long, man-carried rifles ate barrels in heavy combat, and high pressures crystallized steel breeches, and extreme heat from firing expanded the large, empty shell casings, defeating the bolts' extractors. Worst of all was the recoil, which was known to mulch collarbones and jar teeth loose.

The Poles fielded the Model 35 that saw service against early German tanks, and the Germans countered with their 13.5mm Panzerbüchse. Russian tank-killer squads wielded the 14.5mm Degtyarev PTRD, which had an extended life in Korea against early American armor. In the Pacific the Japanese soldiers put up with the 20mm monster Type 97 that could knock a tread off a Sherman tank or punch through the closed ramp of a Higgins boat. As the war saw improved armor clanking across the battlefield, the antitank rifles were replaced by missile launchers such as the 2.36-inch and later 3.5-inch bazookas, the 75mm and 90mm recoilless rifles, and the Germans' iconic panzerfaust, the shaped-charge predecessor of the RPG launcher favored by insurgencies everywhere today.

While these early heavy-caliber rifles were designed for knocking out light armor, they were also used as long-range sniper weapons when conditions permitted. American troops followed suit, adopting the .50 caliber machine gun as a single-shot sniper weapon, though it did require considerable skill for long-range hits. Doping the wind, understanding bullet drift and drop, and estimating the range to target were all skills in their battlefield infancy, unless your great-grandpa handed down his secrets learned with a Sharps on the Montana prairies or at the Creedmoor target competitions.

The future of these big-bore, one-man guns seems limitless, as technology has replaced the Sharps's lead slug with computer-designed Frankenbullets like the .338 Lapua, .416 Barrett, and the .408 CheyTac. For reaching out with superior accuracy, nothing as of this writing surpasses the M200 CheyTac. This sniper rifle brings electronics right to the battlefield with a package that includes a ballistic computer (a personal digital assistant with ballistic software installed on it), a Vector IV laser rangefinder, and a Kestrel 4000 device that monitors wind, temperature, humidity, and atmospheric pressure, all linked to the PDA.[13] Gone are the days of aiming off target

("Kentucky windage"), counting reticule dots in the scope sight, and holding off to place long shots. This computer has ballistic data gathered with Doppler radar at the Yuma Proving Grounds on a wide range of sniper and other combat ammunition. Punch in the ammo, cross-reference the data from the Kestral 4000 and the Vector IV rangefinder, breathe, hold, and squeeze the trigger. The .408 Chey Tac bullet is on target out to 2,500 yards.

As illustrated in earlier chapters, the military's habit of disbanding sniper training and special units after each major conflict dragged down their fighting capability in the next bloodletting. The shopworn idea that a scope sight and a lace-on cheekpad made any combat rifle a sniper weapon also became old. Americans were fortunate that the men behind the guns were far better than their equipment in spite of the available training. The accumulated knowledge and marksmanship of those few surviving snipers finally wrote the book for a full-time job in the U.S. Army and Marines. Competition between our military units improved the breed until the NRA finally resurrected its antique credo of one shot–one kill marksmanship, which became a critical part of an army's tactical success in the field. *American Rifleman* became a catalog for every *Soldier of Fortune* wannabe "fifty cal guy" who wanted to shred an enemy without having to smell him or look into his eyes.

For the military, the recent development of the heavy sniper rifle produced an excellent weapon, and those who master its strict regimen for success deserve praise. The gun's sudden hits have an intense psychological effect on enemy troops. On the other hand, for the SWAT team it can be a liability. Its large, high-velocity round guarantees a through-and-through wound on a human target at most urban distances, and collateral damage stacking up behind such a close shot would be impossible to justify.

On a closing note for military sniping, with every small-arms contractor in the United States jumping on the big-bore sniping bandwagon, a familiar problem arises. Many new designs require unique cartridges: .308 caliber, 7.62mm, .408 caliber, .416 caliber, .50 caliber, and so on. This recalls the Union ordnance chief mentioned earlier. Logistics once again raises its ugly head.

For the civilian "50 cal" shooter, expect to have a Ben Franklin in your pocket for every nine rounds fired down range at those far away critters. Hunters launching shots from distant ridges will find themselves remembering the peacefully unaware bull moose, daydreaming ten-point elk, grazing

Dall sheep, or snoozing grizzly bear as the shooters collect the bigger critter remnants in plastic baggies and dab the rest off rocks and bushes with tweezers and a sponge. At best, the fifty-cal is an expensive curiosity in civilian hands.

Finally, in our single-shot curiosity sweepstakes, we set another super-accurate round on the table top next to the huge .50 caliber cartridge. Yes, it's there. You just have to look closely. It is a .177 lead air gun pellet.

To most readers of this book, having gotten this far coughing through the clouds of gun smoke, to arrive at some kiddy pop-gun may come as a let-down. That's kind of what I thought as I walked up the steps to the darkened high school that allowed the air gun club to use its basement gym for a range. But first, let's review a bit.

My first run-in with a pellet gun is documented earlier in this book and involved my dad's Benjamin air pistol. Decades later, when I read about an air gun range only a few blocks from my house, that old brass and wood pump pistol was taken down from the top shelf of the studio closet. The pellets in their green, flat can were pretty well oxidized a dull, dusty gray from sitting for thirty years, but they fit into the pistol's breech. About ten pumps primed the air cylinder beneath the barrel, and I took a couple of shots, "Pap!" "Pap!" at the empty birdhouse in the snow-covered backyard. Distant raps meant successful hits on the wood that needed painting anyway. Nobody came crashing through the bushes with manacles and arrest warrants, so I figured everything was good.

Why would I consider this form of shooting? Most shooters I have ever met become addicted to the idea of sending a missile of any sort downrange. From hitting targets a mile away with a hot bullet to shuffleboard, a missile is a missile. That's why I still drag out my handmade seventy-five-pound recurve bow once in a while and skewer a hay bale or two getting my eye and muscle memory back. Someday I'd like to build a catapult, but that's another story.

With an air gun, I reasoned I could practice in the backyard, shooting out the open door of our sun room with nobody being the wiser. Sitting at a computer keyboard day after day and pushing words together can produce many fantasies when the engine slows down to idle. It was winter, and I could not fish for largemouth bass in the nearby lake. My writing partner for life, the brilliant and beautiful Janet, deserved to have me out of the house occasionally so she could watch her angst-filled chick flick DVDs and also put her active mind on personal pursuits for a few hours.

A cold Wednesday night found me carrying a small leather case and entering what once had been my daughters' high school but was now a religious academy. I made my way through the deserted halls, went upstairs, and with the help of a cleaning crew person, found the gymnasium. There I met a congenial group of men and a few male and female students. Around the walls were bull's-eye targets.

I went through introductions and laid the case on one of the long tables piled with gun cases, winter coats and Tupperware boxes filled with targets and shooting supplies. I unzipped it, and the older men in the crowd smiled as if they had discovered an old friend. There sat my dad's 1938 Benjamin air pistol, its brass sheen somewhat dulled with patina, but otherwise in working condition.

Confident the brass wheezer would fire, I gave the forepiece pump handle a good ten pumps. Even with the paper bull's-eye target only ten meters distant, I had no idea if the pellets would even be close to the black. The antique went "pap!" five times as I fired, and I reeled back the target to my firing position. I was stunned to find all five shots not only on the paper but fairly well grouped in a cluster at about nine o'clock next to the black bull. All the shots, however, were keyholed, showing the pellets' profiles in the paper, which meant they had tumbled at some point in their flight, making the gun thoroughly unsuitable for serious target practice. But I was content that the old antique still had bite.

The club had guns to loan to beginners, and I tried one of the pistols that used a preloaded cylinder of compressed air, which released a consistently metered amount of air for each shot. The construction of the handgun reminded me of the free pistols designed by Hammerli for international slow-fire shooting at the Olympics. Its sight radius (distance between front and rear sights) was long, and the grip "gripped" my hand with a thumb shelf and index finger groove to the trigger. The members also gave me some unoxidized new target pellets, and I began putting shots downrange.

On subsequent nights I had a chance to use the club's loaner air rifle as well. This rifle was also built along international competition lines not unlike the Anschütz and Walther Olympic guns with laminated stocks, adjustable at every touch point. I found out that no competition-grade air rifles are made in the United States, and there were no stores that sold competition air gun supplies in the Chicagoland area. The only rifles and pistols available are the casual plinking and small-game hunting type made by Gamo, Daisy, Crosman, and Beeman, along with new models by Winchester and Ruger. Most of these are spring-piston designs.

I had the opportunity to teach kids marksmanship at a weekend field day for conservation-minded families. Shooting from under a marquee tent at distant balloons, the kids each got three shots. The Gamo rifles were perfect and easy to reload, breaking the barrel down at a forestock hinge to reveal the pellet breech and cock the spring piston. The accuracy was good enough to take advantage of a 3–9X telescopic sight with crosshairs. Everyone had a ball. That spark of accomplishment was there, together with the understanding that the sport of shooting was not as easy as it appeared.

Back at the air gun club, which taught international competition–style shooting, I discovered a problem. Each night I had no idea if I could get my hands on the rifle to practice, or if I would have to settle for one of the two pistols. All the members owned their own equipment, and the focus of the club was on the young men and women who were, apparently, students at the academy.

In order to have meaningful practice, the sights have to be set for the shooter's hold on the ten-meter target. To advance up through the NRA qualification system, target scores are added up. Borrowed rifles have to be sighted in each time they are fired. The only solution to improving with practice is to buy your own rifle and shooting equipment.

The catch-22 here is cost. For anyone who is serious enough to commit to considerable practice at the international level of competition or who is working up through NRA qualifications, expect to lay out about $3,500 for a decent Anschütz, Beeman, or Walther rifle that is fully adjustable to your body type. Add to that another $300–$400 for a shooting coat with appropriate pads and "hard back" for long hours of support. You will also need carry cases, slings, and a floor stand with offhand spotting scope and rifle rest for offhand shooting. You can be knocking on $5,000 to propel a .177 lead pellet ten meters.

The people at the club were very nice and helpful when asked, and yet I was still using borrowed gear. My groups were tightening up, but I had more fun popping distant balloons with that Gamo spring-piston rifle costing less than $300. In the end, I had to walk away from the international set.

I understand the sport is growing. It is now a regular Olympic event, but I don't have that kind of cash to spread around learning something new. Not when I can take down my Winchester 52C, feel that glass-slick action as I slide in a .22 rimfire match cartridge, and lock the bolt into place. Not when I can tuck that stock into the current edition of my anatomy, smell the linseed oil rubbed into the walnut wood, and bring that sight into alignment with my target. I can still hear Doc Meissner whispering, "Window . . . window . . . any time now . . ." from his spotting scope bench behind the firing line. God, I love it so.

Having reached the modern equivalents of the single-shot ancestors of our sport, there only remain the zero-shot zealots in our American gun culture. These would be the collectors, to whom we owe the preservation of our traditions that have a habit of resurrecting and resuscitating through modern updates of good ideas. Gun collector shows are continually filling hotel conference rooms, county fairgrounds, and exhibition halls throughout the country.

Before proceeding here, understand that this discussion is about museum-quality antique guns, both military and civilian, of all ignition types, calibers, and patent concepts. We are not discussing the "gun shows" heavily sponsored by gunmakers' reps and independent dealers working our of their car trunks, attended by persons who believe owning lots of guns is a collection or frequented by the survivalist crowd touting "strictly legal" assault-type weapons and accompanying accessories.

Having the opportunity to see the collections of firearms lovingly appreciated by their owners and displayed as tributes to American craftsmanship, artistry, and mechanical innovation is a treat for both shooters and other collectors. Restoration of the original gun is often a long and difficult process not unlike restoring a classic automobile. But anyone who has had Granddad's trap door .45-70 Springfield looking like it just came out of the arsenal crate can appreciate the labors and the knowledge required to restore a fine old gun.

Just about all my guns are old. Even my best rifle—the Winchester 52C—is now fifty-five years old. I won't go into my nickel-plated 1890 Winchester with a tang sight or my Smith & Wesson 1909 Hand Ejector, Military & Police, Third Change, Target Model 10, .38 Special revolver in 100 percent nickel plate, because they've already been mentioned. I've even used up my grandfather's .32 Short Iver Johnson and the Quackenbuch-Herkimmer bicycle rifle with collapsible wire stock, wire grip, and ten-inch barrel with a single-shot, swing-out breech. Keeping them preserved and talking about them is as much fun as shooting them. They invariably draw other shooters to my bench wherever I shoot, and that's half the fun of target shooting at public ranges: swapping jargon and knowledge with other shooters.

I very recently talked my arm-candy partner into accompanying me to a Lake County Fairgrounds expedition as "research" for this book. An antique gun collectors association was sponsoring a show—a modest 150 tables—of old firearms, from matchlocks to a hand-built, semiautomatic, .22 caliber replica of a Thompson submachine gun. Janet gamely listened with Oscar nomination–quality interest as I chatted with collectors about salient points concerning their displayed hardware. "Where did the wheel lock shooter stow the spanner needed to wind the lock's spring?" "On a loop of cord around his neck." "That's a fine collection of Savage rifles. What got you into collecting that particular gun?" "I bought one years ago and now I have 450 more at home."

My legs went out before we got to all 150 tables, but the sheer American know-how and ingenuity behind those historical firearms was worth the trip to the fairgrounds. And Janet might be remembering some of the antique hardware as she watches me lug flats of begonias, snapdragons, petunias, and spikes from our car to the backyard's borders and then start transporting sacks of mulch to the front-yard shrubs. Every love has its price.

Instead of maundering on about soulful pleasures of owning and collecting old guns, I will present two cautionary tales. These stories are for anyone who has unearthed an antique firearm from a back-closet hatbox or from behind a couple of mashie or niblick golf clubs with bamboo shafts. The first story has nothing to do with old guns but starts with an old man who owned an old gun and fought in an old war.

The Civil War was churning toward its final year when this middle-aged colonel of the New York infantry who had led his battalion of Union riflemen through a number of skirmishes and a few major battles saw his luck suddenly change. Gen. George Meade (of Gettysburg fame) had personally decorated him. He had been a part of so many sharp and nasty encounters, emerging with wounds and returning to duty so often, that the War Department sympathetically plucked him out of the forward lines and sat him at a desk to work out his enlistment in honorable paper shuffling. He promptly caught the measles and died early in 1865.

Move forward eighty-eight years to an old suitcase full of yellowing letters, fading photographs, and disappearing memories rising like champagne bubbles to burst and leave behind the scent of violets. A wizened grandmother explained the contents of a fiberboard suitcase smelling of garage mold to her daughter. The grandmother fished around in the string- and ribbon-tied bundles until she withdrew a large, fragile-looking envelope and handed it to her grandson.

"I know you're interested in history and the Civil War," she said. "This man was my great uncle."

Inside the envelope, the grandson found the colonel's mustering-out papers presented to his widow along with his death certificate so she could collect his pension from the government. The envelope, yellowed with age, had been mailed to her and bore her address in fine copper point script. It also bore the government logo, and the flap had been sealed with blue wax imprinted with a brass signet. The cancellation on the large, pink stamp in the upper right corner was a signature frank, not a postmaster's hand stamp.

The young grandson also collected stamps. He carefully removed the handwritten forms in the envelope, admired the pink 1865 postage stamp, and then took a pair of scissors and cut the stamp from the envelope, leaving a 2x1–inch hole in a corner of the antique paper. In three strokes the value of that stamp as part of the Civil War muster-out papers was reduced by three-quarters. A piercing shriek went through the world's philatelic force.

The horror of that savage piece of vandalism has followed the grandson for more than fifty years. Its wanton and ignorant brutality was trumped, however, two years later. Any actual gun collectors may want to skip reading this part.

Two years after fellow philatelists were informed of his bloody work, a friend who owned a 10-gauge, thirty-inch-barrel Greener goose gun with exposed hammers dating from the late nineteenth century visited the young man. The double barrels were brown and the wood dark with age, its checkering smoothed by years of use. The actions of both hammers were stiff with congealed grease. The friend asked if the grandson could "fix it up." The shotgun looked awful, but the lad accepted the challenge.

Separating the gun into its component parts, the neophyte gun restorer dunked them in rust remover held in a clever tank made from an old roof gutter sealed at the ends to accommodate their thirty-inch length. The locks were left to simmer in a bath of gasoline to dissolve the grease, and the stock's eroded furniture was also removed from the wood and left to soak in a bath of rust remover. While the metal parts bubbled and hissed, the boy set to work with coarse-grit sandpaper on the wooden stock that had turned dark brown where decades of cheeks had rested and rough hands had gripped. In between brisk rubbings with the sandpaper, the wood was allowed to soak, causing dents and scars to swell and rise for removal. When he was finished, the stock, grip, and slender forestock were smooth as a baby's bottom, though some of the hand checkering had to be sacrificed to get rid of those pesky dents, discolorations, and scratches.

Next, the barrels were dried off, revealing a curious spiral pattern in the steel that the boy had never seen before. Some of the brown from the "rust" remained, and he used a handful of steel wool to remove the last vestiges of the stains. In a few days, the twin 10-gauge tubes glistened brightly.

Locks, hammers, and the breech block with its twin triggers were all expunged of antique grease and freshened up with a buff of fine-grit emery paper to remove scratches and burrs but not too much of the hand-chased engraving. To finish the job, a cold chemical bluing agent was purchased and mixed, and the metal pieces were all submerged in a bath of the stuff. While the pieces took on their new finish, the wooden stock received two coats of Minwax walnut stain and two thinned coats of varnish for a nice hard shine.

The first hint that the young restorer may have erred came when the barrels arose from the bluing soup and dried to the rainbow sheen of an offshore oil spill. In a panic, he fled to the library—where he should have gone before starting the adventure—and in a well-thumbed book on hobby gunsmithing discovered the terms "browning" and "Damascus steel." Sinking into chilled doldrums reminiscent of his Civil War stamp episode, our hero discovered that the curious curly marks on the barrels were caused by two types of steel being wound around a mandrel and welded to form a solid tube, creating a Damascus steel barrel. The "rust" on the tubes was actually a prized patina called browning created by the nineteenth-century gunsmith to prevent surface rust and hold oil.

When all the parts of the grand old Greener goose gun were fitted together, the result was Shotgun Bling. It looked like the gun had been wrapped in oily plastic wrap. The barrels appeared radiantly iridescent, and he could see himself in the wooden stock. Two days later, when he had worked up enough courage to return the vandalized antique to his friend, he slid the shotgun into one of his rifle cases for the trip. When he was finished, he noticed the palms of both hands were oil-slick blue. Would the humiliation never end?

I submit these two cautionary tales to readers who may one day come across a similar antique restoration situation. If any antique-owning friend asks you for a "favor" to "touch up" his old gun, run away. If it is your gun, give it to a professional. Spend a buck. Shouldering the burden of even one historical botch is a soul-sucking experience. Two such experiences can age a person. Like living with a twelve-foot tapeworm, it colors your days.

Epilogue: One good thing did come of that Greener horror. The owner of the shotgun was told—after he stopped throwing furniture at the young gun destroyer—that loading a modern 10-gauge load into the nineteenth-century Damascus steel breeches and tripping the triggers would probably remove his head from his shoulders. That revelation alone is probably responsible for the young gun destroyer reaching his adult years without that shotgun being a permanent part of his anatomy.

And finally, we come to the elephant in the room, the arrival of the assault rifle mythology in America's gun culture. Want to watch a real barroom brawl between guys with $100 haircuts and shiny suits, wearing holstered BlackBerrys, and a bunch of overweight guys in plaid shirts, suspenders, and L.L. Bean "comfort-fit" jeans wearing holstered Glock nines? Just walk into the room carrying a fully tricked-out AR-15 clone sporting a pair of thirty-round banana magazines of 5.56 ammo locked together and drop it on the nearest table. The suits will fight to have it bagged, tagged, and dumped in the nearest deep body of water. The plaids will try to cock it, lock it, and switch on the laser sight.

Neither side will be successful, because this is a metaphor on stereotyping. There are guys who wear suits and use BlackBerrys who spend part of their weekend blasting a crate of sporting clays with their favorite over-and-under shotgun. There are men in plaid who consider a gun to be a curiosity that belongs in a museum next to the sword and the battle-ax. Simplistic profiling is the tool of the extremist, because it makes his job easier. You could label the NRA as a nest of conservative Republican political lobbyists who spend all their time preaching to the choir, but that's not (entirely) true. If all mouth-breathing whack-jobs wore tinfoil hats, it would be easier to speak calmly to them and soften their fevered load, but irrationality does not wear a scarlet letter. In the matter of what has been dumped in our laps as the only two paths of rational gun ownership resolution, the desk-pounding, name-calling, self-styled ideologues look like everyone else.

For the shooting sportsmen who have had their pleasant pastime, their sporting challenge, and their individual pursuit hijacked by self-serving ideologues, some of the fun has been leeched out. If you're not on our side of the line, you're not a patriot. If you don't march with us beneath our signs and shout into our megaphones, you vote for murder and violence. Those conflicting extremes come to a head with the black AR-15–clone rifle.

Before pressing on, let me assure you I'm not a fan of the AR-15. To me, a fine rifle begins with a beautifully figured piece of wood. But that's just me. Every gunmaker who can afford the computer-controlled machines that screw, carve, drill, rout, shave, pierce, and spit out the pieces that bolt, dovetail, fasten, and finally assemble into these plumbers' nightmares is making big money. This is permitted in capitalism. God bless the company that can build a better consumer trap and make a buck. The problem here is not the gun, though it is ugly as sin. It is the marketing, the message, and the perceived value to the buyer.

Here is another cautionary tale—but this one does not bring tears to the eyes like that last one about the old-timey shotgun turned into a lollipop by an ignorant lad who remains nameless. I worked for Motorola Electronics in the 1970s, turning out photography and video and writing for their marketing services department. Those were the days of big cars and big cigars when Motorola owned the two-way communications market. All the department managers were sleek in white shirts with too-tight collars from three martini lunches and tee times at exclusive clubs with golf cart girls delivering booze to the greens. The mobile phone was in the design shop waiting to be hatched in 1983, the pager was a reality, and a new communications opportunity was rising up from the likes of Radio Shack and Cobra. Everybody wanted a CB radio for his or her car and a base station for their home.

Citizens band radio was the cell phone of the 1970s. Its efficiency was driven by five watts of broadcast power and its forty channels allotted by the FCC. The two-way radio had a range of only a few miles if the owner obeyed the rules, but an amped up power supply extended its reach far beyond legal limits. Tinkering with CB radio became a hobby, like brewing your own beer in the basement during Prohibition. Its popularity unleashed a flood of magazines, books, and companies cranking out the fairly simple electronics.

Motorola decided to build a CB car radio, basing its success on the company's leadership in the two-way radio market and the sophistication of its engineering prowess. The resulting radio was state of the art. Once installed with an antenna, all the owner had to do was turn it on, select the channel, and key the microphone. The sleek box had a virtually automated control system and a small footprint beneath the car's dash. Motorola could not give the radio away.

The company, in the throes of its massive marketing ego trip, had ignored the ancient sales axiom "Give the people what they want." Motorola gave them what they should want. A look at the market showed that Americans wanted their CB radios to be studded with dials, levers, buttons, and plug-in receptacles. The case should look like it met military specifications ("MilSpecs") for endurance and had quick-release handles on it and docking bays for a range of accessories, including auxiliary speakers and plug receptacles for strange boxes located in the car trunk that hummed and ran hot enough to fry an egg when the broadcast attenuation extender slide switch was all the way forward. If it didn't look like it should be bolted to the front deck of an armored personnel carrier, it wasn't a CB.

The successful approach to consumer electronics design took a cue from Hollywood—or at least Stanley Kubrick when he launched *2001: A Space Odyssey* in 1968. Until that time, 1950s and 1960s movie spaceships looked all sleek and pointy—like a spitzer bullet but with tail fins. Kubrick's rocket to Jupiter looked like something built out in a weightless environment, constructed at a space station for utility without a cosmetic girder in its body. Consumer electronics designers felt a tremble in the force and the guiding hand of a new consumer trend.

This goes to show how far ahead of his time Eugene Stoner was when he cobbled together the combat rifle that only a mother could love. Kiss the wood good-bye. Its weight-adding bulk only belonged in a quaint exhibition drill platoon—something to slap, something to twirl. Even the classic Mauser bolt-action rifles and pump/autoloader shotguns phased out wood for polymer and polycarbon (the fancy words for plastic) stocks.

The result of the AR-15 military assault rifle, following a natural path of iterations downsized to the current M4 and looking forward to even more unconventional designs, has been an accessory hound's wet dream: the civilian market version. As soon as these ex-military rifles started flying off the shelves when a Democratic congress headed by a liberal president took office, the gun advocates with the big megaphone in Washington knew they had done their job well. Fear was in the conservative saddle, and it was time to ride the horse.

An assault rifle ban had been passed by President Bill Clinton in 1994, but President Bush had let it expire. The NRA and the more rabid gun advocates, with teeth filed to points, went after members and legislators, claiming the antigunners were after all our semiautomatic rifles and shotguns. What's wrong with a bayonet lug on a hunting rifle? No telling what an uppity mule deer might do if only wounded. (If you can't put down a deer with one or two shots, shouldn't you be back practicing at the range rather than slapping in another thirty-round banana magazine?) Imagine a herd of buffalo marching through your neighborhood with signs and megaphones demanding peaceful prairies and better grazing land. You need real firepower to put those big critters in their place.

The assault rifle designed for combat soldiers and police tactical teams joined the flood of new handguns in the civilian market under the banner of self-defense. The self-styled antigun supporters—who, like the Volstead Act perpetrators, claimed to save America from its self-destruction—discovered a new demon. The AR-15–style firearm looked nasty and had terrible potential in the hands of criminals or the mentally unbalanced. Battalions of antigun survey gatherers were dispatched into the streets to ferret out information that used the assault rifle to legitimize their strangely skewed logic.

With both sides jumping up and down with clenched fists, the AR-15–type rifle is with us in a relentless profusion of cookie-cutter sameness, which has become an accepted pattern. In all honesty, the classic lines of the Winchester Model 70 rifle spawned a raft of imitators wedded to a "new and improved" take on the basic Mauser bolt action, a variety of stock barrel bedding techniques, and a plethora of trigger types. The fact that all the AR-15 clones look alike should not be held against them. To make a buck, you follow the winner to the bank. Watching each manufacturer try and distinguish what makes their AR-15 clone king of the hill is as much fun as watching large

American breweries try to convince American beer consumers that they can tell one "lite" lager from another in a blind test.

These rifles are called modular for a good reason. They update the premise of Eli Whitney, who showed John Adams and Thomas Jefferson how he could assemble muskets from random boxes of parts with just a screwdriver and proved the concept of unskilled labor used in mass production. Reading reviews of these clones in *American Rifleman* unearths such comments as "The ACR's construction and design are rugged and reliable, but they are not revolutionary. Most of the components and operating principles . . . are designs with proven histories."[14]

The designers of these rifles are masters of backward engineering—unsnapping a rifle to see what makes it tick and then adding enough small touches to an innovative trick be able to trumpet it as "new and improved." With the Bushmaster ACR rifle built for the military and police markets by Remington and the civilian model tested by Bushmaster, the most revolutionary feature is a quick-change barrel. Why do we imagine a home defender pausing to select an appropriate barrel depending on the size of the intruder? Quick-change barrels are great for machine guns, which tend to overheat in combat situations.

The ads for the civilian model state with authority, "The ACR (Adaptive Combat Rifle) rapidly changes to fit any mission. . . . In a world where survival of the fittest can mean surviving at all, no rifle is a better fit than the one-of-a-kind, all-new Bushmaster ACR." And the tested model can be yours for $3,031.

The same issue reviews the Colt LE6940 carbine, praising its "extensive parts commonality with the M4" and other parts that "follow the proven AR-15 pattern." This rifle is targeted at "Advanced Law Enforcement" use, and except for its seven-pound trigger pull, wobbly collapsible butt stock, and lack of a charging handle extension, it is a "lightweight and robust patrol rifle." If a civilian should happen to yearn for this weapon? Not to worry, they can buy the MT6400R "without a bayonet lug and a muzzle brake instead of a flash hider." All selling for $1,615.

The ads running through these magazines feature Stag Arms's M8 "next generation of piston carbines" for $1,145, and "the finest piston style AR on the market," the Les Baer Piston Rifle. "The Competition can stop trying" with the purchase of the .308 caliber Lewis Machine & Tool LM308MWS, the ad for which urges owners to use the rifle's "knock down, stop your assailant right now power."

The modular concept has also reached into the designs of precision long-range sniper rifles, which gunmakers are also touting for civilian use. Today these big-bore guns designed to take out light armor and as psychological warfare weapons, dropping enemy soldiers at incredible ranges or picking off insurgent after insurgent from a camouflaged location in urban combat situations, have found a civilian market. While long-range shooting is drawing advocates to its stringent regimen, they are well-heeled advocates. For example, the bolt-action Savage Model 110 BA firing the .338 Lapua goes for about $2,267 stripped (no sights, but with Picatinny rails to lard on the accessory scopes, night vision, etc.). It costs more than $100 to reload its five-shot magazine four times with factory ammo.

Like the Barrett line of .50 caliber rifles and its 98 Bravo model that also pushes out the .338 Lapua, the Savage is a combat sniper weapon to be fired from the prone position and weighs about fifteen pounds. The *American Rifleman* review of its mission-based minutiae includes the intense design brainwork that went into its muzzle brake that relieves recoil by venting gasses through a slotted muzzle extension.

While everyone sat around befuddled, some genius suggested that the bottom of the muzzle brake have the gas vents filled in solid. That way, when the gun shoots, the muzzle blast will not be vented down, blowing up dust ("marking") that gives away the position of the shooter. Machine gunners in WWII used to pee in front of their gun to hold the dust down, but that was then. Another brilliant bit of technical explanation that must make rivet-counters foam with delight is the fact that the bolt handle moves straight up and down. This keen bit of legerdemain is justified as maintaining the weapon's "perpendicularity." Oh, we want to play Scrabble with these people.

This is all good fun, and it is understood that these weapons are an economic necessity to keep the gunmakers in business. But there has to be some legitimate use for the semiautomatic civilian versions of combat rifles other than as very expensive toys to keep oiled and sit in the dark corner of the hall closet. Fortunately, the NRA and the gun companies came up with one good solution: the three-gun match. Caution: no slow-and-steady-wins-the-race bull's-eye paper punchers need apply unless they are ready to amp up their game.

The three-gun match requires a competitor to wield a semiautomatic pistol, a tactical shotgun (extended capacity magazine), and an AR-15–type rifle. The object of the three-gun competition is to hit—or "neutralize," in the military/SWAT lexicon—clay, steel, and paper targets in multiple stages, following a set course of fire. Best time with the most hits wins. Ranges vary from one vast stage for all three guns (some courses include an 800–1,000 yard sniper range) or separate ranges for each gun depending on the local geography.

One match, the Superstition Mountain Mystery 3-Gun (SMM3G), began with 67 shooters in 1996 and grew to 275 shooters in 2010. An even earlier three-gun match would be the SOF (*Soldier of Fortune*) match held in Las Vegas. That competition only permitted military or SWAT standard-issue weapons and did not allow International Practical Shooting Confederation (IPSC) race guns.

These semiautomatic race pistols are the equivalent of NASCAR race cars—hand built to the customer's directions or custom designs that have been tweaked for speed and accuracy with special sights, extended magazines, special triggers, and the use of exotic metals, and able to withstand the rapid fire that chews through a magazine of cartridges many times in a single competition. In most three-gun matches, an open category permits anything technology will allow to put rounds downrange.

These matches are exciting to watch as shooters blaze away against the clock in all three disciplines. It is a perfect test of reflexes, shooting skill, and nerves when the adrenaline starts squirting out your ears. Sponsors flock to these shoots with repair facilities, expert consultants, and their own paid shooters, who travel from shoot to shoot, piling up championship points for bragging rights and winning cash prizes that range up to the six figures. At the SMM3G, the sponsors included DPMS Firearms, FNH USA, LaRue Tactical, Bushmaster, Patriot Ordnance Factory, JP Rifles, Dillon Precision, Samson Manufacturing, Nordic Components, Trijicon, and SureFire. Of the group that ponied up over $175,000 in prize money, Bushmaster is the largest and DPMS is the second-largest manufacturer of AR-15–type rifles.

Among American spectator sports, which are usually played with either a stick, a ball, or both, three-gun competitions rank somewhere below curling, Hacky Sack, or lawn darts. Their only public airing comes on the Outdoor Channel with once-a-week half-hours on a couple of *Shooting USA* gun sport shows. Every commentary by the announcers sounds like watching a NASCAR

Chevy roll past showing off its polished blanket of sponsor logos—one loving, tightly edited advertorial. Only the aficionados of the sport are immersed in its culture, as if to justify the huge sack of money laid out to equip themselves for a decent showing at the firing line.

Thousands of spectators used to show up and make a picnic afternoon at Creedmoor and Sea Girt and other long ranges to watch our great-grandfathers lie on their backs with Sharps, Ballard, and Remington rifles, lobbing .50 caliber slugs at distant iron targets, straining to listen for the successful "gong!" announcing a hit. True, in that epoch, six-day bicycle races were considered riveting spectacles. Today's audiences demand a bit more action. Go watch a three-gun match where the winning score may come down to a final round where the target zips across a narrow space and the shooter draws and whangs away six shots in six seconds for the championship. Or imagine the roar of the crowd as a shooter rips a clip of .45 ACP slugs into a flock of clanging steel plates, then it's Knees Up Mother Brown to the next-door shotgun range where he hand-pumps a blitz of pellets into a half-dozen swinging discs and finally dives down behind a long-range rifle to put five rounds eight hundred yards downrange into targets that explode when hit just before cardiac arrest sets in and the clock goes "ding!"

If only there could be a national following of these matches, with scores appearing in the newspaper and online sports pages. But it appears too many people are too busy shouting at each other to channel their energies elsewhere. "Enemies" must be vanquished rather than patrons and viewers won over.

An article on the *American Rifleman* website offers up interesting specs concerning gun use and justification. One of the opening paragraphs leads, "The study, 'Shooting Sports Participation Survey in the United States in 2009' was conducted for NSSF by Responsive Management through a random digit dialing telephone survey of 8,204 U.S. residents ages 18 and older. . . . To avoid confusion, the term 'modern sporting rifle' was further defined as an AR-style rifle."

From there on, the "AR-style" rifle is referred to as "modern sporting rifle." This bit of charming obfuscation is justified by explaining the "AR" does not stand for "Assault Rifle" (boo, hiss), but for "ArmaLite Corporation," for whom Eugene Stoner worked when he cobbled together the first AR-15 modular combat rifle. Then why not "AL?" Okay, we all hear the thousands of tap-dancing feet in the background—sounds like a scene from *42nd Street* or *Top Hat*. If this substitution offends your sensibilities, imagine these semi-automatic appellations: "Garand Modern Sporting Rifle," "Thompson Modern Sporting Rifle," or "Kalashnikov Modern Sporting Rifle."

The study is further justified by Steve Sanetti, president of the National Shooting Sports Foundation, who states, "Those who want to ban these civilian sporting rifles simply because they look like military rifles must acknowledge after seeing this study that AR-style rifles are exceedingly popular with millions of Americans. These rifles are our industry's high-tech, cutting-edge product—rugged, accurate, versatile, fun to shoot and easily accessorized—and they're here to stay."

The survey with a "95 percent confidence level" said that 15 percent of the U.S. population, or 34.4 million people, went target shooting in 2009. In order to eliminate confusion in our use of this survey's findings, the term "modern sporting rifle" will be replaced with the term we've been using, "AR-15–type rifle" (remembering clearly what it doesn't mean). The survey says, "Users of [AR-15–type] rifles were most active nationally and also in every U.S. region."

To understand where these AR-15–type rifle shooters are located, the survey shows 25 percent come from small cities and towns, while the rest are scattered around nonfarm rural areas (25 percent), urban centers (19 percent), suburbs (16 percent), and farms or ranches (15 percent). The ages of 64 percent range from 18 to 44 years, and 86 percent are white, with five percent of AR-15–type rifle owners being African American or Hispanic/Latino. The majority are male (86 percent) with some female participation (14 percent), and 34 percent of the total had some college education. The number of people who shot an AR-15–type rifle in 2009 totaled 8,868,085. The survey concluded that 24,000,000 fired other kinds of rifles, and 22,000,000 shot handguns. The AR-15–type rifle shooters, however, were more active.[15]

In their combat mode (full-automatic and semiautomatic fire, capable of sporting a bayonet or a grenade launcher), they are very useful guns whose primary reason for existence is to keep troops and police alive in firefight situations. But these guns are feel-good pacifiers for the civilians out there who are terrified that a marching barrage of antigun laws and government shock troops are going to do what left Great Britain helpless and begging for small arms in World War II. They fear being herded into terrorist-guarded, liberal-run camps for patriot-dissident conservatives or being helpless to anarchy in the streets. For others—hopefully the majority—the AR-15–type rifle offers an exciting sport that amps up the sedate, somnambulist quality of the Camp Perry and other strictly bull's-eye target matches, which are designed only for the participants and not for spectators.

While the NRA built its reputation and membership base providing organization, administration, and standards for the Camp Perry and other matches, it has notched a piece of the action-firearms scene for itself. The Bianchi Cup is the NRA at its best. The course of fire originated as a law enforcement training match in 1979 by holster maker and former police officer John Bianchi, working with Ray Chapman, 1975 International Practical Shooting Confederation world champion. By 1984 the NRA took over the operation, modestly naming it the NRA Bianchi Cup (officially the National Action Pistol Championship).

For more than thirty years, the sequence of shooting events has not changed. It consists of four stages: practical, barricade, moving target, and falling steel plates that must be knocked down. In 2008 Doug Koenig took home the Bianchi Cup and $8,000 in total prize money. He was also the first competitor to achieve a perfect score of 1,490 points. This four-ring circus is great for spectators, as the shooters draw their holstered pistols, use a two-handed grip in standing and prone positions, and fire for both speed and accuracy against the clock.

Truthfully, we are captives of society, the officials we elected, the police we pay, and the ethnic and religious groups to whom we have committed our support. Gun ownership, once a casual acceptance of responsibility to enjoy the sport it provides and to cause no harm, has become a hot-button topic.

Going out the door every day with a handgun on your hip or in your purse means we have failed our children and our schools, and softened our moral backbone. We have slipped back a few steps in civilization. We've let greed and expediency overwhelm our political process. We've given in to fear. There are more than 200,000,000 guns in American hands. They are not going away. We are stuck with them as we are stuck with automobiles, politicians, and our own daily insecurities.

We are working to correct all of the above, but the guns are still the elephant in the room. The folks who believe in disposing of all guns without first disposing of the aberrations that lead to crime and racial hatred are delusional and should channel their energies to improving education and law enforcement, freeing up the courts, motivating our kids, and helping their neighbors in time of crisis. The NRA has managed to earn itself a reputation as an implacable gun lobby using patriotism as a club, while all these new gun owners are standing around with relatively few programs to learn about the many safe and challenging facets of the shooting sports.

In recent years, to its credit, the NRA has invested time in attempting to protect current rifle and pistol ranges that might be endangered by nearby housing and industrial development. For this purpose, it created the NRA Institute for Legislative Action. The job of this organization is to help defend shooting facilities against zoning and eminent domain lawsuits. Since 1994 their efforts have been successful in expanding range-protection laws from eight to forty-seven states. New facilities such as the Clark County Shooting Park near Las Vegas, are showplaces for work being done to increase multi-discipline shooting ranges to accommodate the growing number of gun owners. This facility offers rifle, pistol, and shotgun sports on a huge acreage that even allows target setups out to 1,200 yards. But not every state can commit 2,900 acres to shooting sports. A greater number of smaller ranges are needed that are accessible to urban populations and that offer instruction and safety programs as well.

Citizen groups and church organizations feared the spread of karate, tae kwon do, jujitsu, and other forms of martial arts because they taught people how to fight. These objections failed to consider the philosophical core of the martial arts' belief culture that taught self-confidence and self-control as goals for character building. The rigorous disciplines of shooting sports have the same objectives.

In trying to build a political base on fear and bullying, the NRA has created a false synergy between the needs of the military and police and those of the civilian population. A gun culture sold to the public on the efficient killing ability of semiautomatic replicas of AR-15 combat assault rifles and hidden handguns is an open door to feudal paranoia and an itchy, nervous society steeped in distrust.

For too many people, guns are scary must-have accessories acquired for all the wrong reasons. Packing a gun all day can push disagreements into confrontations and having to justify carrying a weapon, which often ends in tragedy. Welcome to the Wild West, say the critics.

But as American society has gunned up, murder rates and crime rates have gone down. Cities like Chicago, on the other hand, with a strict gun control law enacted in 1982 and virtually zero handgun tolerance, had a body count of 116 shooting deaths in the first five months of 2010. An estimate of 100,000 guns residing in Chicago homes was made in this same year, and the police have not pressed charges for violation of the gun ban on persons who have defended their families and property against armed thieves. City Hall attempted politically cynical buy-back programs, paying Chicagoans to turn in guns for $100 gift cards. These buy-back efforts always produced a pile of trash, and the gangs got money to buy ammunition.

Finally, on June 28, 2010, the U.S. Supreme Court extended gun rights to every state and city in the country by a 5–4 vote along liberal-conservative lines. This action extended the 2008 ruling that all American citizens have the right to own a firearm. The Chicago handgun ban was overturned. Mayor Richard M. Daley, who was convinced that guns lay at the heart of Chicago's high murder rate even with his gun ban in full effect, began various draconian schemes to make purchasing, owning, and firing a handgun as hard as possible for law-abiding citizens while not affecting the city's gang and criminal element one bit.

Handgun purchasers were required to pay $100 for the privilege every three years. They had to be fingerprinted, could only buy one gun a month, and could only have one gun accessible in the home. All others must be locked and secured out of sight. Each gun owner had to have one hour of handgun training and three hours of safety training for every gun purchased. As for the training and the buying, no gun-firing or training facilities were permitted in the city, nor were shops where handguns could be purchased.

This collection of ordinances had "PUNISH" written all over them. These kinds of laws have the same effect that the original gun ban had: noncompliance and legal overturning. The city hall acolytes went along with this charade so they could have their ward streets cleared of snow in the winter, their garbage picked up in the summer, and their building code variances greased through committee approvals. The main result was sales tax money from gun sales going to the near suburbs. Pistol ranges can flower along the city limits borders, where fees and taxes for gun training and shooting will go to the suburbs to improve their schools and their infrastructure. Chicago's tantrum is the suburbs' windfall, at least until, one by one, these legal obstructions are overturned by clearer heads and these lawmakers can turn their efforts to helping the neighborhoods and kids earn the self-respect they deserve. Other American cities, please take note.

Illinois is a schizophrenic state, divided into two warring cultures. The North is represented by Chicago, the stereotypical Big City, crime-ridden bully, and the South is where the Illinois, Mississippi, Wabash, and Ohio Rivers enclose a cartoon, brooding population of gun-toting rustics. The state capital in Springfield is awash in political hyperbole, polyester politicians hounded by flinty-eyed constituents, and sharply divided pro– and anti–gun control advocates. Even the state police have swung over to favoring "common-sense" gun carry permissions for law-abiding citizens. Being in the middle of the country, Illinois is representative of the issues Americans face and the messy business of geographically and culturally divided government.

The United States is a big country. It is a homogenized brew of mutts who have chosen to live in selected geographies alongside people who share local ideals and beliefs that have been shaped by history, ethnicity, education, and economic opportunity. We are generous in our habits but jealous of our perceived rights. History has shown countless examples of state governments tinkering with laws passed by their representatives elected to Washington. These attempts to skew the work of the government we elected is part of American DNA. Some of this fudging has led to better laws though compromise, while others have hurt our society, as with the civil rights confrontations of the 1960s.

On September 7, 2010, Mayor Daley announced he would not seek another term as mayor. He was the driving force behind Chicago's antifirearms stand, and his successor in 2011, Rahm Emanuel, faces the foaming lobbyists on both sides of the unfortunate delusion that Daley championed. Is it possible that Mayor Emanuel will be able to bridge the chasm created by these polarized factions and seek solutions that confront the actual problems?

So far, Emanuel's speeches, writings, and voting record have placed him firmly in the gun control camp. But, unlike Daley, he does not make a bogeyman of the average gun owner, just the criminal gun owner. He supports the assault rifle ban, which prohibits citizens from owning nineteen models of firearms defined by name including various semiautomatic rifles, pistols, and shotguns classified as "assault weapons" due to having combinations of features such as magazines and combat accessories.

Daley demanded hours of training as a prerequisite for owning a handgun—and then barred training facilities from the city. The most recent city council approved firearms ranges within Chicago city limits where respect for and skill with sporting and defense guns can be taught to all generations.

A minority of young people—fragments of the next generation, who will be running this country or at least shaping our future society—are trying to buy what respect they are denied in schools, at home, in the workplace, and in their drug-soaked neighborhoods at the business end of a firearm. Where should the city's priorities lie? How will the obligations and new responsibilities demanded of parents and politicians affect changes in our way of life? Will anarchy rule, or will a new civility and respect grow?

Two generations currently dominate the argument: the fearful who see guns as instruments of intimidation and death, assassins of presidents, killers of young men and women in law enforcement and the military, glorified and worshipped as brutal decision makers by the other generation. The other group believes that guns are the answer to the "threat" of government rule, to "enforcing" patriotism and propping up persons who received a lousy deal from life and look to even the score. In this vocabulary-ravaged battlefield, guns are the whipping boy or the crutch. Take your pick or see them for what they really are: inanimate objects, manipulated by the best and the worst of our human nature, to teach as well as destroy, to provide as well as take away. They are extensions of our technology that allow us to polish unique senses into skills of which we can be proud.

So, where are we? Is a gun culture that grew alongside our society, reflecting the best and the worst of our decisions, now considered all shot to hell? Do the antigun people turn the country into a giant gun black market? That is what could happen, just like Prohibition made drunks out of people who had never taken a drink. When the British first tried banning all guns a few centuries ago, the people's firearms went into dry wells, corncribs, and barn lofts. During the 1920s in the United States, for all the whiskey and beer cookers hissing and bubbling away, you could get a buzz just driving through some neighborhoods with the car windows open. All that failed experiment did was help fund organized crime in America, blind and kill a lot of incautious drinkers, cause many sober citizens to become alcoholics, and turn the Thompson submachine gun into a romantic icon. The Eighteenth Amendment was the only amendment to the Constitution ever to be overturned. Gun banners face the same inevitable outcome as long as shooting sports are lumped into the same mindset as the needs of the military and police.

I've spent a lot of time teaching art in high school and grammar school, teaching photography in Boys Clubs of America, teaching young men awaiting trial for felonies and disadvantaged kids how to shoot a rifle, and teaching soldiers marksmanship. I've enjoyed watching young people feel accomplishment in learning to do something well and earning the respect and admiration of their peers. Of all my teaching experience, the hours spent instructing courses in the shooting sports have given me the most feedback, because they reflect my own life. Teaching the discipline, the character-building regimen, and the need for practice to overcome natural variables and being a part of their success has been a grand lesson for me.

What are needed are larger venues to expand these lessons learned and grow shooting sports into, for want of a better name, a National Shooting Sports League. Create a positive application of shooting skills on a larger scale than the current club matches. Action pistol contests, three-gun matches, practical shooting events, Western shooting competitions, and trick shooting exhibitions are all spectator-friendly and highly visual, with dashes of drama thrown in. Tell me, is a shooting sports college scholarship too strange to consider? Why can't these sports be presented on the same scale as tennis, golf, or bowling in Olympic-style venues? And why not present them on network television?

On April 10, 1971, ABC broadcast the first flag-to-flag NASCAR race, the Greenville 200. Everyone feared empty grandstands because the race would be on TV. The Greenville-Pickens Speedway was jammed, and later *Wide World of Sports* began a long relationship with that "southern" sport to become a billion-dollar broadcast staple.[16] Granted, action pistol shooting is no careening, flame-belching stock car swapping paint down the home stretch, but exposing larger audiences to the masters of shooting sports has to create new role models for our next generations.

Impossible Shots has already migrated from the Outdoor Channel to the more mainstream History cable channel. In June 2010 History launched *Top Shot*, a show pitting two teams of shooters proficient in various disciplines from archery to pistol and long-distance rifle sports. Renewed into 2011, it is a decathlon-type competition both of skill with a variety of historical and contemporary guns and antique missile launchers and the ability of team members to support each other in the stress of combined-effort competition. Seeing and hearing targets that explode, shatter, and move, the audience experiences instant results and can feel the tension when there is a miss and feel the exhilaration of a perfect score.

Shooting USA on the Outdoor Channel sets the bar for a shooting sports magazine-type show featuring firearms, archery, impossible "trick" shots, and the latest technology. Jim Scoutten is a good host, comfortable in front of the camera and keeping a fair balance between sports shooting and "self-defense" regimens with guns-as-weapons touted by combat range owners and manufacturer-sponsored touring ammo burners. *Shooting USA* is two-thirds of what a great shooting show could be if the sport had a wider audience appeal.

The NRA should be a leader in popularizing televised shooting sports, but instead it offers *American Rifleman Television* and misses a great opportunity. Watching this show actually makes shooting and the study of firearms uninteresting. Its well-intentioned hosts and narrators are amateurs at communications and have that deer-in-the-headlights constipated style of delivery. A Toastmasters public speaking course should be mandatory for all the show's on-camera talent. Expertise is not enough. The stock music is ponderous, as are the CAP (cheap as possible) camera setups. Gratuitous field trips to manufacturers, many of which are also sponsors, produce boring looks at computer-driven machines splashing oil as they churn out parts assembled by workers on the assembly line over and over again. The interviews are softball affairs, along the line of, "Well, sir, what do you think of this new gun you are trying to sell?" Is the interviewee going to reply, "Frankly, it's a piece of shit, but just wait until we iron out the bugs in next year's model"? "I Have This Old Gun" is the most interesting feature, and the narrator sounds like a 1950s TV hair tonic salesman. Hang the suits in a closet, dump the seamless paper backgrounds, visit real shooters, and drop this educational format that went out with the 1960s.

What are my creds? I have fifteen years as a television and commercial video producer, director, and writer, creating programs that earned a long list of industry awards. The NRA show appeals to just enough members who feel compelled to watch, but any audience outside the very small niche of True Believers is put off by low-rent content selection, delivery, and production values. With the NRA's enthusiastic membership base, revenue streams, and gung-ho support of America's shooting sports tradition, it can do better, and with their resources, it should.

For too long, shooting has been narrowly equated with killing. That is why a disconnect is needed between the aspects of shooting as required by the military and law enforcement and the sporting skills practiced by millions of Americans. Create shooting programs at high school and college levels. Not one student was injured at South Shore High School when we had a .22 caliber competition shooting team. My two daughters and my son all learned to shoot in their early teens, and they learned safety and responsibility as well. I like to think those times spent on the range helped them move on to find paths of their own. I get to be the proud dad here because it is my book. Our oldest, Damienne, excelled at gymnastics and went on to compete in triathalons while becoming a successful businesswoman and world-class mom. Allison is an accomplished horsewoman and a project designer for McGraw-Hill. Collin is a teacher, film critic, and documentary filmmaker.

So how do we create that disconnect between peoples' squeamishness over guns as killing machines instead of sporting implements? Centuries of wars, violence, and crime involving firearms are hard to replace with a clean slate. However, a few former moonshine entrepreneurs did something similar with stock car racing. They gave kids and low-wage family men a place to race their hot cars for cash prizes instead of risking death or jail time trying to run corn whiskey past the cops and feds. Today, kids with engineering degrees are sitting behind the wheels of those expensive racers.

Is there a Wii trapshooting game with flying clay targets? Must video games glamorize bloody violence instead of sharpening eye-hand coordination with skill-based challenges rather than ripping the head off your adversary? Rifles, pistols, and shotguns are part of the American scene, and it is about time they joined the American lifestyle as challenging sports with rewarding outcomes.

Backing away from positions based on instilling fear is not easy, especially when the tub-thumping exaggerations have been successful in pitting "us" against "them." But creating a positive image of shooting sports on a large scale is one way to change the way people respect each others' rights and responsibilities in future generations. Maybe that's asking for Utopia. Maybe so, but there are smarter people than me who could make it happen.

I've got a lot less time ahead of me than I have behind me, and I'll keep going to the range as long as I can see past the end of the muzzle. I still get the same kick out of sliding that first cartridge into the breech as I did when I was twelve years old in that damp crawl space under Pat Brady's house. Now, though, I enjoy watching other people discover the fun and become trapped in the experience like a bug in amber. I take a friend of mine, Dave Kastner, who lives a few doors from me, out to the Illinois State Rifle Association range at Kankakee, Illinois—a great facility with shotgun, rifle, and pistol ranges. We always start at the shotgun trap range, and he has steadily improved with his younger, faster reflexes. Dave generally breaks more clay targets than I do now, but then I take him over to the hundred-meter rifle range and crush him on the bull's-eye targets. Dave, however, is probably the most relentless person I know. Eventually, he'll get better there too, but I have a half-century of practice behind me, so I can let that carry my performance for the time being.

As C. S. Lewis once observed, "Experience: that most brutal of teachers. But you learn my God do you learn."

That is the way it has been. The life experiences have always been harder, and only one shooting experience still brings a pang of regret. If you've read this far, you know which one it is. That's a pretty good average for any support system. I've found out a lot about my sport and myself as I've written this, which makes me even happier to have been a part of such rich traditions. Memoirs are ego trips, and if you're lucky you only have to do it once. After that everyone's heard your stories so you can, like the actor Charlton Heston, shut up, stand by the mantelpiece, and look like Moses.

APPENDIX A
National Shooting Sports League

Imagine opening the sports page of your local newspaper to read about how your city's NFL football team burned its hereditary rivals by a field goal just before the two-minute warning in the fourth quarter. Then on page three, the NHL hockey franchise blew its third in a row, unable to score on an empty net. Finally, you check the NSSL three-gun match competition, where your team won by six seconds, going clean on the shotgun and steel target handgun competitions before a cheering crowd.

Why not? Does a National Shooting Sports League have to be a fantasy in a country where the shooting scene is sanctioned and directed by so many organizations: Amateur Trapshooting Association, Civilian Marksmanship Program, Cowboy Mounted Shooting Association, National Muzzle Loading Rifle Association, National Rifle Association, National Skeet Shooting Association, National Sporting Clays Association, Single Action Shooting Society, USA Shooting (Olympics), United States Practical Shooting Association, AIM (Academics, Integrity, Marksmanship), Collegiate Shooting Sports Initiative, National 4-H Shooting Sports, Scholastic Clay Target Program, Scholastic Steel Challenge, and the Boy Scouts of America, to mention the most prominent.[1]

Shooting participation had been on a downhill decline since its peak of 24 million target shooters in 1993, dropping to 18 million in 2005. Much of this plummet had been attributed to creeping urbanization and lack of firearm's exposure to young people by veteran sportsmen as shooting facilities and training diminished.[2] However, during 2009, that number for target shooters jumped to 15 percent of the U.S. population, or roughly 34.4 million people firing on America's ranges.[3] Also take into account the millions of hunters licensed every year and the approximately 200 million firearms owned by American citizens. A National Shooting Sports League can appeal to a much wider audience than the niche events staged by these organizations for the participants. The competitions can be made more spectator friendly. Marketing must be aimed at building gun ownership motivation through the appeal of sporting skills rather than the fear of attack and menace that now fuels most of the gun industry advertising and political posturing.

Mastering any of the shooting sports is both character building in its rigor and in keeping with the longest sporting tradition in the United States. Demonstrating accuracy with a firearm has been a praiseworthy attribute since the Pilgrims stepped ashore. Today both sides of the gun ownership issue shout at each other while all that energy could be spent picking up the pieces of our sport and creating an NSSL that can stand next to any NFL, NBA, or NASCAR headline on any sports page in America.

APPENDIX B
Exhibition Shooters

People were scratching to get by after the 1920s rolled over into the 1930s and the Great Depression shut down the country's economic engine. With the Old West abandoned to the pages of pulp fiction by the turn of the century, only the daily headlines splashed with bootlegger gunfights and bank robberies kept firearms in the public eye. People needed diversions to lift their spirits. Flagpole sitters spent weeks perched high above city streets. Barnstorming pilots rolled and looped surplus World War I biplanes above cow pastures to draw a crowd and sell rides. Airplane and automobile races pushed these new technologies to their limits.

Shooting sports were no different. Ammunition and gun manufacturers fielded teams of trick shooters performing for crowds to show off rifle, pistol, and shotgun skills that harkened back to marksmanship feats of our ancestors. American patriotism showed in these gun masters' abilities to win out over seemingly impossible odds.

At the Lead Cube pistol range in South Dakota on August 20, 1932, Ed McGivern punched out five .38 caliber slugs into a group the size of a silver dollar in 45/100ths of a second, measured by an electric timer. And he did it *twice*. That sounds impossible until you see the film of the event, the target with the witnesses' signatures, and the timer's paper strip tape. During the Depression era, shooting exhibitions became a large audience draw, especially in rural communities where gun ownership was a fact of everyday life. Ammunition and gun manufacturers hit on the advertising truth that "showing is better than telling."

The synergy was a natural one. The gun and ammo makers provided the weapons and bullets, and the gun handlers perfected their trick shots and made the crowds forget for a couple of hours that they were broke so they would drop a half-dollar into a coffee can. It takes thousands of bullets to perfect certain tricks, and ammo costs money. There has to be some "show business" patter to go along with Mom shooting a cigarette out of Dad's mouth while Sis explodes clay targets with a shotgun and a mirror.

From 1901 to 1945, Adolph and Plinky Toepperwein (sponsored by Winchester) of San Antonio, Texas, were in great demand for their shooting skills. Capt. A. H. Hardy of Denver, Colorado, and Rush Razee, an exhibition shooter for Remington Arms, could both hold audiences of town and farm folks spellbound with shooting stunts. But one exhibition shooter stood out. He could do all the standard stunts: hitting disks on edge thrown into the air, hitting a dime in the air, and keeping a tin can bouncing in the sky with the shots from two revolvers. Ed McGivern had one specialty, though, that none of the other stunt shooters ever copied or equaled. He fired with incredible speed.

A Montana native, McGivern was hardly the tall, rangy gunslinger. He looked like an Idaho baking potato turned on end wearing a high-top sombrero. He would have looked at home taking tickets on a trolley or slicing a ham behind an apron at the corner butcher shop. But he preferred to teach police forces how to draw and shoot their revolvers when he wasn't entertaining crowds of admirers.

What made McGivern's performances even more incredible were his tools. Many exhibition shooters used the abrasive quality of toothpaste to polish the interior workings of their guns' mechanisms, worked with emery paper to smooth any friction spots to achieve slippery speed, or hand-loaded special ammunition to reduce recoil and improve accuracy. McGivern just opened a box. He used unmodified factory guns and ammo bought at the hardware store. His guns were mostly police revolvers: Smith & Wesson Military & Police models or Colt Official Police or Police Positives in .38 caliber. The ammo he fired was the same as in the boxes on the local hardware store shelf. Using out-of-the-box weapons and bullets showed that what he did was actually available to the cop who set his mind to shoot better and faster.

His feats also took the wind out of the sails of those competition target shooters who swore that thumb-cocking the revolver for every shot (single action) was the only way to achieve medal-winning accuracy. McGivern just pulled the trigger that rotated the cylinder and dropped the hammer (double action). Now, why couldn't anyone else repeat his five shots fired in two-fifths of a second? Chances are Ed had a pair of hands that could squeeze two grapefruits until dust came out. The secret of trigger control is a very firm grip so the index finger can move independently of the gripping action. The gun cannot "float" in the hand, nor can the trigger-squeezing action shift the handgrip, pulling the shots left or right.

The fact that McGivern was built like a fireplug gave him a low center of gravity when he leaned forward into the recoil of the revolver.[1] It is also a credit to the revolver manufacturers that their products could sustain that blurring speed over and over again. Today's high-speed competition and exhibition shooters such as Smith & Wesson revolver champion and speed record holder Jerry Miculek owe a lot to McGivern's pioneering work.

The Depression-era exhibition shooters and demonstrators continued the nineteenth-century tradition of Annie Oakley, A. H. Bogardus, Frank Butler, William Frank "Doc" Carver, and other marksmanship entertainers during a time when our spirits were dragging and we needed heroes. They were the down-to-earth shooting sport counterparts to pilot Amelia Earhart, race driver Barney Oldfield, and movie star Tom Mix. Rivalries among shooting stars were legendary, drawing large crowds to trick shot matches such as the twenty-five shotgun matches between Bogardus and Carver over two months in 1883 to prove who was top gun. Carver won nineteen of the competitions.

Exhibition shooters have carried over into the modern era. Bob and Becky Munden, like the Toepperweins, do a husband-and-wife act, performing either with blank ammunition showing fast shooting or with live ammunition, if a range or safe open field is available. Munden claims to be the fastest living quick-draw-and-shoot champion and has broken some of Ed McGivern's old records. Herb Parsons puts on a good show, helped at times by his young son, but some of his records, like shooting thousands of two-inch square wood blocks tossed in the air without a miss, do not suggest that the audience hung around after the first two or three days. Spectators drifted away, but agonizing curiosity brought them back to check the tally and maybe be there when he finally missed. John Huffer and Tom Frye did the same wood block routine with .22 rifles continually reloaded by assistants.

All these shooters could cut a playing card edge-on with a bullet or drill a dime thrown in the air. With a shotgun, Parsons broke seven clay targets that he threw into the air. Tom Knapp, an exhibition shooter who fires fifty thousand shells a year, came along and busted eight with one toss. And so it goes. Going back to William Tell popping an apple off his son's head with a crossbow, there was probably some jasper who came along later and tried the trick with a walnut. Another truth is their ability to draw a crowd, because these grassroots pistol, rifle, and shotgun crack shots are pretty much just folks like us.

Exhibition shooters like Knapp and Miculek work crowds of five hundred men, women, and kids. Their skills, plus many fast-draw and Western shooters, have regenerated the game. Television has grown their audience with cable TV shows such as *Impossible Shots* and *Extreme Marksmen*. These shooters are all sponsored by the gun industry, and their ability to draw families to their shows is more valuable than advertisements in gun magazines that draw mostly male readers. Family shooting teams like the Topperweins and, in the next generation, the Mundens open up shooting to a more varied audience.

Shooting sports need more skill spectacles to lift firearms' appeal beyond their centuries of use as weapons.

APPENDIX C
Hitting the Target

America's gun culture is based on one result guided by both style and technology—hitting the target. Everything else is style and technology. To loose a projectile from one location to arrive at another location with sufficient affect to satisfy the need for the action is about all anyone can expect. The trick is to predict the point of arrival to produce a maximum result. Back when a firearm was little more than a lethal plumbing project propelling something like a stove bolt through armor designed to fend off sword thrusts, many of the most primitive matchlocks were aimed using a sighting aid. As the aiming devices and schooling in their use became more sophisticated, the firearm's efficiency increased.

Shooting is all a matter of alignments, and firearms are designed to aid the human body to configure itself, support the mechanism, successfully touch off a round, and guide it toward the chosen target. While some aiming devices are an integral part of the shooting process, others are essentially window dressing. The cap-and-ball percussion pistol used to assassinate President Abraham Lincoln was only six inches long and had a three-inch barrel, and yet the designers gave the barrel top a few licks with a file to produce a notch rear sight and cut a mortise slot above the muzzle to tap in a blade front sight. Affixing some form of sight to a firearm suggested a certain cachet, a qualification that the piece was capable of producing a degree of precision marksmanship.

The evolution of the firearm sight says as much about the users as it does the technology employed. The earliest gunpowder weapons were shock tools whose bark and flaming display were as important—probably more important—than the missiles they propelled. Aiming was a group effort. The gun made a splendid club after its discharge, or a blade could be plugged into the still smoking muzzle for close stabbing work. The musketeers of Europe waded into conflict draped with bandoleers of preloaded powder charges, coils of slow-burning cord impregnated with saltpeter, and sacks of lead balls. They moved and fired as a body, thrusting the matchlocks at the enemy like spears, bracing against the resounding slam of recoil, muzzle blast of flame, and billow of smoke.

An aiming device added to an early firearm reflected the conceit of the gunsmith who built the weapon or the order of the wealthy gun purchaser. It suggested that every element of the gun was correctly assembled and aligned, and if the shooter used the sight correctly, the distant target should be accurately struck. This, of course, was not always true. However, simple notch-and-blade open sights are found on matchlocks dating back to the sixteenth century and even more so on the expensive and better-constructed wheel locks enjoyed by sporting royalty.[1]

The wheel lock's use of flint gripped in a doghead striking against a rotating wheel producing sparks to ignite powder in the flash pan led to the simpler but more efficient flintlock. When coupled with the rifled barrel introduced from Europe and applied in the American colonies to the Pennsylvania or Kentucky long rifle, the flintlock muzzle-loader finally made an accurate sight useful. The eastern settlements in the Appalachian Mountains teemed with wild game, and a good rifle fed the families until enough domestic livestock became available.

The military continued to be mired in the volley-fire mob-action shooting that dominated the eighteenth-century battlefield, but during the American Revolution, the success of hunters shooting the accurate rifles instead of smoothbore muskets seeped into the consciousness of many field-grade colonial officers. After the British officers and sergeants were shot, their subordinates lost direction, and whole units fell apart. Using Virginia "long shirts" with their rifles sighted out to two hundred yards, aimed fire was directed at individual, tactical targets. British officers began tumbling from their saddles, and noncoms pitched over dead before the distant shot was heard. The British countered these murderous assassinations—which is how the Euro - peans characterized the surgical attacks—with their own sharpshooters. The Hessian Jaegers were accurate hunting rifles in competent hands, as were the British Ferguson breechloading flintlocks.[2]

While the sharpshooting rifleman was held in esteem in civilian life where the turkey shoot or target shoot for a prize was a village entertainment, the military saw the skill differently. Among the officers, war was still a gentleman's conflict where fair play was a chivalrous standard. Sending skilled snipers out to kill specific men with long-range shots—murdering the target from a hiding place—was distasteful. Whenever a sniper was captured alive, they were often treated like criminals and executed with bayonets.

War was and remains a dirty business. When the average colonial was discovered to be a mediocre shot, the army gave him buckshot-and-ball ammunition to spray more lead among the enemy lines. When American officers and sergeants were still learning their trade under fire, militia snipers with rifles were sent in to shoot experienced British officers and sergeants to level the playing field. Considering the conventions of the time, both acts were considered war crimes, but both sides were guilty of combat brutalities. The use of shotguns and snipers with sighted rifles helped Americans win a country of their own.

Eighty years after the British ran out of money, patience, and public support for their colonial war and sailed away, Americans took a shot at destroying the country with a first-class civil war. This time they had even better tools to get the job done: the steam frigate, the Dahlgren breechloading cannon, the ironclad warship, giant mortars, the railroad, the telegraph, and the rifled musket.

At last, the Springfield Model 1861 .58 caliber rifled musket was available to all Union troops. It was a percussion-fired muzzle-loader, but its rifling gave it long-range accuracy. Mounted on the barrel top was a graduated, open notch sight with flip-up leaves for one hundred–, three hundred–, and five hundred–yard ranges. There was no windage adjustment to shift the sight left or right to accommodate breezes blowing across the bullet's path, but a good rifleman using a Kentucky windage guess could make a long-range hit. To the narrowly focused military, of course, these muskets only meant they could begin their unsighted volley fire from a greater distance. Napoleon's dicta were still taught at West Point.

The Confederacy's soldiers shouldered the Enfield .577 rifled musket, which could also fire the Union .58 caliber Minié ball until the bore became too fouled and had to be cleaned. They also used the British Whitworth rifle, which mounted a three-power refractor telescopic sight that recorded kills on

Union officers at ranges close to eight hundred yards. Besides the scope sight, the rifle employed a twisted hexagonal bore that fired a similarly shaped .45 caliber bullet. That combination raised the weapon's effective range to fifteen hundred yards.

The Union army employed its own special rifle for trained snipers. It was built by J. F. Brown of Haverhill, Massachusetts, as a single-shot, percussion weapon with a thirty-two-inch octagonal barrel that fired a .45 caliber bullet, The sight, developed by L. M. Amidon of Vermont, was a telescopic system as long as the barrel, mounted near the fore end and rear end with controls back by the shooter. Another Union sniper gun was a fifteen-pound rifle designed by Edwin Wesson. This "bench gun" had a full-length telescope that allowed accurate shots out to unheard of ranges.

But the champion of Civil War–era long-range hits on a distant target went to an Englishman in 1865. William E. Metford and Sir Henry Halford built a .50 caliber telescope-sighted rifle that weighed about fifteen pounds and fired a 700-grain bullet ahead of a charge of 150 grains of powder. The great chunk of lead traveled two thousand yards to be the only hit on the 6-inch square target fired at Wimbledon that year.[3]

The technology developed during the Civil War added considerable precision to the industry of turning soldiers into casualties. No invention did more to polish the luster of this achievement than the self-contained brass-or-copper-encased cartridge. Finally, the lead bullet, gunpowder propellant charge, and ignition primer were simply plugged into the rifle or pistol and fired out the barrel. One major result of this invention was consistency. Until cartridges arrived, each shot was at the mercy of the gun owner's ability to properly load all the components into the rifle the same way each time—often under extreme stress and bad weather conditions. Following the battle of Gettysburg in early July 1863, some rifles were collected from the battlefield with as many as ten loads jammed down their barrels. In the panic of facing a charging enemy, soldiers had loaded and fired, loaded again, and pulled the trigger without putting a new percussion cap on its nipple to discharge the weapon.

However, in that same battle during its first day, dismounted U.S. cavalry under Brig. Gen. John Buford fought a successful retreat against a much larger Confederate force through the town of Gettysburg. The Union troopers kept up their firepower with the Sharps .52 caliber carbine. This short-barreled weapon was a transition gun between the muzzle-loader and the cartridge repeater. It loaded from the breech but used a paper cartridge, which had its end snipped off by the closing breechblock and was ignited by a separate percussion cap. The Sharps could fire up to five shots a minute, compared to three for the Confederate muzzle-loaders in competent hands. The later Spencer repeaters issued as rifles and carbines gave a soldier seven shots loaded into a tube in the gun's butt

The end of the war left the country flooded with lethal weapons and with men to whom life was cheap and land to the west was wide open with opportunity. Helped along by the evolving industrial age of mass production, assembly lines, and an endless stream of migrant workers to work the simple machines, gun manufacturers had cranked out tens of thousands of guns of all types. Now, they had to face the usual dumping of military stockpiles into the civilian market. The government arsenals began converting the Springfield 1863 muzzle-loader rifles into breechloading, "trapdoor," single-shot weapons firing the .45-70 cartridges. After Smith & Wesson came cap-and-ball revolvers made by Colt and Remington, who converted their cylinders to fire fixed ammunition and began designing new guns around the expanding variety of cartridge calibers.

Gunsights remained static in their development until long-range target shooting began drawing crowds and participating rifle clubs in the East. The rolling hills and flat prairies of the West also caused a need for long hunting shots. The 1870s through the 1880s saw the design of the sight to match the long reach of the new .40–.50 caliber high-energy cartridges designed to punch paper consistently at a thousand yards across windswept rifle ranges and to bring down buffalo one after another without stampeding the whole herd with up-close gunshots. Longer-range scales were etched on the steel flip-up sight rails and fine screw adjustment allowed for minor corrections, which translated into major shifts of impact way downrange.

The National Rifle Association was responsible for the growth of the target sport, and those developments are covered elsewhere here. Out West, the long-barreled, heavy-caliber, breechloading rifle became the signature tool of the meat and hide hunter. Their job was twofold. There was a market in the East for buffalo hides. The bones were crushed for fertilizer, and the tongue was a dining delicacy. On the other hand, every buffalo killed was one denied to the Plains Indians who depended upon the herds for their existence.

Railroad crews pushing west needed feeding, as did soldiers in their forts along the immigrant trails. Whole companies of buffalo hunters with their wagons and hired skinners rolled out of Dodge City and Wichita on the prairie's edge. These communities became cow towns once the buffalo were driven off valuable grazing land that was free for the taking.

With his Sharps .50 caliber rifle, the hunter set up a stand about two hundred yards from a standing herd of bison. If he had enough of a grubstake, he had a pair of rifles of the same caliber. He made himself comfortable, sometimes with a small stool or just a double roll of blankets, and propped up a forked shooting stick on which he set the heavy octagonal rifle barrel. With the wind quartering toward him, he reached into his leather sack of .50-70 caliber cartridges he hand-loaded himself to save overhead, opened the breech with a downward sweep of the steel trigger guard, and inserted the brass tube and a lead slug about the diameter of a nickel. Next, he raised the sight from the shoulder stock's grip just behind the cocking hammer.

The sight looked like a narrow railroad track with a tiny metal disk riding up and down between the rails. An aperture had been drilled in the disk, and screws were turned to adjust its position left or right to correct for the wind, or up and down to set the distance to the target. Satisfied with the sight setting, the hunter settled the front blade sight on a distant buffalo, centered the combination in the rear aperture, cocked the hammer, blinked away the spiderwebs caused by his heartbeat and silver spots from eyestrain, and fired. The buffalo disappeared behind the cloud of black-powder gun smoke, and it was a moment before the breeze cleared the air. The "buff" was down with a shot through the lungs. And so to work. Hours later, the pile of empty brass cartridge cases glittered in the sun where they had gathered at his feet, and he took a break to pour water down his gun barrel and let it cool. His face had become a mask. It wore a gray patina of gunpowder smoke except where he had wiped his eyes and mouth with his bandanna. In front of him, the prairie hillside was littered with buffalo corpses, pierced and still, and the skinner wagon had arrived with the men in greasy overalls carrying axes and large knives to begin carving up the profit for the day. The hunter collected his empty brass to reload with powder and lead and thought about lunch.

By the 1880s the open and aperture gunsights had matured to their final pattern and would remain as such for coming decades. The latest telescopic lenses produced wider fields of view and greater magnifications that reached farther, and the tubes were filled with nitrogen gas to eliminate fogging. The latest versions are zoom models that allow variable power with the twist of a ring. Better glass led to more light-gathering power and fewer distortions. Range-finding reticules allowing the shooter to compensate for wind, spin drift (movement off target caused by the bullet's direction of spin produced by the rifling twist), and bullet drop from the tug of gravity result in miraculous hits on targets over a mile distant.

The notch-and-blade sight added one feature using light-gathering photoluminescent pigments that glow after being exposed to light. Companies such as Trijicon have made use of a tritium phosphor lamp to create illuminated reticle and floating dot optical (unmagnified) sights that don't require a battery and will burn for up to fifteen years.

Today's technology reflects advances in the study of light waves and frequencies that allow optics to see specific reflected spectrums. Beginning in the years after World War II, infrared spotlights were shined into the dark, and a scope sight mounted on the rifle saw heat signatures reflecting the varying absorptions of the infrared spectrum. This concept of "seeing" heat signatures evolved into "night-vision" scopes that produced soft but discernable green images moving in the dark. An improvement on that technology is the Starlight military scope that operates on four AA batteries but provides much higher-resolution night-vision images.

The laser has created by far the most interesting gunsight. These sights can be retrofitted to most popular handguns and also rifles that offer a rail system of attaching accessories. They project an adjustable red or green dot on any target. The laser beam is matched to the gun's point of aim at a given distance, and the bullet will strike wherever the dot appears depending on wind, bullet drop, and the shooter's twitchy trigger finger. This true point-and-shoot accessory typified by the series created by Crimson Trace is fast and accurate without ever raising the weapon to eye level. In self-defense, the adversary, just seeing the dot on his or her body, will often surrender.

The gunsight migrated from an implied suggestion of accuracy to technological guarantee that hitting the target has never been easier. Its evolution has matched improvements in every stage of firearm development.

APPENDIX D

Guns in a Big, Dark Room

Revolvers blazed, horses galloped, fists flew, and music soared as audiences cheered the celluloid heroes who appeared every week at the local movie theater. If one unique thread has woven together America's gun culture, it is the motion picture, specifically the Western. All countries have a cultural heritage based on heroes, myths, great historical events, and a literary evolution. In the United States, following the Revolution and the exploration of the Louisiana Purchase, the War of 1812 and the settling of the western continent shaped our nation's character. The war showed we could stand fast and overcome a really bad situation, and the western migration proved we could face the unknown if the expected reward was big enough.

For all its drama and romance, the reality could be both brutal and unforgiving. The westward migration created larger-than-life people and events, some swollen with hyperbole and vivid imagination, while others occurred in virtual isolation, passed along by semiliterate survivors. By the time the actual lurid and mundane events were concluded after the turn of the century, Americans had inherited a body of stories to accompany the identities of the mythic names and events gleaned from the pages of newspapers and magazines of those not-so-distant times.

Pulp novels churned out by writers who had never been west of the Mississippi River described in detail extraordinary feats of Western marksmanship, horsemanship, and savagery that defied both belief and physics. Historians waded in to try and separate fact from fiction—and mostly failed, falling under the thrall of sincerely retold fantasies. When fact contradicted

the fiction, people trusted the legend because it was bigger and more exciting. Matching that need for a bigger, more vivid telling of these tales, the
motion picture, with its bright screen shared with others in a big, dark room,
offered the most saturating, involving experience. When Edwin S. Porter shot
his film *The Great Train Robbery* in West Orange, New Jersey, in 1903, he
had no idea of the huge floodgate he had kicked open. While the 740-foot
silent film flickered onto its screen, actor Justus D. Barnes, playing the part
of a train robber, turned and fired his revolver directly at the audience.
Women shrieked, and men bolted from their chairs. From the moment that
film ended, the motion picture's ability to tell a dramatic story was never in
doubt. The fact that *The Great Train Robbery* had a Western theme was not
lost on other potential filmmakers, and its budget of $150, with prints sell-
ing for $11, each made it a good financial bet.[1]

From *The Great Train Robbery* to the 1950s, the "programmer Western"
became standard fare for movie houses across the country. Eventually, they
became "B" Westerns to separate them from the film studios' mainstream
"A" fare with big budgets starring major actors. While some stars such as
Tom Mix, John Wayne, Gary Cooper, Roy Rogers, and Gene Autry moved
on to fame, wealth, and honors, most of the cowboy stars remained with the
assembly-line Westerns. Often shot in a few days or a week, the plots came
from Western novels or were copied from earlier films; sometimes scenes
from past movies were extracted and inserted into new productions to save
money and time. Do you need a wagon going over a cliff, a cattle stampede,
a town in flames, or an Oklahoma land rush? Once it was produced for a
film with a decent budget, the scene was fair game to be edited into future
projects for a fraction of the original cost.

But the big attractions were the shootouts. Guns were everywhere.
Certainly, there were gangster and police movies. *Scarface* and *The Roaring
Twenties* filled scenes with gun smoke. In Westerns, however, everyone—
including some of the "cattle queen" women—wore big revolvers in holsters
on their hips. You could always tell the bad guy. He wore a black hat and a
raggedy-ass gun belt. The hero's dumb sidekick wore a gun but never had
sense enough to use it, so the big Peacemaker Colt spent the film dangling
from his belt, below the buckle, more often than not pointed at his crotch.

Most Western gunslingers wore silver-trimmed, studded belt-and-holster
combinations to protect their nickel-plated Colts. Ken Maynard wore a tall-

crowned white hat, filigree-trimmed boots, tight pants, and ironed shirts, but he was a superior horseman and rodeo star and sometimes played the fiddle when singing cowboys began making inroads in the late 1930s. Buck Jones and Harry Carey were strong and silent, while Hoot Gibson often added comedy to his characters. These men were all real horsemen and personified the Western "good guy": law-abiding, tough, no time for girls, and wearing leather gloves everywhere day and night.

And then there were the aberrations. Tom Mix really had led a life of adventure, from fighting in Cuba in 1898 to rodeo and trick-shot demonstrations at circuses. He was a peace officer, and his acting career spanned the early days of filmmaking from silent productions to the "talkies" of the 1920s and 1930s. He had no problem with having old western towns and stagecoaches share a movie with fast sports cars and airplanes. He wrapped his final scene with a broken neck in a fast convertible at the bottom of an Arizona ditch. Autry couldn't ride, couldn't shoot, couldn't fight, but could sing and play the guitar. Stuntman Cliff Lyons made a career out of making Autry look good in fights and in the saddle, keeping Republic Studios in the black. Autry died in bed worth millions of dollars. John Wayne played in B Westerns and fast-paced serials that showed an episode each week until the evil menace was brought to justice. He even sang in one film, portraying a gunfighter called "Singing Sandy" who always sang a song before he shot down his opponent. Anyone who heard his song quaked in fear. They dubbed Wayne's singing voice with an operatic baritone who trilled his Rs. In reality, any gunfighter who heard Wayne's actual voice would have been so hysterical with laughter that he could have been beaten to death with a stick.

Bob Steele, Johnny Mack Brown, Lash LaRue, George O'Brien, Charles Starrett, Whip Wilson, and the legendary Tim McCoy were champions of justice and let their six-guns do their talking. McCoy was a genuine Western character, a former army scout who knew Indian sign language, was a crack shot, and always carried himself like an avenging angel, as did the early silent film cowboy William S. Hart. Hart had earned his chops on the legitimate stage spouting Shakespeare. Regardless, McCoy often snapped off his shots with a flick of the wrist—an affectation that would not have hit the horse let alone the rider. Cowboys "fanned" the hammers of their revolvers, spraying the general vicinity of their targets, but on screen managing to shoot the gun from the evildoer's hand. For actors who could not master the intricacies of the single-action Colt, for far-away shots double-action (no hammer-cocking required) revolvers were substituted, miraculously becoming single-action guns in close-up or in the holster. Gene Autry was so gun-shy that he kept his gloves draped over his holstered gun grips. "Wild" Bill Elliot wore his Colts with grips facing forward, as Wild Bill Hickock did when he carried his revolvers tucked in his belt. Even so, Elliot was considered by studio stunt-men as the fastest gun handler of the movie westerners.

The kids knew the names of every Western star's horse. Hopalong Cassidy (William Boyd, who hated kids) struggled to stay aboard Topper. Tom Mix rode Tony. Ken Maynard had trained Tarzan. Roy Rogers sang in the saddle on Trigger, and Gene Autry yodeled away to Champion's clip-clop. These horses got screen credits, private trailers, silver-mounted bridles, and mono-grammed nose-bags.

Since the audience for this gunfire and mayhem was largely small boys with a sticky quarter to spend and considered everything female to be "icky," women in the film were often screen credited as "The Girl." These same boys were sometimes frisked at the theater door for loaded cap pistols, peashoot-ers, or squirt guns that could take the action to a whole new level. The weapons were returned at the conclusion of the program.

These films circulated throughout the country by studio theater chains and independent distributors, who changed the feature every week. So, how many bloodthirsty monsters did these weekly six-gun killing sprees create? Probably not very many, because the Western was always a morality play; all the elements were fixed in place, starting with the hero ("A stranger rides into town . . . "). The town or ranch is a victim of some kind of oppression (the nasty cattle baron, banker, saloon owner, hired gunman, et al.). The girl is the owner of the business in trouble or daughter of the enfeebled business owner who faces foreclosure, is plagued by cattle rustling, has water access cut off, or has unknown valuable minerals on property. Possibly her father, stepfather, or kindly uncle (disposable victim to motivate further action) is gunned down. The only real variables were the occupation of the hero (who often has a secret identity as a federal marshal or Texas Ranger), and the depth of depravity of the villain. The end was a foregone conclusion. Goodness, telling the truth, helping your friends, defending the weak, and standing against tyranny were spelled out before rolling the end credits.

Many cowboy heroes never shot to kill—only to wound or disarm their grizzled, bad-to-the-core opponent. Most bad guys were pounded into whimpering, cowardly submission by our two-fisted champions. Though the Western was a uniquely American product, they were hugely popular overseas with dubbed dialogue. Into the 1940s the people of many nations saw the United States as a Wild West kept safe by six-gun-toting, guitar-plucking supermen who loved their horse more than the girl.

When the movie studios had to divest themselves of their chains of theaters, the profitable B Westerns disappeared, and the genre continued as less frequent, big-budget feature productions. Westerns had always found room on the radio dial as Tom Mix talked kids into asking Mom for Ralston Cereal. *Bobby Benson and the B-Bar-B Riders* galloped into many dangers, and the Lone Ranger, with his Indian companion Tonto, fought for justice while explaining the Ranger's black mask and the ballistic efficiency of solid silver bullets. Some of the old B Western movie scripts were recycled into more serious dramatic radio shows such as *Gunsmoke*. That show migrated to television, with tall, rugged actor James Arness playing Marshal Matt Dillon instead of William Conrad (short, fat, and with a mustache and a tough-as-nails voice) at the radio microphone. Television Westerns aimed for a more adult audience, using the same old plot and character devices but with more complex motivations, such as *Maverick*, *Cheyenne*, *Sugarfoot*, *Wanted: Dead or Alive*, *Have Gun—Will Travel*, *Bounty Hunter*, *Yancy Derringer*, and *The Rifleman*, and family sagas "in living color" such as *Bonanza* brought all manner of firearms and crack shots into American living rooms.

Then along came *Star Trek*—essentially a remake of the Western *Wagon Train* but set in deep space with aliens and rocket ships—and everything changed. Openly lusty Star Fleet commanders, miraculously good-looking female space aliens, and the United Federation of Planets switched six-guns for phasers and photon torpedoes. Soon callow youths wielding lightsabers challenged the Empire for freedom of oppressed peoples. This set of rousing adventures led to intellectually challenging video games on computers, creating a generation of youth with nanosecond eye-hand coordination.

Today, the highest grossing film in history, netting ticket sales in the billions worldwide, is *Avatar* by James Cameron. A stranger with a secret agenda rides into town and meets a girl whose father runs a large organization threatened by an even larger organization. The stranger takes the side of the girl's father, falls in love with the girl, and leads the oppressed in a revolt against the forces of evil in a huge, victorious battle at the end. *Avatar* is a B Western with a somewhat larger budget.

"I just pointed my rifle at him . . . and let him have the big one right through the third button on his shirt. If he ever figured to sew that particular button on again he was going to have to scrape it off his backbone." Louis L'Amour wrote those words in *Ride the Dark Trail* (1972). The Big, Dark Room of the imagination does not need flickering images on a screen to conjure up vivid scenes. Authors paint with words, and we walk down the dangerous trails and streets that rush from their synapses to their fingertips. Between weekends, when the movie theaters screened "adult" films of love and lust, redemption and retribution, kids read books and comics.

Sure, there were Archie and Jughead, Li'l Abner, and enough superheros to save the planet a dozen times over, but the real stories were written and drawn for EC Comics. Entertaining Comics artists John Severin, Wally Wood, George Evans, and Jack Davis knew how to draw action adventures from the Knights of Ancient Briton to the dusty streets of Dodge City or Tombstone. They knew the horses and guns and implements of warfare and the emotions of their pen-and-ink players who marched and blasted their way from panel to panel.

When the latest issue of *Two-Fisted Tales*, *Frontline Combat*, *Shock SuspenStories*, or *Aces High* arrived in the mail, all activity in neighborhoods stopped. There was a reality in those pages that did not talk down to kids. Wounds were accompanied by pain, death seeped blood, loss created sorrow, and with their only nod to fantasy, evil deeds brought justified retribution.

The kids also read *Terry and the Pirates*, *Steve Canyon*, *Little Orphan Annie*, and *Dick Tracy* in the Sunday newspaper comic pages. Bookworms paged through editions of *Treasure Island*, *The Last of the Mohicans*, and *Riders of the Purple Sage*. Some even took down the books that had entertained their fathers and grandfathers: *Don Sturdy among the Gorillas* by Victor Appleton (1911) or the stories of the intrepid inventor Tom Swift in books such as *Tom Swift and His Electric Rifle* (1910). A high school personal reading list (well-thumbed copies buried in the bottom of the underwear drawer) included anything by Mickey Spillane, anything featuring detective Shell Scott, and a dog-eared, underlined, disintegrating copy of *Battle Cry*. So much for great literature.

These were the kids in midwestern Chicago, but they represent variations on a microcosm at a post–World War II time when the tastes we share today were being formed. The bucolic rural days of the United States were ending, and sweeping social changes were upon us as media technology sped up everyone's absorption rate. Comics morphed into video games and graphic novels. Movies and television brought hyperrealism to the viewing experience, first with color and then with computer graphics, high-definition images, and 3-D visualization. *Avatar* continued the tradition of the B Western programmer, and books began the long transition into Kindle, Nook, iPad, and other screen-based text readers.

Along with all the other aspects of culture—music, fine arts, performance, automobiles, architecture, financial, sports, etc.—the gun culture has kept in step.

That Big, Dark Room between our ears is aware of the program every day, as we have come to live with it.

APPENDIX E

Them's Fightin' Words: Video Games

Since after World War I, American youngsters had to rely on the radio and later on movies and television for their audio, and then audio-visual, taste of shooting mayhem. They role-played their detective, law enforcement, and cowboy adventures after they had absorbed the story over the airwaves. The kids became the Lone Ranger, Dick Tracy, or Flash Gordon in their imaginations as they battled evil with cap pistols in the vacant lot next door. Who could possibly have anticipated that one day, young game players—and eventually adult game players, too—could enter the imaginary worlds of their heroes and terrifying villains and actually control the action within the story? It was like jumping inside your TV screen and battling the Hawk-People alongside Flash, Dale Arden, and Dr. Zarkov on the planet Mongo.

The emergence of video games definitely belongs in a story of America's gun culture. Today's young people have their relationship with guns colored by their exposure to the vivid and often brutal gun-filled video games. Parents are concerned that these war, crime, and supernatural game themes, realistically portrayed and involving their children's' participation in the violence and carnage, are strongly influencing the kids' lifestyles and values. These violent fantasy worlds created in color pixels celebrate guns in their most savage role as weapons of destruction.

The very earliest video game, patented by Thomas T. Goldsmigh Jr. and Estle Ray Mann in 1948, was titled *Cathode Ray Tube Amusement Device* and featured a missile whose path could be aimed by knobs to fall on a target affixed to the face of the screen on a clear plastic overlay—a shooting scenario.[1] By 1961 the earliest team game was created by MIT students on the

DEC PDP-1 computer. *Spacewar!* allowed two players to each control a spacecraft that fired missiles while dodging screen hazards. The game was traded all over the early bulletin-board version of the Internet and, because of a number of spin-offs, is considered to be the first truly influential video game.

By 1978 computer games migrated to the shopping mall in coin-operated arcade consoles, each hardwired into a single game. *Space Invaders* by Taito was an instant success and spawned a number of near clones that required the shooter to prevent the landing of alien spaceships. In *Asteroids* the player used a zapping ray gun, aimed with a knob, and fired with a button as the enemy rained down from above.

Other games required dexterity and advanced eye-hand coordination like Roland Bushnell's *Pong*, and the incredibly addictive *Donkey Kong* established one genre, while driving games that put the player in a racecar began developing their own arcade audience. Shooting games, however, gave an implied power to the player, along with high point scores to compete with and dazzle peers. Arcade games packed hardwired speed with a dedicated microprocessor and vivid color graphics to suck in game players' quarters.

The early to mid 1970s saw the first home "arcade" consoles: stand-alone boxes with hand controls that hooked up to the television screen. The games came in cartridges that plugged into consoles such as the Magnavox Odyssey, which sold two million units, and the ColecoVision, which arrived in 1982.[1] One of the hottest console games was *Top Gun*, based on the Tom Cruise movie involving Navy fighter jet training and shooting down enemy aircraft.

Existing at a different level from the visceral shooting scenarios were role-playing games that offered the player a fantasy identity and the ability to interpret clues, solve puzzles, and collect artifacts with special powers in order to fulfill a quest or arrive at a destination. Many of these games were designed to run on early home computers by Apple, Tandy, Commodore, Texas Instruments, and Atari. The earliest role-playing game, *Dungeons & Dragons*, evolved in the late 1970s, as did *Akalabeth: World of Doom*.

I created my first computer game in 1984, the same year I wrote my first published book, a third-party manual about the Franklin Computer. That machine was wrapped in a legal struggle with Apple over the interpretation of the read-only memory (ROM). Was it a mechanical device or intellectual property? Apple's intellectual property agument won, and Franklin tanked, but not before my book, published by Scott-Foresman, sold out its run because it was the only third-party book on the Franklin computer for the owners of the thousands of machines that had been sold. Timing is everything.

My computer game also used timing. It was written as I attended computer programming classes at Harper Community College at night. I had three Franklin computers given to me by the company to write the book, and besides testing every known piece of Apple software for compatibility, I felt the text needed some remarks on programming with the Franklin in Applesoft BASIC, a noncompiled language for the drooling knuckle draggers (DKDs) who populated the shadowy periphery of the true Nerd Hierarchy of sophisticated hackers and code freaks. I included myself among the DKD lowerarchy, but the urge to create something with the simple code and its childlike protocols was too strong.

My effort was call *Danger—UXB*, named after a BBC TV series about a detail of British soldiers in WWII whose job was to disarm unexploded bombs dropped on London by the Luftwaffe during the Battle of Britain in 1940. "UXB" stood for "unexploded bomb," and my game gave the player a choice of bombs, from 500-pound aerial parachute mines to 150-pound iron bombs, each with a unique timing device or clockwork fuse and each with a variety of booby traps ("I say, Geoff, do I nick the red wire, the blue wire, or the—"). I employed a matrix and random number generator plus a real-time clock and vector graphics on the simple, green text screen. Today *Danger—UXB* would be to *Resident Evil 4* as the Ford Model T is to the Space Shuttle. I can only say I had 64kb of memory to work with and saved the whole game to a 124kb floppy 5-1/4-inch disk.

My second, and final, shot at video game immortality was a war game called *Blimp Wars*, set in a postapocalyptic world. A self-contained colony of humans circle the ravaged earth in search of other surviving civilizations aboard great helium-filled dirigibles and smaller blimps. I drew all the characters, the dirigibles, and some of the aggressor civilizations they encountered. I was working with Konami—a fledgling company at the time—on a Las Vegas multimedia reveal of their latest gaming products for arcades and home computers. While the show came off quite well, my game languished as being too "cerebral" for a market that was just beginning to blast bad guys and alien robots to bits. I couldn't compete with the Teenage Mutant Ninja Turtles.

Video games such as *Grand Theft Auto* that glamorized crime and killing caught the attention of adults just as comic books in the 1950s galvanized parents into censorial action. From pulpits and op-ed columns to TV specials, shoot-'em-up video games are held responsible for the decline of youthful morals. The games became insidious, migrating first from arcades to home computers, then to laptops, Xbox and Nintendo consoles, pocket game players, and cell phones. They materialized everywhere. Even the movies embraced the format, and Spider-Man leaped from comic book to computer game to movie screen.

Now entire role-play sagas combing the quest scenario with the shooting and killing action scenes enhanced by superior computer-generated graphics have filled sixty-foot movie screens in shopping mall multiplexes with live actors. Amid all this blood and thunder, how do us creaky fogies and the NRA turn around the image of guns as killing machines, keep the excitement, and drain away the gore?

As a victim of the 1950s Comic Code Authority that stripped *Shock SuspenStories*, *Tales from the Crypt*, *Two-Fisted Tales*, *Frontline Combat*, *Aces High*, and the original color version of *Mad* magazine off the shelves, I can only offer a small clue. When I finally left home at age twenty-one to seek my fortune out west, my sainted mother condemned my comic book collection to the trash. Along with it went all my *Playboy* magazines (including the first issue, with the Marilyn Monroe photos), but that is another grim and tear-stained story.

My point is, after sailing off in a ballistic rage, calling up the demons of Hell, and summoning scourges from the bowels of the earth that would make the Black Death seem like a kiddies' balloon party, five minutes later I had a cool drink, and life moved on. By the time I learned of my mother's innocent depredations, I had outgrown the comics. I had discovered the chilling joys of H. P. Lovecraft, Edgar Allan Poe, and Ambrose Bierce when I needed a horror fix.

Parents today have the same worries as those befuddled souls in the 1950s. Only the medium has changed. The pace of life has increased incredibly. Today's kids are smarter, taller, stronger, and possess deep wells of stamina and intellectual curiosity that my generation can only admire from our DKD status. The heavy-duty violent games will reach market oversaturation and become the next generation's Rubik's Cube or hula hoop, and the Xbox will go on a shelf until the next neighborhood garage sale.

As far as the video game's impact on our current gun culture, kids are smarter than most grown-ups think. Overscheduling kids—especially in the summer—takes away their power, the very thing they look for in those games. Giving kids the chance to discover what they enjoy at their own pace without keeping them on the same schedule they are forced into at school gives them a chance to develop initiative.

My mother was certain I was damned to a life of sloth and idleness when she came out to the park one sunny afternoon when the air was perfumed with the fresh flowers growing abundantly in the nearby Park District garden, the squirrels were chittering in the trees, and a lazy breeze wafted in off Lake Michigan to tousle the tops of the tall elm trees. She stopped short at the line of dense bushes that obscured the view of the near edge of the park from her back-porch observation post. There were my pals and I, each with our back to our favorite tree, reading the latest edition of *Tales from the Crypt*. There was always some disturbed guy on the cover plunging a blood-dripping, rusty ax into somebody—usually a dame who had wandered into the toolshed in her nightie.

Even without her dishrag, Mom was formidable. We scattered like a covy of quail, snatching up baseball mitts, basketballs, roller skates—anything we had dropped in the grass—and became hyperbusy as she stalked off, muttering under her breath. My life has been anything but a languid treacle of sloth and idleness, and those stories, even the ax murders, made me want to tell stories of my own.

Maybe the NRA could spend a buck or two producing video games that feature the mental and physical challenges of shooting sports or, better yet, show the kids a real target range where the reality is so much more exciting. How about a new version of *Space Invaders* that involves hitting the aliens with a .22 before they drop to earth? Don't get me started. Janet inherited Mom's dishrag.

Notes

Foreword

1   Despite the fact that the U.S. Supreme Court has declared the Second Amendment right to own a gun a personal right like other rights set out in the Bill of Rights, the controversy continues. For a historical background, readers should consider the following: Michael A. Bellesiles, *Arming America: The Origins of a National Gun Culture* (New York: Knopf, 2000). This book was repudiated for its faulty research but set off a controversy with national significance. Also see Joyce Lee Malcolm, *To Keep and Bear Arms: The Origins of an Anglo-American Right* (Cambridge, MA: Harvard University Press, 1994); Lee Kennett and James LaVerne Anderson, *The Gun in America: The Origins of a National Dilemma* (Westport, CT: Greenwood, 1975); Stephen P. Halbrook, *That Every Man Be Armed: The Evolution of a Constitutional Right* (Albuquerque: University of New Mexico Press, 1984); and Rudolph B. Lamy, "The Influence of History upon a Plain Text Reading of the Second Amendment to the Constitution of the United States," *The American Journal of Legal History* 49, no. 2 (April 2007): 217–30.

2   Robert V. Remini, *The Battle of New Orleans: Andrew Jackson and America's First Military Victory* (New York: Viking Penguin, 1999), 142.

3   See Richard Slotkin, *Gunfighter Nation: The Myth of the Frontier in Twentieth-Century America* (New York: Atheneum, 1992).

4   T. Lindsay Baker and Billy R. Harrison, *Adobe Walls: The History and Archaeology of the 1874 Trading Post* (College Station: Texas A&M University Press, 1986) and Mike Venturino, *Shooting Buffalo Rifles of the Old West* (Livingston, MT: MLV Enterprises, 2002). In Part IV, Ch. 28 of *Shooting Buffalo*, "Legend of Billy Dixon: Life & Times of a Long Range Hero," reprinted with permission from the September 1994 issue of *Shooting Times*, 223–235.

5   See Joseph H. Alexander, *Edson's Raiders: The 1st Marine Raider Battalion in World War II* (Annapolis, MD: Naval Institute Press, 2001); Jon T. Hoffman, *Once a Legend: "Red Mike" Edson of the Marine Raiders* (Novato, CA: Presidio, 1994); and James Brady, *Hero of the Pacific: The Life of Marine Legend John Basilone* (Hoboken, NJ: John Wiley & Sons, 2010).

6   See Laura Brower, *Women and Guns in America* (Chapel Hill: University of North Carolina Press, 2006).

7   See Glenda Riley, "Annie Oakley," in Gordon Morris Bakken, ed., *Icons of the American West*, vol. 1 (Westport, CT: Greenwood, 2008), 209–230.

8   Mark V. Tushnet, *Out of Range: Why the Constitution Can't End the Battle over Guns* (New York: Oxford University Press, 2007), 104.

9   Ibid., 124.

1. A New Culture Shaped by Old Fears

1   Harold L. Peterson, *The Treasury of the Gun* (New York: Golden Press, 1962), 35.

2   James Burke, *Connections: From Ptolemy's Astolabe to the Discovery of Electricity; How Inventions Are Linked—and How They Cause Change throughout History* (Boston: Little, Brown, 1978), 225.

3   Peterson, *Treasury of the Gun*, 48.

4   "Rifle," Merriam-Webster, http://www.merriam-webster.com/dictionary/rifled.

5   Michael Lenz, *Guns, Culture and the Roots of the Second Amendment* (Cologne, Germany: University of Cologne, 2004–2005), 31.

6   Ibid.

7   Ibid.

8   Alexander Rose, *The American Rifle* (New York: Bantam Dell, 2008); History of Black Powder, The First Foot Guards, http://footguards.tripod.com/06ARTICLES/ART28_blackpowder.htm.

9   Joyce Lee Malcolm, *To Keep and Bear Arms: The Origins of an Anglo-American Right* (Cambridge: MA: Harvard University Press, 1994), 10–11.

10 Ibid., 40–45.

11 Amos Barrett, letter of April 19, 1825, Vincent Kehoe Collection, *We Were There! The American Rebels* (Worcester, MA: American Antiquarian Society, 1999).

12 J. Hammond Trumbull et al., eds., *The Public Records of the Colony of Connecticut*, 15 vols. (Hartford, CT, 1850–1890).

13 Eli Whitney, "The Manufacture of Firearms," Eli Whitney Collection, http://www.eliwhitney.org/new/museum/eli-whitney/arms-production.

14 Pamela Lowry, "The Development of American Machine Tools," Schiller Institute, http://www.schillerinstitute.org/educ/hist/devo_machine_tool.html.

15 Peter Baida, "Eli Whitney's Other Talent," *American Heritage Magazine*, May/June 1987.

2. Heading West: Prophets of Individualism

1   Fred L. Israel, ed., *1897 Sears, Roebuck Catalog* (Philadelphia: Chelsea House, 1993), 581.

2   Bruce Wexler, *The Wild West Catalog* (Philadelphia: Running Press, 2008), 118–22.

3   Joseph G. Rosa, *Age of the Gunfighter* (Norman: University of Oklahoma Press, 1995), 110.

4   David Dary, *Cowboy Culture* (New York: Knopf, 1981), 305.

5   Duncan McConnel, "Suicide Specials," *American Rifleman*, February 1948.

6   Silas Casey, *Schools of the soldier and company, Instruction for skirmishers and music* (D. Van Nostrand, 1865).

7   C. B. Lister, Executive Director, *Background of Your Association*, Annual Report to the NRA, January 1947.

8   Ibid.

9   N. H. Roberts, "Long Range Rifles of Yesterday," *American Rifleman*, March 1948.

10 "History of Adobe Walls," The Faultline Shootist Society, http://www.faultlineshootistsociety.com/?page_id=907.

11 Dick Culver, "In Distinguished Company,"Civilian Marksmanship Program, http://www.odcmp.com/Competitions/In_Distinguished_Company_Culver_2000.pdf.

3. It's a Small-Bore World after All

1   Frank C. Barnes, *Cartridges of the World* (Iola, WI: Krause Publications, 2000).

2 "218 Bee," The Reload Bench, http://www.reloadbench.com/cartridges/218b.html.

3 Winchester Repeating Arms Company, miscellaneous correspondence concerned mainly with .22 firearms and ammunition 1917–1919, Winchester Arms Collection Archives.

4 Herbert G. Houze, *The Winchester Model 52: Perfection in Design* (Iola, WI: Krause Publications, 1997), 37–48.

5 Winchester Repeating Arms Company, miscellaneous correspondence concerned mainly with .22 firearms and ammunition 1917–1919, Winchester Arms Collection Archives.

6 Ibid.; Houze, *Winchester Model 52*, 65.

7 Jose Poncet, with Patrick McSherry, "The Spanish 7x57mm Mauser, Model 1893," The Spanish American War Centennial Website, http://www.spanamwar.com/spanishmauser.htm.

8 During my years living on Chicago's South Side, my address was *3006* E. 78th Street. Make something of that if you will.

9 "Camp Logan National Guard Rifle Range Historic District, at Illinois Beach State Park, Lake County, Illinois," Division of Resource Review and Coordination, Cultural Resource Program, http://dnr.state.il.us/OREP/cultural/cmpLogan/camplogan.htm.

10 James E. Serven, ed., *Americans and Their Guns: The National Rifle Association through Nearly a Century* (Harrisburg, PA: Stackpole, 1967).

4. "A Simply Operated Machine Gun . . ."

1 "The Gun that Made the Twenties Roar," http://www.gangstersandoutlaws.com/Tommygun.html.

2 "Timeline in FBI History," Federal Bureau of Investigation, http://www2.fbi.gov/libref/historic/history/historicdates.htm.

3 Advertisement, *National Geographic*, January 1924.

5. A-Hunting We Did Go

1 Gerry Souter and Janet Souter, *The Founding of the United States Experience* (London: Carlton, 2006), 58.

2 Rose, *The American Rifle*, 136.

3 ".22 Hornet," The Reload Bench, http://www.reloadbench.com/cartridges/22h.html.

6. World War II: The Game Changer

1 Michael Mullin, "Preparing for War: Chrysler Military Production, 1940–1942," Allpar, February 1965, http://www.allpar.com/history/military/preparing.html.

2 Raymond J. Stan, "Editorial: The NRA and National Defense," *American Rifleman*, September 1941.

3 David K. Yelton, *Hitler's Home Guard: Volkssturmmann* (Oxford, UK: Osprey, 2002).

4 Ben-Ami Shillony, *Politics and Culture in Wartime Japan* (New York: Oxford University Press, 1981), 82.

5 "Blackshirts," Wikipedia, last modified September 6, 2011, http://en.wikipedia.org/wiki/Blackshirts.

6 Editorial page notice, *Cook County Herald*, April 9, 1943.

7 Gerry Souter and Janet Souter, *The Founding of the United States: 1763–1814* (London: Carlton, 2006), 43.

8 "The Rifle Squad," Bayonet Strength, http://www.bayonetstrength.150m.com/Tactics/Formations/rifle_squad.htm.

9 "M-1 Carbine Semi-Automatic Carbine," Military Factory, http://www.militaryfactory.com/smallarms/detail.asp?smallarms_id=54.

10 Michael Lee Lanning, *Inside the Crosshairs: Snipers in Vietnam* (New York: Ballantine, 1998), 156.

11 David Le Page, "Harry Patch, Slam Marshall and the Death of Humanity," *Leaves Caution Behind* (blog), September 1, 2009, http://lepageblog.wordpress.com/2009/09/01/harry -patch-slam-marshall-and-the-death-of-humanity/.

12 S. L. A. Marshall, *Men Against Fire: The Problem of Battle Command* (Norman: University of Oklahoma Press, 2000).

13 C. F. Vernon, "The Johnson L.M.G.," *American Rifleman*, October 1942.

14 F. C. Ness, "Dope Bag," *American Rifleman*, May 1940.

15 H. P. Sheldon, "The Rifle Is Finished," *American Rifleman*, May 1940.

7. Gathering the Reins in a Runaway World

1 Christopher Jensen, "Employee Engagement and the Desire to Unionize," http:// employeeengagement.ning.com/profiles/blogs/employee-engagement-and-the-1?xg_source =activity.

2 NRA Staff, "Mission Accomplished!" *American Rifleman*, December 1945.

3 Brian Trumbore, "Taft-Hartley," Buy and Hold, http://www.buyandhold.com/bh/en /education/history/2002/taft_hartley.html.

4 David T. Zabecki, "Stand or Die: 1950 Defense of Korea's Pusan Perimeter," HistoryNet.com, May 1, 2009, http://www.historynet.com/stand-or-die-1950-defense-of-koreas-pusan-perimeter.htm.

5 David Halberstam, *The Coldest Winter: America and the Korean War* (New York: Hyperion, 2007), 110.

6 Ibid., 125.

7 Zabecki, "Stand or Die."

8 George Kennan, "The Sources of Soviet Conduct (1947)," The History Guide, http://www .historyguide.org/europe/kennan.html.

9 NRA advertisement, *American Rifleman*, February 1948, 5.

10 C. B. Lister, "Passion for Crisis," *American Rifleman*, March 1948, 10.

11 Ann Coulter, *Treason: Liberal Treachery from the Cold War to the War on Terrorism* (Crown, 2003).

12 Chuck Hawks, "The Dark Side of Smith & Wesson," Guns and Shooting Online, http:// www.chuckhawks.com/smith-wesson_dark.htm.

13 Charles Askins, "Why America Lost the Olympics," *Guns Magazine*, April 1957.

14 Robert Dyment, "Whose Fault Is It if Cops Can't Shoot?" *Guns Magazine*, August 1957.

15 Ibid.

16 William C. L. Thompson, "Guns Are Big Business," *Guns Magazine*, March 1955.

17 Ibid.

18 "Unintended Consequences: Pro-Handgun Experts Prove That Handguns Are a Dangerous Choice for Self-Defense," Violence Policy Center, November 2001, http://www.vpc.org/studies/unincont.htm.

19 Ibid.

8. The Me Generation under Fire

1 General Social Survey, "GSS Cumulative Data Set (1972–2004)," http://gss.norc.org/.

2 Gary Kleck, "Measures of Gun Ownership Levels for Macro-Level Crime and Violence Research," *Journal of Research in Crime & Delinquency* 41, no. 1 (February 2004): 3–36.

3   Clayton Cramer, "Gun Laws under the Influence," *Shotgun News*, November 18, 2002.
    Cramer is quoting Civil Code §1714 from the California legislature.

4   Lisa O'Neill Hill and John Welch, "Gun Maker Named in Suit Over Shooting," *Riverside
    (CA) Press-Enterprise*, April 7, 2000.

5   Pamphlet texts quoted from Josh Sugarman, *National Rifle Association: Money, Firepower,
    and Fear* (National Press Books, 1991).

6   1991 Shooting, Hunting, Outdoor Trade (SHOT) Show program.

7   "The New Equality" in Sugarman, *National Rifle Association*.

8   Franklin Zimring and Gordon Hawkins, *A Citizen's Guide for Gun Control* (New York:
    Macmillan, 1987).

9   "More Women May Be Turning to Firearms," *Washington Times*, March 30, 2010,
    http://www.washingtontimes.com/news/2010/mar/30/more-females-may-be-turning-to-
    firearms/.

10 According to the FBI's *Uniform Crime Report*, justifiable homicide is defined as "the killing
    of a felon, during the commission of a felony, by a private citizen." See "Expanded Homicide
    Data," U.S. Department of Justice, http://www2.fbi.gov/ucr/cius2009/offenses/expanded
    _information/homicide.html.

11 "Self-Defense: The Great Myth of America's Gun Industry," Consumer Federation of
    America, http://www.consumerfed.org/pdfs/self_defense.pdf.

12 "James Connolly: A Rebel Song," *Petes' Radical Poetry Site* (blog), March 28, 2007, http://
    wwwpetepoetry-bullybuster.blogspot.com/2007/03/james-connolly-rebel-song.html.

13 "M16 5.56mm Rifle," GlobalSecurity.org, http://www.globalsecurity.org/military/systems
    /ground/m16-history.htm.

9. Put the Gloves on the Bosses and Let 'em Duke it Out

1   Steve Chapman, "False Fears about Concealed Guns," *Chicago Tribune*, March 31, 2011.

2   Frederick Law Olmstead, *A Journey in the Back Country* (1860; repr., Manchester, England:
    Cornerhouse Publications, 1972), 414.

3   Clayton E. Cramer, *Concealed Weapon Laws of the Early Republic* (Westport, CT: Praeger,
    1999), 24.

4   Mark Erickson, *Antique American Switchblades: Identification and Value Guide* (Iola, WI:
    Krause, 2004).

5   "Horrible Rencontre," *Natchez Daily Republican Banner*, October 7, 1837.

6   "Political Assassination: The Violent Side of American Political Life," Digital History, http://
    www.digitalhistory.uh.edu/historyonline/assassinations.cfm.

7   Jack K. Williams, "Georgians as Seen by Antebellum English Travelers," *Georgia Historical
    Quarterly* 32, no. 3 (September 1948): 168–169.

8   William Stevens, *Pistols at Ten Paces: The Story of the Code of Honor in America*
    (Cambridge, MA: Riverside, 1940).

9   Essinger, James, *Jacquard's Web: How a Hand Loom Led to the Birth of the Information
    Age* (Oxford, England: Oxford University Press, 2004).

10 John Bodnar, *The Transplanted: A History of Immigrants in Urban America* (Bloomington:
    Indiana University Press, 1985).

11 Randy Wakeman, "Smokeless Powder Muzzleloading," Guns and Shooting Online, http://
    www.chuckhawks.com/smokeless_powder_muzzleloading.htm.

12 Geoffrey W. Norman, "The Real Hatfield," October 1, 1990, http://www.inc.com/magazine
    /19901001/5391.html.

13 "CheyTac Intervention M200 Sniper Rifle – .408 Caliber," Future Weapon Technology, http://www.futurefirepower.com/shooter-movie-cheytac-intervention-m200-sniper-rifle.

14 Glenn M. Gilbert, "Bushmaster ACR: A Transformative Firearm, *American Rifleman*, May 2010, 53.

15 NRA Staff, "Target Shooting Grows in Popularity," *American Rifleman*, April 20, 2010.

16 Gerry Souter, *The Earnhardts* (Santa Barbara, CA: Greenwood Press, 2008), 77–78.

Appendix A. National Shooting Sports League

1 Scott Walker, "U.S. Hunting and Shooting Trends: Sharp Reductions in Hunting Participation, Target Shooting in U.S," Suite 101, December 8, 2009, http://www.suite101.com/content/us -hunting-and-shooting-trends-a82906#ixzz15qZro34d.

2 Ibid.

3 Debbie Thurman, "Target Long Guns," *The Shooting Industry*, August 1, 2010, 33; Responsive Management, "Sport Shooting Participation in the United States in 2009," National Shooting Sports Foundation, 2010, http://nssf.org/PDF/research/NSSF-Shooting -Participation-2010-Report.pdf.

Appendix B. Exhibition Shooters

1 Ed McGivern, *Fast and Fancy Revolver Shooting* (Chicago: Follett, 1975).

Appendix C. Hitting the Target

1 Harold L. Peterson, *A Treasury of the Gun* (New York: Golden Press, 1962).

2 Bruce Lancaster, *The American Revolution* (New York: Simon & Schuster, 2003), 246.

3 Civilwarguns Forum, Civilwarguns.com, http://www.civilwarguns.com/board/viewtopic .php?id=1&t_id=13.

Appendix D. Guns in a Big, Dark Room

1 John Tuska, *The Filming of the West* (Garden City, NY: Doubleday, 1976), 3–5.

Appendix E. Them's Fightin' Words: Video Games

1 "History of video games," Wikipedia, last modified August 25, 2011, http://en.wikipedia.org /wiki/History_of_video_games.

2 "ColecoVision History," ColecoVision.dk, http://www.colecovision.dk/history.htm.

Bibliography

Burke, James. *Connections: From Ptolemy's Astrolabe to the Discovery of Electricity; How Inventions Are Linked—and How They Cause Change throughout History*. Boston: Little, Brown, 1978.

Cramer, Clayton E. *Concealed Weapon Laws of the Early Republic: Dueling, Southern Violence, and Moral Reform*. Westport, CT: Praeger, 1999.

Dary, David. *Cowboy Culture: A Saga of Five Centuries*. New York: Knopf, 1981.

FMG Publications, *Guns Magazine*: Ed McGivern, "My Challenge to Hollywood Hotshots," January 1957; Larry Moore, "Toughest Shooting Sport of All," January 1957; Col. Charles Askins, "Why America Lost the Olympics," April 1957; Robert Dyment, "Whose Fault Is It That Cops Can't Shoot?," August 1957; Arvo Ojalla, "The Truth About Hollywood Hotshots," December 1955; M. E. Fuller, "Shooting Irons of the Old West," December 1955.

Fowler, Will, ed. *Encyclopedia of Guns*. London: Anness, 2007.

———, Anthony North, and Charles Stronge. *The Illustrated Encyclopedia of Pistols, Revolvers and Submachine Guns*. London: Anness, 2007.

Grennell, Dean A., and Mason Williams. *Law Enforcement Handgun Digest*. Northfield, IL, Digest Books, 1972.

Hogg, Ian V., and John Weeks. *Military Small Arms of the 20th Century.* 4th ed. Northfield, IL: DBI Books, 1981.

Houze, Herbert G. *The Winchester Model 52: Perfection in Design.* Iola, WI: Krause Publications, 1997.

Israel, Fred L., ed. *1897 Sears, Roebuck & Co. Catalog.* Philadelphia: Chelsea House, 1993.

Lanning, Michael Lee. *Inside the Crosshairs: Snipers in Vietnam.* New York: Ballantine, 1998.

Lenz, Michael. *Guns, Culture and the Roots of the Second Amendment.* Cologne, Germany: University of Cologne, 2004–2005.

Malcolm, Joyce Lee. *To Keep and Bear Arms: The Origins of an Anglo-American Right.* Cambridge, MA: Harvard University Press, 1994.

Marshall, S. L. A. *Men against Fire: The Problem of Battle Command.* Norman: University of Oklahoma Press, 2000.

McCullough, David. *1776.* New York: Simon & Schuster, 2005.

McGivern, Ed. *Fast and Fancy Revolver Shooting.* El Monte, CA: New Win Publishing, 1984.

National Rifle Association. *American Rifleman Magazine*, issues 1939–2010.

Nemerov, Howard. *Four Hundred Years of Gun Control . . . Why Isn't It Working?* Contrast Media Press, 2008.

Peterson, Harold L. *The Treasury of the Gun.* New York: Golden Press, 1962.

Rosa, Joseph G. *Age of the Gunfighter: Men and Weapons on the Frontier, 1840–1900.* Norman: University of Oklahoma Press, 1995.

Tuska, Jon. *The Filming of the West.* Garden City, NY: Doubleday, 1976.

Utley, Robert M., ed. *The Story of the West: A History of the American West and Its People.* New York: DK, 2003.

Wexler, Bruce. *The Wild West Catalog.* Philadelphia: Running Press, 2008.

Zimring, Franklin, and Gordon Hawkins. *A Citizen's Guide for Gun Control.* New York: Macmillan, 1992.

About the Author

Gerry Souter received his bachelor of art education degree from the Art Institute of Chicago and the University of Chicago. He has worked as an art teacher, a security guard, a rifle instructor, and a deckhand in the U.S. Merchant Marine. His creative experience as an international photojournalist, filmmaker, and award-winning video director, producer, and writer has been extensive. He and his wife, Janet, have authored or coauthored more than forty books in the areas of history, biography, young adult fiction, art, military history, business, and the Internet. Recent titles include *The Chicago Air and Water Show: A History of Wings above the Waves* (History Press, 2010), *The Vietnam War Experience* (Carlton Books, 2008), *Military Rifles: Fierce Firepower* (Enslow, 2006), and *American Realism: 10 American Painters* (Sirrocco, 2009). They live near Chicago.